TELLING
TRUE STORIES

Navigating the challenges of writing narrative non-fiction

Matthew Ricketson

ALLEN&UNWIN

SYDNEY•MELBOURNE•AUCKLAND•LONDON

Allen & Unwin
83 Alexander Street
Crows Nest NSW 2065
Australia
Phone: (61 2) 8425 0100
Email: info@allenandunwin.com
Web: www.allenandunwin.com

Cataloguing-in-Publication details are available
from the National Library of Australia
www.trove.nla.gov.au

ISBN 978 1 74237 935 7

Index by Puddingburn
Set in 12.5/15 pt Granjon by Midland Typesetters, Australia
Printed and bound by Hang Tai Printing Company Limited, China
10 9 8 7 6 5 4 3 2 1

For Gill, again, always

Table of contents

Chapter 1

Why true stories matter

The truth isn't always beauty, but the hunger for it is.
Nadine Gordimer, Nobel Prize-winning South African writer

Our very definition as human beings is very much bound up with the stories we tell about our own lives and the world in which we live. We cannot, in our dreams, our daydreams, our ambitious fantasies, avoid the imaginative imposition of form on life.
Peter Brooks, *Laws' Stories: Narrative and Rhetoric in the Law*

Telling true stories is a powerful form of public communication. Researching what is going on in people's lives and in the world around us unearths fresh, even revelatory, information that at its sharpest will speak truth to those in positions of power and authority. A well-crafted true story explores events in their complexity and people in their full humanity. Using a timely, narrative approach to write about actual people, events and issues for a broad audience produces works that lodge deep in the reader's gut and resonates in their mind. They prompt reflection; some true stories stay with the reader for months, even years. Some spur readers to action. That action may mean simply sharing the true story with friends and strangers. It may mean the upending of long-held views. It may mean joining a group or even setting one up to address a particular issue. It may mean even more far-reaching changes in a person's life. However a reader might be affected by reading true stories, the act of researching and writing true stories and of readers engaging with them is of profound importance in a democratic society.

True stories may be published in newspapers or magazines, or in multimedia online productions; they may be written at book length or they may be its visual equivalent—the documentary film. 'True stories', which is a broad term for an activity that goes by various names—such as long-form journalism, literary journalism, narrative non-fiction and creative non-fiction—has a longer history than is often thought, is more widely practised than is recognised and, in my experience, produces some of the most vibrant writing available today. True stories can encompass a variety of forms, including bestselling, agenda-setting work from high-profile journalists, like David Marr's *Power Trip*, his 2010 *Quarterly Essay* about the then prime minister of Australia, Kevin Rudd. It can include deeply researched, explanatory books, such as Gitta Sereny's account of Mary Bell's murder of two small boys in England, *Cries Unheard*. It can also take in beautifully written ruminative works, such as Anna Funder's Samuel Johnson award-winning *Stasiland*, which excavates the experiences of ordinary East Germans since the fall of the Berlin Wall in 1989. These are but three examples among thousands, many of which are discussed in this book. This field of writing is most developed in the United States but is practised across the English-speaking world. It is also found in numerous non-English-speaking countries, as two studies, *Literary Journalism Across the Globe* (2011) and *Global Literary Journalism* (2012), illustrate, but except for the few that are translated, these true stories are less well known in English-speaking countries among those of us who don't have any other languages.

I come to this field both as a practitioner and as an academic. My interest, which has long since become a passion, stems from experience early in my career when I began to see what journalism struggled to communicate. In 1983, soon after completing a cadetship at *The Age* newspaper, I was among several staff sent to cover what became known as the Ash Wednesday bushfires, the worst natural disaster in Victoria in nearly five decades. After interviewing survivors in Lorne and Anglesea, on the coast south-west of

Melbourne, what struck me most and what I still remember today is the gap between the enormity of the event and the means at my disposal to communicate it—a short news article. The people I interviewed, which included a builder and a family with two teenage children who had lost their homes, were in what I now see was a state of shock. They could not find the words to express how they felt, but emotion was fairly radiating from them in waves. Confusion, emptiness, a sense they had been picked up like a flake of ash and thrown helter skelter—that's what I intuited, but that could not be put in a news piece so I pushed more questions on them and eventually got some 'quotes', as they are known in the news media industry, and duly filed. As 'quotes' they were fine, but they fell far short of conveying what I thought needed to be reported that day, which was at least some sense of the intense emotions survivors experienced.

By its nature the inverted pyramid form of the hard news article prioritises not emotion but information, and certain kinds of information at that—election results, natural disasters, burglaries, gold medals, company takeovers, scientific breakthroughs and the like. Hard news focuses on the concrete rather than the abstract, and on action rather than reflection. It has proved an extraordinarily durable means of conveying important information quickly and concisely. Even the most recent communication form—the 140 character-long tweet—is used by journalists to report news as it breaks. The rapid dissemination of important information in hard news and in journalistic tweets, though, strips out emotion and vaults over analysis; it fails to attend to the breadth of readers' needs and tastes.

In time I learnt that numerous other journalists had bumped their heads on hard news' low ceilings, and some had spoken about it publicly. As a young reporter working on *The New York Herald Tribune* in 1963, Tom Wolfe was sent out to get person-on-the-street reactions to the assassination of the American president, John Kennedy. He found people of various ethnic backgrounds blaming each other for the killing and faithfully reported their comments, only to find that those comments never made the paper. He realised that, almost by osmosis, a 'proper moral tone' for a presidential assassination had been decided upon. 'It was to be grief, horror, confusion, shock and sadness, but it was not supposed to be the occasion for any petty bickering. The press assumed the moral tone of a Victorian gentleman' (Flippo 1980, p. 56). David Simon, a former crime reporter for *The Baltimore Sun*, now best known for creating a brilliant, innovative drama for television, *The Wire*, expresses a similar view. 'For four years I had written city murders in a cramped, two-dimensional way—filling the back columns of the metro section with the kind of journalism that reduces all human tragedy, especially those with black or brown victims, to bland, bite-sized morsels' (1991, p. 627). His experience prompted him to take a leave of absence from his newspaper to spend time observing the inner workings of the city's homicide squad. The result was a landmark work of book-length journalism, *Homicide: A Year on the Killing Streets*.

After working in Australian newsrooms for eleven years I had experienced the tangible excitement and pleasures of journalism and still strongly believed in the news media's fourth estate role, but had become frustrated by the gap between the richness and variety of what I saw, heard and felt on the road and the narrowness and sameness of the forms in which I was allowed to write. It was only after I began teaching and studying journalism, in 1993 at Royal Melbourne Institute of Technology (RMIT), that I began to appreciate the depth of its history and just how supple and enlivening are the various forms of journalism.

I began incorporating what I learnt into my own work, first as a freelancer and years later as a staff journalist when I returned to the industry as *The Age*'s media and communications editor. Like many before and since, I imitated Tom Wolfe's 'hectoring narrator', in a 1996 profile of playwright Hannie Rayson for *The Weekend Australian Magazine*, in ways that make me cringe today. More successfully, researching and writing a biography published in 2000 of Australian author Paul Jennings enabled me to explore a subject in depth. In recent years the stories I have probably most enjoyed doing are those where I was able to spend time hanging around with the subjects and then write the pieces in a narrative style, such as one about television journalist Ray Martin, for *The Monthly* in 2005, and another about *The Chaser* comedy team, for *The Age* in 2007.

Over those years I also saw the virtuous circle that can be formed between practice and theory. Reflecting on my practice improved it; researching and writing stories raised questions that prompted more study. This in turn also made me see the narrowness of what I had been taught at the university where, as an undergraduate, I did honours in English. The only kinds of writing we had studied were poetry, drama and fiction. If journalism was mentioned at all the adverbial 'mere' was welded to it. The idea that there could be anything creative about non-fiction was not even discussed. I still enjoy reading fiction, but in the last two decades narrative non-fiction has provided some of the most intense and enlightening reading experiences of my life. I remember being deeply moved reading John Hersey's *Hiroshima* half a century after it was written and half a world away in the Australian bush one summer holiday. I was in awe of Ted Conover's commitment to discover the reality of America's prison system by working undercover as a guard for a year to produce *Newjack*. And after reading Chloe Hooper's *The Tall Man* I felt shame at my apathy about the lives of many Indigenous Australians.

These are only three examples among hundreds of articles and books I have read that have opened my eyes to the sheer variety and richness of writing beyond poetry, drama and fiction. Some of these articles and books investigate the issues of the day while others are moment-by-moment excavations of processes as mundane as building a house. Some are biographies of people who are still alive while others are accounts of journeys that take the writer inward as well as outward. Others still are books that explore a particular idea, as English-born, Canadian-raised Malcolm Gladwell's *The Tipping Point* famously did. Many of these articles and books are written by journalists, but many are written by novelists. One background is not necessarily better preparation for writing true stories than the other; nor does the field belong to one or the other. In that way of thinking lies energy-draining turf wars. Much more useful, I think, is to see what various backgrounds enable practitioners to bring to the task, and what they can learn from each other.

I discovered in my own work, as well as in others', that because so much of journalists' energy is taken up with finding the news, they have less energy, not to mention little time, to devote to the subtleties of storytelling. This shortcoming can be disguised in a 1500-word feature article hooked to big news events, but the demands of a book-length narrative exposes it to a harsh light. Novelists understand storytelling, but most have had little experience with the demands of finding and verifying information people don't want you to know. Beneath experience and training lie the temperaments that characterise practitioners in the two fields. Burning curiosity drives journalists out into the world to discover what is really going on; a novelist's curiosity is more often directed inward. What they observe goes into creating their own imaginary worlds. A prime focus on the external world, coupled with precious little time to reflect on what they do, leaves journalists under-prepared to make sense of or express with any sophistication how they feel about the subjects of their stories. Conversely, novelists can become so preoccupied with their emotional and imaginary worlds that it overshadows the needs and desires of the actual people, events and issues they are writing about. These are, of course, generalisations; there are journalists such as Conover who have an acute sense of their subjectivity, and novelists such as Hooper who venture out into forbidding terrain. It is an observation, though, that helps when analysing the issues that arise in this area of writing practice.

The combination of practice and reflection has led me to the view that the finding and telling of true stories provides a solution to problems besetting the news media and public debate. Not the only solution, and not a total solution, but one solution to two of the news media's particular problems. First, the limited time and space available to print and broadcast media necessarily means daily coverage is superficial. A good journalist can cover a lot of territory in one day, but it is those journalists able to spend more than a day on an issue who provide the most searching coverage. Second, the internet's virtually unlimited space dissolves one of journalism's perennial limits, but its capacity to be updated instantly has yoked the news media to even tighter deadlines, which has had the effect of creating what Dean Starkman calls 'the hamster wheel' (2010). That is, newspaper journalists write many more news articles than they did a decade ago. They also need to be able to produce audio and video reports as well as those for the next day's newspaper, and they use Twitter to gather and present news. At the same time, the threat posed by the internet challenges the business model that has long sustained mainstream media and has forced newspapers to shed many staff. Fewer journalists filing more news reports on more platforms intensifies conditions in the news media that lead to superficial coverage. Critically, Starkman identifies that news organisations have a choice about jumping on the hamster wheel or deploying their resources to focus on finding and writing stories other outlets do not have; this would give them a chance of drawing audiences to them ('the hamster wheel').

I may be a strong believer in the virtues of telling true stories, but the power inherent in the form throws up important and knotty issues. For instance, how do practitioners balance their need to maintain editorial independence with the closeness to key sources that comes from gaining the deep level of trust usually required to construct a narrative non-fiction work? Are there any limits to the kinds of narrative approach practitioners can take when representing actual people and events? Can you, for instance, write interior monologues, or are a person's innermost thoughts and feelings the province of fiction? Is the omniscient authorial voice appropriate in narrative non-fiction when, by definition, practitioners cannot know everything about the people and events they are writing up? And, how do people read true stories in books as distinct from reading them in newspapers or magazines or on websites? If practitioners present their book in a narrative style, is their work read as non-fiction or, because it reads *like* a novel, is it read *as* a novel?

Overwhelmingly, the books written about this form of writing are either scholarly analyses or how-to guides. Scholarly works have certainly made important contributions to understanding the history of narrative non-fiction (Tom Connery's *A Sourcebook of American Literary Journalism*, 1992), have charted the extent of its practice (Norman Sims's *True Stories: A Century of Literary Journalism*, 2007), and have theorised its particular aesthetics (John Hartsock's *A History of American Literary Journalism*, 2000), but these works were not written primarily for current or aspiring practitioners. How-to guides—such as Lee Gutkind's *The Art of Creative Nonfiction* (1997), Peter Rubie's *The Elements of Narrative Nonfiction* (2009) or Jack Hart's *Storycraft* (2011)—provide much useful advice, but such advice comes primarily from the individual author's perspective, with little context or discussion of competing views. The key difference with the book you have in your hands is that it combines the two. That is, it is a practical guide to researching and writing narrative non-fiction and it is underpinned by an understanding of the critical debates and practice issues surrounding this form. The former is grounded in my experiences as a practitioner, the latter in academic study including, but not limited to, a doctoral thesis.

These issues are complex, as is evident in the controversies surrounding earlier landmark works of narrative non-fiction (such as Truman Capote's *In Cold Blood*), in the journalistic books of Bob Woodward, in Janet Malcolm's excoriation of Joe McGinniss's *Fatal Vision* in her work *The Journalist and the Murderer* and in the furore sparked by Helen Garner's *The First Stone*. Crucially, these controversies were about questions of ethics as well as aesthetics. Or, to put it another way, a question threaded through this book is: does the ability to write well resolve all the issues inherent in telling true stories?

Some good scholarly attention has been devoted to these controversies. In 1997 literary scholar Daniel Lehman developed a framework for understanding the complex series of relationships that exist in non-fiction: 'writer (outside text) to event; writer (through text) to event; reader (outside text) to event; reader (through text) to event; event arbitrated by text; text arbitrated by event and interpreted by writer and reader' (p. 36). Lehman's work was important to the field; it was also, as the quotation suggests, dense: 'the transaction among writer, reader and subject forces the nonfictional narrative onto a multireferential plane that I would call "implicated"' is another example (1997, p. 4). Accordingly, I have developed what I hope is a more accessible framework for understanding the practice issues in true stories, from the project's conception to its eventual reception. The issues begin in the research phase of a project and are present throughout the writing phase, both in how the writer represents what they found in the research phase and in how they establish a relationship with their reader. The kind of expectations readers themselves have of a piece of narrative non-fiction is an important element in the framework.

Apart from explicating these issues through an accessible framework, I have interviewed leading Australian practitioners—John

Bryson, Helen Garner, Chloe Hooper, Malcolm Knox, David Marr and Margaret Simons. The work of a seventh, Estelle Blackburn, has also been examined, but it was less important to interview her because she has written a book, *The End of Innocence*, about how she went about researching and writing her investigative book *Broken Lives*. These practitioners were chosen for several reasons: because they have produced landmark or controversial works, because they have written both journalism and novels, because they have spent time reflecting on their practice, or for a combination of these reasons. Unless otherwise noted, quotations come from my interviews with them.

I have also drawn on reflections from other practitioners, notably those interviewed by Robert Boynton for his book, *The New New Journalism: Conversations with America's Best Nonfiction Writers on Their Craft*. Boynton is a journalist and journalism academic whose work has been published in magazines such as *Harper's* and *The New Yorker*, and who is director of New York University's magazine journalism program. Published in 2005, *The New New Journalism* includes interviews with nineteen leading practitioners, all of whom have written at least one work of book-length journalism and most of whom have written several. They are Ted Conover, Richard Ben Cramer, Leon Dash, William Finnegan, Jonathan Harr, Alex Kotlowitz, Jon Krakauer, Jane Kramer, William Langewiesche, Adrian Nicole LeBlanc, Michael Lewis, Susan Orlean, Richard Preston, Ron Rosenbaum, Eric Schlosser, Gay Talese, Calvin Trillin, Lawrence Weschler and Lawrence Wright.

Boynton's comprehensive interviews—the book runs to nearly 500 pages—explore a range of topics, from how the writers generate ideas, how they gather material and how they write, to ethical issues, such as how they gain access to the people they write about and the nature of the relationship they form with them. Preceding each interview is an introduction, including critical reception to the writers' works, but Boynton does not offer his own assessments beyond what is implicit in the book's subtitle. Nor does he analyse what his interviewees have told him. Boynton's lengthy introduction to the volume is aimed at locating those he has chosen in the history of American journalism rather than espousing a particular approach to the various issues discussed by the writers. The interviews in *The New New Journalism*, then, offer a rich source of primary material for analysis. Where any of these nineteen writers are quoted in the text, unless otherwise noted, the source is *The New New Journalism*. What I found is that Boynton's interviewees have learnt from the earlier controversies, and they have found workable solutions for many of these thorny practice issues. Their solutions were reached project by project, however, and they have not generalised from their experiences. Nor have they found solutions to all the issues that arise for writers of true stories.

There is value, then, in gathering a broad range of writers' reflections, analysing them and incorporating them in my suggested framework. I have also developed workable solutions to practice issues not considered by others. I have concentrated on those issues I consider the most important or that consistently trouble current and aspiring writers, but space prevents me from dealing with every possible issue that does or could arise. Who knows, for instance, whether the hyperconnectedness we are experiencing through the mass of new communication technologies will in time rewire our brains away from immersive reading or whether it will induce a craving for moments to disconnect and reflect, as William Powers argues for in his thought-provoking 2010 book *Hamlet's Blackberry*. Many of these practice issues arise in whichever medium the true story is published. The difficulties practitioners experience in reconstructing scenes they did not witness are common to newspapers, magazines, books and online media. Some issues, however, are felt more urgently in one medium than another. The problem of maintaining editorial independence while working closely with principal sources over an extended period arises often in book-length projects and rarely in daily journalism. And some issues, I would argue, are distinctive to a particular medium. When readers pick up a newspaper or magazine, they expect to read journalism. When they pick up a book, they overwhelmingly associate a narrative storytelling style with fiction. Hence the need for writers of narrative non-fiction to think more carefully about how they present their work to readers.

This book, then, offers guidance about true stories published in newspapers, magazines and books. Documentary films are true stories told visually; their value as a medium and the issues inherent in their making parallel those in the print media. I will have less to say about them, though, partly because it is outside the scope of this book and partly because there is already a sizeable professional and academic literature about documentary. Long-form true stories told online is an emerging area of writing, but to date much of it originates in newspapers and magazines; there may well be issues particular to the rapidly developing online medium but that too is a field to be explored at another time. This book, then, will discuss newspapers, magazines and, indirectly, online media, but emphasises book-length narrative non-fiction for a couple of reasons; first, because it is a rapidly expanding area and, second, because the issues particular to it have so far received less attention either from practitioners or scholars. I've developed the framework in this book partly from theories about narrative and applied ethics, with the needs of current and aspiring writers in mind. As such, the book is shorn of much of its theoretical root system but anyone wanting to dig into that further can consult my works listed in the bibliography, particularly the doctoral thesis. As I explore the multi-faceted issues around telling true stories I use case studies of various works to illustrate how practitioners have resolved them—or not.

Chapter 2

What makes a true story?

I've never liked the word 'non-fiction'. 'Non-Christian' hardly encompasses all the rich and various traditions of Judaism, Islam, Confucianism, Shinto, Hinduism, and the many other religions of the world, and 'non-fiction' hardly does justice to the many kinds of writing it lumps together ... It defines a major category of human endeavor—encompassing essays, historical narrative, contemporary narrative, autobiography, biography, and reportage—with an empty negative.

Richard Rhodes, *How to Write: Advice and Reflections*

If you ask most people how well the news media served society in the war on Iraq, the most likely answer is not well at all. At best, too many media outlets reverted to stenography in reporting claims by the Bush administration that Saddam Hussein had close links to those responsible for the 11 September 2001 terrorist attacks, and at worst newspapers and television stations in Rupert Murdoch's global media empire became cheerleaders for the American president's plans to topple Hussein's regime. Media scholars have cemented this view, notably David Dadge, who wrote in his 2006 book *The War in Iraq and Why the Media Failed Us* that even those outlets that did question the official reason for going to war 'often reported them in such a way that they gave credence to the Bush administration's view, while downplaying the view of those who disagreed' (p. 2).

What has so far escaped the attention of most scholars is just how well served society has been by those writing longer articles and journalistic books about the war, beginning with Mark Danner, who was commissioned by *The New York Review of Books* to go to Iraq, and who sent back two lengthy despatches headlined 'How Not to Win a War' (September 2003) and 'Delusions in Baghdad' (December 2003) that combined vivid, on-the-ground reporting with historically informed analysis (Danner 2009, pp. 372–91). Danner had been among the minority of journalists questioning the case for going to war, and what he learnt in Baghdad confirmed his scepticism and deepened his fears for the war's disastrous long-term consequences. Some other works contained news that had eluded the daily media, such as Ron Suskind's account in *The One Percent Doctrine* that an al-Qaeda jihadist claimed by the White House to be the organisation's chief of operations on his capture in 2002 turned out to be a mentally ill minor functionary. Abu Zubaydah was subjected to waterboarding and soon began telling his captors of all kinds of invented terrorist plots. So, writes Suskind, 'the United States would torture a mentally disturbed man and then leap, screaming, at every word he uttered' (2006, p. 111).

Thomas Ricks, like Suskind, benefited from lifting his gaze above the daily deadline parapet. Researching the war for his 2006 work *Fiasco*, he was given thousands of pages of government documents, including the classified plan for the invasion. In 2003 the documents would have been deemed too sensitive, but 'two years later, who cares?' he told one interviewer. He was able to write an authoritative—and scathing—account of an invasion that, he writes, was 'launched recklessly, with a flawed plan for war and a worse approach to occupation. Spooked by its own false conclusions about the threat, the Bush administration hurried its diplomacy, short-circuited its war planning, and assembled an agonizingly incompetent occupation' (2006, pp. 3–4).

Beyond disclosing news, though, some authors have substantially enlarged our understanding of the war. The abuse of prisoners at Abu Ghraib by American soldiers provoked a global furore in 2004, and rightly so, but four years later Philip Gourevitch and Errol Morris collaborated on a book and documentary film, both entitled

Standard Operating Procedure, that asked other, equally confronting questions about Abu Ghraib. 'We are all implicated, I'm afraid, because we haven't wanted to see ourselves clearly', Gourevitch told me in an interview. Most found it easier to vilify what the Bush administration characterised as 'seven bad apples' than recognise that worse atrocities were happening regularly as a matter of policy.

'We wanted to react with outrage at what the soldiers had done, but we also like to identify with the lone whistleblower and that, at least partly, was what soldiers like Sabrina Harman had done too. I don't condone what the soldiers did at Abu Ghraib, but given the way the chain of command works, and the explicit praise they were receiving from superior officers for how they were treating the prisoners, where was the space for them to voice any protest against their orders? If you fight terror with terror, how can you tell which is which?' (Ricketson 2008).

There are many other noteworthy works about the war in Iraq; some have won awards (*The Looming Tower: Al-Qaeda and the Road to 9/11* won the Pulitzer Prize for general non-fiction), some have become bestsellers (*The One Percent Doctrine* topped *The New York Times* list) and some have been acclaimed for the quality of their writing (Sebastian Junger's *War* is one among several).

If this brief survey allows us to see the potential scope and influence of this field of writing, it also brings us to a question that needs addressing before going any further: what, exactly, is this field of writing and what should it be called? There is a veritable phalanx of names deployed, but broadly they fall into two groups. The first includes the word journalism, or something like it, as in literary journalism, narrative journalism, long-form journalism, book-length journalism and reportage. The second group includes the word non-fiction, namely literary non-fiction, creative non-fiction, narrative non-fiction and, Capote's invention, the non-fiction novel. In 1973 Tom Wolfe advocated for a 'New Journalism' that he believed was set to not only revolutionise journalism but also dethrone the novel as 'literature's main event'. But even Wolfe recognised that any title containing the word new was destined to be consigned to 'the garbage barge of history'.

This profusion of terms has several implications. The first, obvious one is that none of them has won wide acceptance among either scholars or practitioners, despite considerable debate. The reasons for this include the prickliness of journalists towards notions of literariness; the historical hostility of literary critics towards journalism; a belief that the field stretches beyond news journalism; a frequent conflating of a narrative approach with literary merit; resistance to defining a field in the negative (non-fiction); and vigorously contested philosophical debates about the nature of truth that bear directly on a field in which practices to verify facts and a narrative approach are central (Boynton 2005, pp. xi–xxxii; Forché and Gerard 2001, pp. 1–4; Hartsock 2000, pp. 1–20; Lehman 1997, pp. 1–39; Ricketson 2001b, p. 150).

The second implication of the profusion of terms is that all are groping towards naming a writing practice that is not only about actual people, events and issues, but is also literary or artistic. The criteria critics choose to define a field have ramifications for what is included and what is excluded. Raymond Williams has shown in *Keywords* how since the mid-eighteenth century the term 'literature' has come to mean 'well-written' books that are 'creative' or 'imaginative' writing. But as Andrew Milner asks in *Literature, Culture and Society*, who defines what is well written, and why is creative or imaginative literature regarded as superior to other forms of writing? 'The implicit premise that philosophy, science and history are somehow neither imaginative nor creative is very obviously indefensible' (2005, p. 2). The notion that literature inherently equates to fiction, poetry or drama is also questionable, because there may be factual material in imaginative literature, argues Milner, citing John Milton's sonnet on his blindness that, according to the available biographical information, contains accurate information about the poet's condition and his response to it. From late in the nineteenth century, however, influential literary figures began exulting 'imaginative literature' in prose—by which was meant fiction—as the most important form of writing and ignored or devalued other forms of prose, according to John Hartsock in *A History of American Literary Journalism*.

Whether this area of writing practice is or can be art or literature, however that may be defined, is an important question, but not one central to this book. When literary or artistic criteria are used to define an area of writing, however, people are pushed into certain choices about what to read or study. I resist such a push, and not simply because I might want to argue with various critics' assessment of the literary or artistic qualities of various pieces of journalistic writing, but more importantly because such arguments have the effect of obscuring three key issues: first, the extent to which this field of writing is practised at book length today; second, the ethical issues that arise in this area; and third, the conflating of a narrative approach with notions of literary merit. Taking these issues one by one, scholars have understated the extent to which such journalism is practised at book length. Journalism written in a narrative style can certainly be found in newspapers in the English-speaking world, but it is more likely to be found in magazines and, it appears, most likely to be found in books. I say appears because without universal agreement as to what constitutes this field, and because what I would call book-length journalism is subsumed into the broad publishing category of non-fiction, it cannot be enumerated exactly.

An early study of the New Journalism noted that much of it was published in book form (Murphy 1974, pp. 17, 26). Edd Applegate drew on seventeen anthologies and scholarly works to compile, in 1996, *Literary Journalism: A Biographical Dictionary of Writers and Editors*, which included journalists and editors working in newspapers, magazines and books. Even so, of the 172 people listed, 112, or about two-thirds, had written at least one work of book-length journalism. In 2007, the Nieman Foundation collated contributions from journalists and editors reflecting on their practice at its annual Narrative Journalism conference. Of the fifty-three contributors in this collection, also called *Telling True Stories*, thirty-six had written at least one work of book-length journalism; many had written several. In 2009, Sarah Statz Cords compiled a readers' guide to investigative non-fiction entitled *The Inside Scoop* that contains more than 500 titles, most of them published in the United States since 2000. These figures show the practice of book-length journalism is more widespread than has been recognised.

The second issue—that ethical concerns are inherent in the finding and telling of true stories—is almost self-evident, but needs to be stated explicitly because of the third issue, which is the conflating of a narrative approach with literary merit. I would not argue that scholars in the literary non-fiction, literary journalism and creative non-fiction fields have ignored ethical issues, but that they examine them within the context of work that they argue is literary or artistic (Weber 1980, pp. 43–55; eds Sims & Kramer 1995, pp. 3–34; Cheney 1991, pp. 217–32; ed. Gutkind 2005, p. xix–xxxiii). This has led most of them to blur the question of whether the ethical issues inherent in representing people and events in a narrative style of writing are magnified or diminished by the practitioner's literary or artistic skills, or whether it is in the initial taking of a narrative approach that the ethical issues are triggered. This issue is central to this book.

It plays out in the differing critical receptions to the work of Bob Woodward, a newspaper reporter who has become a prolific practitioner of narrative non-fiction, and Truman Capote, a novelist who wrote a 'nonfiction novel', as is discussed in detail in Chapters 3 and 4. Woodward's work has not been included in any of the seven major anthologies of what is termed either literary journalism (Sims 1984; Sims & Kramer 1995; Kerrane & Yagoda 1997; Chance & McKeen 2001) or creative non-fiction (Talese & Lounsberry 1996; Gutkind 2005; Williford and Martone 2007). Woodward's newspaper reports, co-written with Carl Bernstein, on the implications of the break-in at the Watergate Hotel have, however, won a place in two anthologies of investigative or muckraking journalism: *Muckraking! The Journalism That Changed America* and *Shaking the Foundations*. The notion that ethical issues would be present in a work of narrative non-fiction acclaimed by many literary critics—Capote's *In Cold Blood*—but not in the work of Woodward, whose books are excluded from literary journalism anthologies, is, plainly, nonsense.

Continuing debate about what to call this field of writing does seem to exemplify political scientist Wallace Sayre's maxim, 'The politics of the university are so intense because the stakes are so low', but according to Hartsock, absence of any unity about the name of the field and its boundaries has left it without a natural home or a champion within the academy. Universities are susceptible to the creation of moated fiefdoms, but readily identifiable departments or centres have access to institutional funding and recognition—to build a field, or to block it. As members of interpretive communities, scholars have a role to play in finding and disseminating new knowledge.

What, then, to call the field? Roadblocks appear everywhere. 'Journalism' certainly describes a sizeable chunk of it, but the word has its roots in the day's news, and a good number of practitioners cast their nets wider both in what they write about and how. The same applies to 'reportage', which has the added problem of sounding pretentious (especially by those placing emphasis on the third syllable). 'Narrative' is relatively well understood, but within narrative studies the word carries multiple, carefully delineated meanings. For narratologists—a ghastly word, I know, but that is what they call themselves, which means they only have themselves to blame—a hard news article is one kind of narrative, a feature article another, which is not particularly helpful here. Still, I like the word narrative as it says storytelling has a key role to play. It also makes no judgement about the literary or artistic worth of the work. Like many others, I resist 'non-fiction' on the ground that it is better to say what something is than what it isn't. 'Non-fiction' also fairly drips dullness, but the word is widely used and instantly recognisable, which is more than you can say for long-form or book-length journalism. For this reason I can see why some use 'non-fiction' and attach 'creative' to it as a way of signposting that reading such work won't feel like eating a bowl of dry bran. Like Milner, I believe creativity is not confined to poetry, drama or fiction, but the word connotes invention or even fiction, which is an issue that is both central and controversial in this field, as is discussed in Chapter 5. The same problem applies even more to 'non-fiction novel', which, as critic Sven Birkerts tartly remarked, is an oxymoronic term and a moronic idea. 'Literary' invites the question: says who? Terms like 'literary non-fiction' sound pretentious and boring; that is, the exact opposite of the writing the terms seek to describe, as Ira Glass remarks in his introduction to an anthology he edited, *The New Kings of Nonfiction*. 'Calling a piece of writing "literary nonfiction" is like daring you to read it' (2007, p. 12).

For these reasons I have arrived at 'true stories'. I acknowledge that if 'creative' carries many meanings and is open to misinterpretation so does 'true', but the word does also make clear that it is actual people, events and issues that are being written about. 'Stories' signals that the account of these actual people, events and issues will have been made into a story and one that promises to engage the reader fully. There is an additional, important benefit with the term: whenever I talk to everyday readers, 'true stories' is the one they best understand. The rest induce eyes either to roll or glaze over. I will also refer to narrative non-fiction as it, too, encompasses the field, albeit less pithily.

Whichever term is chosen, it inevitably excludes as well as includes. It suggests a clear distinction exists between journalism written for newspapers; journalism written for magazines; and journalism, or other forms of non-fiction, that is published in books. There are differences but there are also similarities; it is preferable, in my view, to see journalism practised in the three print forms existing along a continuum. That enables us to see there are also points on the continuum at which book-length journalism intersects with other kinds of books that, like journalism, are about actual people and events, and points at which it diverges too. Wolfe may have predicted any term containing the word 'new' would end up gathering dust, but the New Journalism remains important in any discussion of this field, not least because, in becoming its chief advocate and a leading practitioner, Wolfe began talking about the inner workings of journalism in ways rarely seen before. In his famous essay entitled 'The New Journalism', Wolfe outlined four writing devices normally associated with fiction: constructing the article or book as a series of scenes; using dialogue rather than quotations from interviewees; narrating from various points of view, whether the journalist or the people being written about, and even as an interior monologue; and recording status details.

The New Journalism was not a movement in any formal sense. It is generally dated from the early 1960s, with Gay Talese's remarkably intimate profile of former heavyweight champion Joe Louis, to the late 1970s, when controversies over the extent of fictionalising clouded Wolfe's assertion that the form's distinguishing virtue was that '*all this happened*'. The idea of taking a narrative approach to writing about actual people and events was never as new as Wolfe liked to claim, but for a variety of reasons there was a flowering of work in the 1960s that was far livelier to read than earlier journalism, that challenged the orthodoxies of objective journalism and upended the narrow range of topics and people considered newsworthy. Works by its leading figures—including Wolfe, Joan Didion, Norman Mailer and Hunter S. Thompson—are still read today. It also sparked controversies about whether it was fact or fiction, whether it was acceptable to create composites or whether it was possible to report seemingly from inside someone's skull that contributed to the tainting of the term 'New Journalism'.

That is one reason why other terms have been pushed forward since. Another is that, even though the term 'New Journalism' faded from view, the writing of true stories did not. At the same time, the sharp debates surrounding the New Journalism prompted work by scholars and practitioners to clarify the nature and boundaries of this area of writing; this book aims to build on that work (ed. Sims 1984, pp. 3–25; ed. Connery 1992, pp. 3–37; Sims & Kramer 'Breakable Rules for Literary Journalists' 1995, pp. 21–34; eds Talese & Lounsberry *Writing Creative Nonfiction: The Literature of Reality* 1996, pp. 29–31; Boynton 2005, pp. xi–xxxiv; eds Keeble & Tulloch 2012, pp. 1–19). Because true stories straddle various media forms as well as book publishing, it is useful to outline the six main elements and compare them between newspapers, magazines and books.

The first, core element of book-length journalism is that it is about actual events and people living in the world, and concerns the issues of the day; given that a book takes longer to research and write than a newspaper report, journalists try to choose events or people or issues that merit such an investment of time and energy. Most articles published in newspapers are quickly forgotten because of their sheer number; because newspapers are 'constantly revisiting the familiar', as Australian practitioner David Marr puts it; and because news, as media historian Mitchell Stephens writes, is about 'what is on society's mind', and that changes continually. A former editor of *The Age* newspaper, Graham Perkin, once said that only news reports that have their roots in the past and a stake in the future have any lasting impact. This idea also applies to book-length journalism. There are books that are produced to deadlines almost as tight as those for newspapers and magazines. Known in the publishing industry as 'quickies', these books are produced to capitalise on urgent, widespread public interest, such as the trial of Bradley John Murdoch in 2005 in central Australia for the murder of English backpacker Peter Falconio. One book was published within forty-eight hours of the announcement of the jury's decision to find Murdoch guilty. As speed of publication is the key to a successful quickie, it gives away the biggest single advantage a work of book-length journalism has over newspaper and magazine work—time.

The second element of book-length journalism is extensive research. Newspaper journalists are trained, or become experienced, in gathering information quickly and unearthing information that people and institutions may not want revealed. With more time they are able to uncover substantially more information that may itself make news to be reported by the news media. Woodward, an associate editor of *The Washington Post*, is the best-known and most consistent exponent of this approach. Time spent also enables journalists to understand the context in which the subject of the book occurs. Some journalists also engage in 'saturation reporting', to use the term coined by Wolfe in 1970 (Murphy 1974, p. 10), where they spend long periods of time observing, interviewing and simply being around those they are writing about in the belief this will yield rich, below-the-surface material usually unavailable to journalists bound by daily deadlines. It is relatively common for journalists working on book-length projects to research a topic as intensively as a PhD student, according to Norman Sims, an editor of two anthologies of literary journalism and a scholarly book about the topic.

The third element of 'true stories' is taking a narrative approach. Scholars of narrative may find narrative in a wide range of writing, but in the field of journalism a distinction is drawn between articles written in an expository or hard news report form and those written to read as if they were a novel, which can be described as narrative journalism. It is possible to write a work of book-length journalism in expository form, but the majority of them are written predominantly in a narrative style, because the various devices outlined in Wolfe's essay enable practitioners to more fully engage their readers.

The fourth element of book-length journalism is the range of authorial voices, which is much broader than that allowed to daily news reporters who are tethered to the institutional voice of their newspaper. As the sole author of a work of book-length journalism, the journalist can choose their style and tone of voice. Some choose to remain in the background of their books while others foreground their presence. A journalist's choice of voice may differ from book to book, but it is usually driven by their stance on the philosophical question of whether it is possible to represent reality in their work or whether, as Michael Schudson writes, while they believe 'The world may be "out there," as so many of us commonsensically believe', no individual and no instrument apprehends it directly. 'We turn nature to culture as we talk and write and narrate it' (1995, p. 52).

The fifth element is exploring the underlying meaning of an event or issue. For journalists, the aim of spending more time on a project is to plumb its depths and to report and analyse it from a range of perspectives. The aim is to develop an overview of the issue that may include a coherent argument about it; though because journalists seek to attract the broadest possible audience, they try to find a balance between making an argument that is intellectually challenging and writing in a narrative style that engages readers emotionally as well as intellectually. As Margaret Simons says: 'You have more room and space for ambiguity and ambivalence in a book. You don't have to serve it all tied up with a pussy bow. Or, to put it another way, it has to have a theme, or why are you writing a book rather than another feature story?'

The sixth and final element of book-length journalism is its impact. As these works focus on events, people and issues that stand out from the daily crush of news coverage, and as more time and energy have been devoted to the research and writing, it is likely to have a greater impact on readers, whether they are the subject of the book or members of the general public. If the book concerns a topic of public debate (such as, say, asylum seekers or climate change) it may influence policy-makers and others in positions of authority.

Comparing the six elements of book-length journalism with newspaper and magazine journalism illuminates how the three areas of print media operate along a continuum. The subject matter of the three is the same, as are the research methods. Journalists gather material through three main methods: documents (whether in print or online), interviews and firsthand observation. The point of difference comes from the time given to researching a book, which means the journalist will be able to get documents by means such as the *Freedom of Information Act 1982* (Cwlth), whose long lead times make requests (and contesting appeals in court) impractical or off-putting for many, but by no means all, daily print journalists. The vast amount of government, commercial and personal information that is publicly available online has made it easy to examine, say, legal judgments the moment they are delivered without needing to be in court, which makes the work of newspaper journalists easier. Those working on books take the time to read full reports rather than executive summaries and to analyse them against other documents. Journalists working on books tend to do more interviews face to face rather than by telephone or email, and do longer interviews. They also have more time to observe events and people at first hand than is available to most magazine and, especially, newspaper journalists, who today spend most of their working day tethered to a computer and a mobile phone.

Where the majority of works of book-length journalism are written in a narrative style, the majority of articles published in newspapers are in expository form. Hard news reports are in expository form; feature articles can be written in a combination of expository and narrative style. It is common for features to begin with a description of a scene relevant to the article, and equally common for them to revert to exposition for the bulk of the article. When a newspaper journalist is reconstructing a major news event they may choose to present the feature as a chronological narrative. The use of a narrative approach is more common in magazines than newspapers. The average news report runs to five hundred words and few run longer than eight hundred words. Newspaper feature articles begin at around a thousand words and rarely run more than two thousand five hundred words. Magazine features range between two and ten thousand words, occasionally longer. It is pieces of this kind that find their way to sites like www.longform.org or www.byliner.com, where they are shared with readers beyond their home publication. In Australia, the *Quarterly Essay* series gives its contributors around 25,000 words to look into a topical issue. In English-speaking countries, publishing houses have set up imprints for short, topical books, some of which are published in print while others are available for the growing market of those reading on tablets and other e-readers.

Newspaper and magazine journalists are yoked to a house style. The conventions of the news report have changed little since it emerged as a journalistic form in the mid-nineteenth century, which testifies to its resilience as a vehicle for conveying information quickly and clearly. What distinguishes the work of one journalist's news report from another is less the tone of voice or use of language than the newsworthiness of the information. By putting information in pride of place, though, news reports exclude or minimise emotion, context and analysis. As Mitchell Stephens puts it: 'When words are herded into any rigid format—from news ballad to two-minute videotape report—their ability to re-create events in their fullness may suffer' (1988, p. 242). There is some evidence that distinctions between various news forms are becoming more fluid. Those writing features are given some, but not much, latitude to write in a voice other than that stipulated for hard news reports. It is primarily among columnists that an individual voice is valued, and this applies less to expert than to opinion columnists and to personal columnists. An example of the former is Andrew Bolt of the *Herald Sun*, who has a strong following and is perhaps the best known—and certainly the most controversial—columnist in Australia. An example of the latter is Sandra Tsing Loh, whose idiosyncratic columns for *Buzz* magazine in Los Angeles were gathered together in 1996 in the drolly-titled *Depth Takes a Holiday*.

Daily journalism puts greater store in astonishing readers than in leading them to understanding (Schudson 2005). Newspaper journalists work under acute deadline pressure, especially in the twenty-first century, when they may also be filing and updating online reports as well as producing audio and video reports; magazine journalists work under marginally less deadline pressure even though they, too, may make video pieces or write blogs. Where a newspaper or magazine journalist can be satisfied with making sharp observations, they rarely have time to explore the underlying meanings of an event or issue. A work of book-length journalism needs to be grounded in an overarching argument or a compelling narrative style, or a blend of the two. Finally, newspapers, magazines and books can all have an impact. At the micro level, most newspaper or magazine articles do not have the same impact on a reader as a book. At the macro level, a newspaper can, over a period of time, use its institutional weight to campaign on an issue and make an impact on the body politic in a way that generally is beyond the reach of individual journalists who write books.

In drawing the distinctions between journalism in the three print forms, it can be seen that magazines provide a bridge between the two other forms. They are periodic publications but less driven than newspapers by the news agenda of the day; they provide more space and time than newspapers for journalists who in turn need to develop their skills in narrative in order to keep readers' attention for the duration of a longer article. In numerous cases, works of book-length journalism have been either reprinted from magazines or have begun life as magazine articles and then been expanded to book length. A well-known example of the former is Lillian Ross's *Picture* and of the latter is Thompson's *Hell's Angels*. Once journalism becomes part of the book publishing industry, however, it is subsumed into non-fiction, a category that unhelpfully is defined by what it is not and which contains a vast range of genres that includes almost everything apart from fiction, drama or poetry.

In bookshops, non-fiction books may be shelved in a category entitled non-fiction, but more often they are spread across numerous categories, some of which, like cooking and gardening, do not normally contain works of book-length journalism. Other non-fiction categories (such as politics, philosophy, psychology, true crime, science, the environment, sociology, sport, travel, history and biography) commonly house works of book-length journalism (Cords 2006). These categories will also contain the work of other authors: perhaps a novelist writing, say, a travel book; a freelance author; or, more often, a specialist in the field, usually an academic. In libraries, non-fiction books are usually catalogued according to their subject matter, whereas fiction is catalogued according to author, which hinders the likelihood of readers becoming aware of particular writers of non-fiction. When William Howarth, a literary academic, decided to edit a collection of long-time *New Yorker* staff writer John McPhee's articles he found his work scattered throughout his university's libraries and wondered why. In his assessment, McPhee's books had 'stretched the artistic dimensions of reportage' and qualified as 'literature'. In 1999 McPhee won the Pulitzer Prize for a general non-fiction book for *Annals of the Former World*. Nor are publishers always clear about how to describe what they are offering. Some editions of George Orwell's *The Road to Wigan Pier* have been categorised as fiction, while Bernard Hare's 2006 work *Urban Grimshaw and the Shed Crew* is listed as fiction when it is a true story, according to journalism scholar Jenny McKay (eds Bak & Reynolds 2011, p. 55).

Moving from comparing the proposed six elements of book-length journalism with newspaper and magazine journalism to comparing them with various non-fiction genres, the first point is that the subject matter may be the same, as it concerns actual events and people, but where the journalist is interested in the issues of the day, an historian is interested in the past. Traditionally, biographies have been about people already dead, but it is relatively common for biographies of living people to be published, and many of these biographers are journalists. Academics are trained to study issues dispassionately and in depth, which intersects with the book-length journalist's aim to explore the complexity of an issue, but their background also means the majority of academics are less attuned to events and issues of the day and to making a timely contribution to public debate. Journalistic training usually means that even with more time to work on a book project, a journalist is driven by the impulse to write something sooner rather than later, and for a broad rather than a specialist audience.

Most authors of non-fiction books do extensive research. There is some overlap with the research methods used by journalists and some points of difference. Almost all researchers draw on documents, and some interview those they are writing about and some observe events and people firsthand. Historians are skilled at finding and interpreting primary documents, sociologists are skilled at framing questionnaires and interviewing large numbers of people and anthropologists are skilled at gaining access to groups of people they want to study and observing them firsthand for long periods of time. Most academic or freelance authors are less experienced than journalists in persuading people who do not want to be interviewed to be interviewed, and in persuading them to reveal material that may not be in their best interests. Stephen Oates, an American academic historian, has told how difficult he found it to behave like an investigative journalist while researching a biography of Martin Luther King Jr. 'Nothing in graduate school had ever prepared me for this. I was terrible at it. I hated to intrude on other people's privacy, to ask them to remember things that could be painful' (Weinberg 1992a, p. 2).

In trade, as distinct from academic publishing, it is common for non-fiction books to be written in a narrative style, to improve the likelihood of engaging the reader and of increasing sales. Novelists who write non-fiction are considered to be well placed because they will already have highly developed writing and narrative skills. Truman Capote is an obvious example, but in English-speaking countries there are numerous other novelists who have written book-length journalism, including Didion, Orwell and Helen Garner. Academic authors are accustomed to writing for a specialist rather than a general audience, which is also why the majority of them are less conversant with the wide range of possible narrative approaches available to authors of non-fiction. Novelists, by comparison, are used to this. Academic authors are trained to explore an issue in depth, to analyse it from a range of perspectives and to mount a coherent argument set within a theoretical framework. A novelist writing a non-fiction book may or may not be equipped to mount a coherent argument, but will probably be alive to the underlying meanings in an issue or event. Finally, the novelist's writing ability, and perhaps their reputation, will in all likelihood ensure their non-fiction book makes an impact on readers, though they may be less aware than a journalist of the possibility of their book influencing policy-makers and others in positions of authority. Most academic authors are interested in the broad political and social impact of their work.

Journalism written for newspapers and magazines sits in the context of a well-established practice that is widely known in the community and has attracted a sizeable body of scholarship. The same can be said of the various genres of non-fiction books already listed, especially those such as history, politics and sociology that are also recognised academic disciplines. A journalist may write a book that is described as history or biography or sociology, or any of the large number of genres within non-fiction, and be described by their publisher as an historian or biographer or sociologist. Alternatively, the journalist may conceive of, research and write as a journalist and produce a work of book-length journalism. For both projects, the journalist uses the same methods to gather their material, the same writing style and has the same aim of reaching the broadest possible audience. What, then, distinguishes the two? There is no obvious answer. It depends on how the publisher markets the book, where the bookseller displays it, how a librarian categorises it, how the audience reads it and, finally, whether the author identifies themself as a journalist or as a practitioner of a particular non-fiction genre. For example, in Australia, Les Carlyon, an experienced journalist and former editor of two daily newspapers, has written two comprehensive historical works—*Gallipoli* in 2001 and *The Great War* in 2006—but is he to be seen as a journalist writing book-length journalism, an historian or a 'popular', as distinct from academic, historian? In 2007 the latter book was both a co-winner of the Prime Minister's history prize and a finalist in the best non-fiction book award made by the Australian journalists' union, the Media Entertainment and Arts Alliance. Alternatively, a writer normally identified as a novelist, such as Garner, may use the journalistic methods just described to produce a work of book-length journalism, but may well describe their work with another term. Garner called *The First Stone* 'reportage' in an author's note, but told me she was comfortable with the term book-length journalism.

By the criteria developed for this book, Carlyon's books are history and Garner's *The First Stone* is book-length journalism, as Carlyon writes about events that took place more than eighty years beforehand while *The First Stone* concerns contemporary events. Interviewing participants was not available to Carlyon, nor could he observe at first hand the events he was writing about, though he did revisit the battlefields. Book-length journalism concerns contemporary events, but the definition allows more flexibility than in daily journalism, which predominantly reports what happened that day or the one before. Similarly, book-length journalism deals mostly with people still alive but incorporates the recently dead; practitioners writing about crime could scarcely survive without that qualification.

Biographies of living people can be seen as book-length journalism if the practitioner uses journalistic research methods and writes in a narrative style for a broad audience. Such biographers encounter many of the issues discussed in this book, as I experienced writing about Paul Jennings, and have discussed elsewhere (2000b). History, biography, sociology and numerous other genres within non-fiction are established among publishers, booksellers, reviewers and readers; book-length journalism is not. The term is not in common use perhaps because it describes an activity that comprises only part of journalism in the print media and only part of non-fiction in publishing. Nor are the terms listed earlier well known beyond the academy, though at least the journal *Creative Nonfiction* can be found in some bookshops. As mentioned above, 'true stories' is a well-known term, though its association with films has tainted it. Hollywood studios may say a film is based on a true story, but it might be more accurate to say, paraphrasing Groucho Marx's crack about Chico and Harpo: 'Any resemblance between these two and living persons is purely coincidental'. Some films, such as Steven Spielberg's 2005 *Munich*, even say in the credits: 'Inspired by real events'. Well, what isn't?

Books hold a different place in the cultural landscape to films, and to newspapers and magazines, which affects the status of the journalist and the expectations readers have of the different media forms. The relationship between journalists and newspapers and magazines is that of employee and employer. The masthead is more important than the individual journalist. The editorial identity of a newspaper or magazine, or a broadcast media outlet for that matter, is undeniably moulded by individual journalists, but it is made up of the sum efforts of many individuals over decades, even centuries. As Al Pacino, playing television producer Lowell Bergman in the film *The Insider*, comments when contemplating leaving journalism over a thwarted interview with a tobacco company whistleblower: 'I'm Lowell Bergman, I'm from *60 Minutes*. You know, you take the *60 Minutes* out of that sentence and nobody returns your phone calls.' Newspapers and magazines are, to a greater or lesser extent, institutions. Readers develop a relationship over time with the institution even though they may grow fond of, or dislike, individual journalists' writings. The relationship between a journalist and a publisher is not one of employee–employer, though it is a commercial relationship. The journalist, or journalists in the case of teams such as Woodward and Bernstein, is responsible for the entire content in a book, compared to single newspaper or magazine articles. Most readers understand that newspapers and magazines are produced to unyielding deadlines, leading inevitably to at least some errors; they generally expect greater accuracy from a book that has taken at least a year, and often more, to produce.

The value of true stories derives from its constituent elements outlined above. To be specific: the immediacy and urgency of the practitioner's probing of events, issues and people that affect society; the fresh information and insights yielded by in-depth research that may influence public debate; the opportunity for the reader to be shown something about the world and its people that they know little about; the level of engagement for the reader offered by a book written in a narrative style; and the pleasure for the reader if the practitioner writes in a distinctive or memorable style. Of the numerous works of narrative non-fiction available, most exemplify many or all of these qualities.

To provide some examples, Barbara Ehrenreich, in *Nickel and Dimed: On (Not) Getting By in America*, had the idea in 1998 of testing American President Bill Clinton's belief that people could survive earning US$7 an hour. She took a succession of low-paid jobs in diners, at Walmart and as a house cleaner, which showed her fierce commitment to investigating policy arguments about poverty through on-the-ground reporting that echoed Orwell's project half a century earlier in *The Road to Wigan Pier*. Published in 2001, her book was studded with footnotes, as might be expected from a long-standing social critic and author, but her approach to the subject on this occasion was determinedly journalistic, yielding a book that was by turns gritty, personal, informative, trenchant and penetrating. She found that many people earning low wages needed to take a second job just to pay basic bills, which added further stress to their lives and those of their families. She concluded that affluent people such as herself should not so much feel guilt about the level of poverty but shame: 'Shame at our *own* dependency, in this case, on the under-paid labor of others' (2001, p. 221).

Narrative non-fiction that yields newsworthy information, such as Woodward's books routinely do, clearly carries the value that accrues to news, but it is higher-grade ore, as it owes its existence to the journalist's ability to unearth it as distinct from the simpler, and more common, journalistic activity of reporting an event that has happened or a media conference or release of an official report. It is also important to note that the act of drawing a newsworthy item from a full-length book can be fraught, as it (necessarily) reduces the material to the form of the daily news report. Chris Masters's *Jonestown*, for instance, which the Walkley Awards's judges said balanced a 'rigorous study of the role and pervasive influence of radio talkback on government and policy makers—and the potential for media corruption—with a richly detailed and human picture' was reduced to a news report and ensuing controversy about Alan Jones's sexuality. The gap here between the practice of daily and book-length journalism highlights one of the values of the latter: setting news-worthy events in their context. One of Hersey's several achievements in *Hiroshima* was to be able to provide a more accurate number of dead (100,000) and injured (as many again) than the United States government had released, and to confirm the cause of death of many victims—radiation sickness (Lifton & Mitchell 1995, pp. 53–55, 88; Yagoda 2000, p. 192). Wilfred Burchett, an Australian, was the first western journalist to assert this, describing what he saw as 'the atomic plague' in his exclusive report for *The Daily Express* in London in September 1945, but the deputy head of the Manhattan Project, Brigadier General Thomas Farrell, had strongly denied Burchett's report at a press conference and accused him of falling victim to Japanese propaganda. When Hersey's *Hiroshima* was printed in book-form by Penguin in November 1946, it was banned in Japan for two years by the American Occupational Authority under the command of General Douglas MacArthur (Sanders 1990, pp. 19–20).

Newsworthy disclosures in a book-length true story can make a substantial impact, which mirrors the kind of impact that is the aim of investigative journalism, and which sits within the news media's role as a watchdog on institutions and people in positions of power in society. An early, famous example is Ida Tarbell's two-volume book entitled *A History of the Standard Oil Company* that was published in 1904, just after it had run in nineteen monthly parts in *McClure's* magazine. Her articles and book painstakingly documented the extent to which the company, co-founded by John D. Rockefeller Sr, had monopolised the oil industry through both enterprising business skills and ruthless, even illegal, activities. Tarbell's work cut through the secrecy surrounding Standard Oil and laid bare its convoluted structure in clear language that prodded readers to outrage and made Rockefeller one of the most hated figures in the country, according to his biographer, Ron Chernow (*Titan* 1998, pp. 425–65). The then United States President, Theodore Roosevelt, had been working to break up the anti-competitive behaviour of trusts in American business, and Tarbell's work not only exposed Standard Oil, but also built a broad base of support for action. In 1906 his government filed an anti-trust suit against Standard Oil that led to a Supreme Court order to dissolve the company. In a dual biography of Rockefeller and Tarbell, *Taking on the Trust*, Steve Weinberg argues Tarbell's 800-page book is perhaps 'the greatest work of investigative journalism ever written', while another Rockefeller biographer, David Freeman Hawke, writes that it was one of very few books to change the course of history (Weinberg 2008, p. xii).

Where the work of Tarbell underlines the value to society of true stories, it is more common for works to contain information that in all likelihood will be new to readers but not necessarily newsworthy; that is, the information fulfils a common newsroom definition of news, namely, 'tell me something I don't know', but either does not have the hard edge necessary for a newspaper report or is not reducible to the inverted pyramid formula. The ability of practitioners to unearth sizeable amounts of relevant, interesting information is easily overlooked in true stories, where information is presented without a tag signalling its newness as is implicit in a daily newspaper report. Most book-length true stories contain much information new to readers unless they are already specialists in the field. Some of the new information stems from the practitioner's witnessing of events that the reader probably will not have seen for themselves, especially if the event took place overseas or is outside the reader's range of experience. In *Stasiland*, Anna Funder reveals what life was like for ordinary East Germans after the collapse in 1989 of the Berlin Wall. East Germany had been a closed society ruled by its secret police, the Stasi. She reports, for instance, that where in Hitler's Third Reich it was estimated there was one Gestapo agent for every 2000 citizens and in Stalin's Soviet Union a KGB agent for every 5830 people, in East Germany there was one Stasi officer or informant for every sixty-three people. Surveillance was not only widespread, but creepily invasive, she writes, as the Stasi had developed a 'quasi-scientific' method of 'smell sampling' in the belief that surreptitiously taking samples of citizens' clothes, often their underwear, would help them find criminals.

Many readers value true stories that help them make sense of newsworthy events. When Woodward and Bernstein published *All the President's Men*, among the hundreds of letters they received from readers were scores thanking them for explaining what had been a confusing, hotly contested issue that played out incrementally over months (Shepard 2007, p. 95). Much more common today than in 1974 when *All the President's Men* was published are the media events that permeate every corner of the public sphere for a short period then disappear from view. Sometimes it can take years for all the relevant information about these events to become public and for their meaning to become clearer. For instance, Dave Cullen was one of many journalists who rushed to Columbine High School on 20 April 1999 where two students, Eric Harris and Dylan Klebold, killed twelve of their schoolmates and one teacher before committing suicide. Books about mass shootings are common in the United States (at least partly because mass shootings are common); what distinguishes Cullen's *Columbine* is that he spent almost a decade researching and writing it, which means he can dispel many myths that still cling to the event, and he makes good use of the thousands of pages of official documents that have been released gradually over the years after court orders, and this helped his quest to answer the question of why Harris and Klebold committed the crime.

Cullen has provided readers with solid means to check the book's veracity: twenty-five pages of endnotes, a fifteen-page bibliography and a thoughtful note on sources at the front of the text to tell readers how he is able to present the two killers' thoughts and feelings—he drew on the extensive journals and videos they made. He has also made freely available on his website (www.davecullen.com) copies of or links to thousands of pages of documents and pictures gathered in official investigations, including lengthy excerpts from the killers' journals and photographs of them and the crime scene. In the context of a mass shooting, drawing on such personal material is volatile; some might think that collecting and cataloguing such a comprehensive archive of primary source material is overly invasive, but Cullen provides extensive material on his website about the need to identify depression among teenagers, which he calls the lost issue of the Columbine shootings. He also exercises care by not reproducing on his site photos of the two killers' dead bodies. 'They were never officially released, but leaked. They are graphic and horrific. You can easily google them but I won't post them here' (http://columbine-online.com).

Columbine calmly demolishes the main myths of the shootings: that they were committed by the so-called Trench Coat Mafia who were taking revenge after being bullied by the school's 'jocks'. Harris and Klebold wore duster coats but were only loosely aligned with those dubbed the Trench Coat Mafia. More important, they were not bullied and were not loners. The pair had a plan to set a bomb in the school cafeteria and detonate it when students were gathered there. Their goal was to kill more people than Timothy McVeigh had in Oklahoma four years before. There were other myths, but you get the picture; a book-length work of narrative non-fiction enables practitioners to counter the errors that are an inevitable part of daily news media coverage. Equally if not more important, *Columbine* shows the value of persistent digging in its handling of the story of one of the victims, Cassie Bernall. A student who survived the shootings, Craig Scott, told how he had heard one girl profess her faith in God before being shot dead and his story reached the news media a few days later after it first spread among evangelical Christians.

Amid the national outpouring of grief for all the victims, Bernall, an evangelical Christian, was singled out for martyrdom, with religious scholars predicting she could become the first officially designated Protestant martyr since the sixteenth century, and her pastor, George Kirsten, telling his congregation of a vision he had had of seeing Cassie and Jesus hand in hand after they had just been married. 'And Cassie kind of winked over at me, like, "I'd like to talk, but I'm so much in love". Her greatest prayer was to find the right guy. Don't you think she did?' The problem was that the story was not true. Two female students who had witnessed Cassie's death had told police she had not said a word before being shot, but their statements were not released at the time. Scott had not made up his account, but it may well have been another female student, Valeen Schnurr, he heard, and somewhere along the line the story was tied to Bernall. Cullen reconstructed Schnurr's experience from her police statement, eyewitnesses and his interview with Schnurr and her mother. Shot and injured by Klebold, Schnurr dropped to her knees:

'Oh my God, oh my God, don't let me die,' she prayed. Dylan turned around. This was too rich. 'God? Do you believe in God?' She wavered. Maybe she should keep her mouth shut. No. She would rather say it. 'Yes. I believe in God'. 'Why?' 'Because I believe. And my parents brought me up that way.' Dylan reloaded, but something distracted him.

He walked off. Val crawled for shelter (2009, pp. 224–5).

Schnurr's story reached the news media after Bernall's. Instead of being accepted as another faith-affirming story, it was labelled a copycat. 'The bigger Cassie's fame grew, the more Val was rejected', writes Cullen. Schnurr and her two fellow students were placed in an invidious position: out of respect for Cassie's grieving parents, they did not want to say the story was wrong but they were also disturbed that myths rather than facts were circulating, especially about an event that they too had been part of. Eventually, investigating police intervened when Cassie's mother was about to publish a memoir repeating the error. Misty Bernall told them the martyr story was not central to her book and agreed to put in a disclaimer opposite the table of contents referring to 'varying recollections' that meant 'the exact details of Cassie's death ... may never be known'. The evidence against martyrdom was overwhelming, Cullen writes, but those at Cassie's church said they would stay with the martyr story regardless. And they did; websites were set up defending the story while others repeated it without even mentioning that it had been debunked. Misty Bernall's memoir went on to sell more than a million copies, which reinforces the observation that if the strength of faith is its power to believe in the absence of evidence, that is also its weakness. This qualifies but does not disqualify *Columbine* as a shining example of the virtue of long-term digging for information and insight.

More visibly, readers value works that lead them to parts of the world of which they have little experience or knowledge. In 1966 Hunter S. Thompson drove readers into a subculture on the fringe of American society by writing about a notorious motorcycle gang for his book *Hell's Angels*. Before that, Thompson had written a magazine article for *The Nation* that was limited to a critique of the mainstream news media's alarmist and ill-informed coverage of the gang's activities. The article is sharp but contains little of the material he gathered while riding with the gang on and off for about a year. Bill Buford, when editing the English literary magazine *Granta*, reprised and extended Thompson by running with groups of soccer fans in *Among the Thugs*. In a less determinedly macho vein, John Lahr, drama critic for *The New Yorker*, takes readers backstage for a season at the Royal Drury Lane in London of one of Barry Humphries's shows, in *Dame Edna Everage and the Rise of Western Civilisation*, offering a rare insight into the life of a performer and his relationship with his audience.

Turning from the quality of the information disclosed to the style of the prose, it is clear that true stories written in a driving narrative style appeal to many readers. Certain events (such as disasters, rescues and crime) lend themselves particularly well. Examples include *Alive*, in which Piers Paul Read, a successful novelist, reconstructed the ten-week-long struggle for survival by people stranded after a plane crash in the Andes mountains in 1972. The survivors had to make an agonising decision whether to eat those who had already died. Jon Krakauer's account of an ill-starred climbing expedition to Mount Everest in 1996 that saw eight climbers die, entitled *Into Thin Air*, is equally gripping. Read's book was adapted for film and was included in Kevin Kerrane and Ben Yagoda's historical anthology of literary journalism, *The Art of Fact*: 'What finally makes *Alive* such an extraordinary document is that Read, in his calmly straightforward yet riveting prose, does what the great works of literature have always done. He provides a singular look at the workings of the human spirit, and an illuminated path to the great questions—in this case, what does it mean to be alive?' (1997, p. 183). Krakauer's book was a finalist for both the Pulitzer Prize for general non-fiction and the National Book Critics Circle award. With such dramatic events, the temptation for the practitioner is to focus on recounting what happened and to strip out any complications, such as conflicting versions of events, and avoid analysing any issues prompted by the event. That does not occur in *Alive* or *Into Thin Air*, but true stories about crime appear particularly susceptible to this last problem.

True stories that focus narrowly on a dramatic event are what Nicholas Lemann, dean of the Columbia School of Journalism, calls 'yarn-spinning'. To him, 'the marriage of narrative and analysis is the fundamental project of journalism' (eds Kramer & Call 2007, pp. 112–16). Lemann's book-length journalism testifies to his belief: both *The Promised Land: The Great Black Migration and How It Changed America*, published in 1991, and *The Big Test: The Secret History of American Meritocracy*, published eight years later, blend an idea with how that idea is driven by policy-makers and how it is experienced by ordinary people. The first book concerns the migration of African-Americans from the south after the introduction of cotton-picking machines rendered their labour redundant and how—and why—the cities that received them, such as Chicago, struggled and failed in their 'war on poverty' in black communities. The latter book examines how, soon after the end of World War II, educational bureaucrats set up the Educational Testing Service, creator of the Scholastic Aptitude Test (SAT), with the aim of creating a pure meritocracy that would wash through the entire democracy; the test soon became pervasive and with that came a rash of unintended consequences. Short summaries do not capture the nuance of the arguments Lemann develops in both books, nor do they convey how difficult it is for a practitioner to make engaging reading out of such abstract material as the spread of an educational testing system. As Lemann writes, however: 'Purely analytic work or purely narrative work is conceptually cleaner than the blending of the two. Narrative married to idea is complicated, difficult, and somewhat messy. So what? Life is, too. If it weren't, there wouldn't be any need for journalism' (eds Kramer & Call, 2007, p. 116). Another prominent example of such work is Ron Rosenbaum's *Explaining Hitler: The Search for the Origins of His Evil*, which combines his obsessive quest to understand the Nazi leader with his accounts of meetings with historians and filmmakers in a book that is not only thoroughly readable and stimulating, but as one reviewer writes: 'Its personal, freewheeling qualities enable Rosenbaum to get closer to the demonic element in Hitler than he would have done if he had been a professional historian' (cited in Boynton, 2005, p. 327).

Relatively few journalists are read primarily for their prose style, but those who are have become some of the best-known practitioners. The most obvious example is Wolfe. His idiosyncratic and attention-grabbing use of punctuation was the first thing many readers and critics noticed, followed soon after by other elements of his narrative voice, which even in a piece of cultural criticism was loud and sassy. In 'The New Journalism' Wolfe writes that from early in his career he would do anything to avoid 'coming on like the usual non-fiction narrator, with a hush in my voice, like a radio announcer at a tennis match'. To Wolfe, this understated voice was the great problem of non-fiction writing:

> You can't imagine what a positive word 'understatement' was among both journalists and literati ten years ago. There is something to be said for the notion, of course, but the trouble was that by the early 1960s understatement had become an absolute pall. Readers were bored to tears without understanding why. When they came upon that pale beige tone, it began to signal to them, unconsciously, that a well-known bore was here again, 'the journalist,' a pedestrian mind, a phlegmatic spirit, a faded personality, and there was no way to get rid of the pallid little troll, short of ceasing to read (1973, p. 31).

Few people stopped reading Wolfe, then or since.

Thompson's *Fear and Loathing in Las Vegas* is an extreme example. Not many readers remember the actual assignment Thompson was supposed to be covering, but most remember the book's opening lines:

> We were somewhere around Bartsow on the edge of the desert when the drugs began to take hold. I remember saying something like 'I feel a bit lightheaded; maybe you should drive ...'

And suddenly there was a terrible roar all around us and the sky was full of what looked like huge bats, all swooping and screeching and diving around the car, which was going about a hundred miles an hour with the top down to Las Vegas. And a voice was screaming: 'Holy Jesus! What are those goddamn animals?' (1971).

For the record, it was *Rolling Stone* magazine that sent Thompson out to Las Vegas to cover a motorcycle race and a district attorneys' convention about drugs. Whether *Fear and Loathing in Las Vegas* is a true story is not quite the point here; Thompson's idiosyncratic style, equal parts apocalyptic self-dramatising, vivid description and razor-sharp insights, is found, too, in his more obviously journalistic work, such as *Fear and Loathing on the Campaign Trail '72*. If Thompson and Wolfe's narrative voices draw attention to their individuality, others are less showy but equally distinct, such as that of Didion, Orwell and Garner, all of whom draw readers for their authorial voice as well as for what they have to say about a subject.

What emerges from this analysis is that the value of true stories derives as much from the material disclosed as from how it is written. Where in news journalism more value is set on the information disclosed than how it is presented, and in novels more value sits in the quality of the prose and the story told than in the information content, true stories sit in the middle of the continuum between daily journalism and novels. Along this continuum, of course, the claim on our attention of some true stories is made more by the material disclosed than the prose style, and vice versa, just as some daily journalism is arrestingly written and some novels dense with well-researched information. The examples given above demonstrate that what is being offered in a true story is fresh information, more information, information set in context and information whose meaning has been mined and shaped into a narrative that fully engages readers' minds and emotions. Value deriving from information disclosed sits within well-established claims about the free flow of information and ideas in a democratic society; by that criterion alone, true stories carry weight. Housing all this information in a well-constructed narrative magnifies the work's potential impact on readers and, for that reason, it can also magnify potential problems, for writers and for readers.

Chapter 3

Learning from the journalistic method

We are all haiku writers in newspapers but in a book you have a different relationship with the reader, and you have to use different language. I think a useful image is the maze. You are saying to the reader, 'Stick with me, we'll get to some tricky spots and some dead-ends and we'll even, I'm afraid to warn you, get to some boring bits but the journey will be worth it and I'll get you to the other end.'

David Marr, journalist and author

One of the beauties of writing is that it is open to anyone—no licence required—but that does not mean all writing has equal value. As the German novelist Thomas Mann once said: 'A writer is someone for whom writing is more difficult than it is for other people', which seems a smartly ironic way of encapsulating writing's elasticity and its punch. The same notion applies to true stories: no licence required but its practice throws up many issues, with many potential solutions. Most commonly, true stories are written by those with a background either in journalism or in fiction. As mentioned in the introduction, my purpose is not to argue one is better preparation than the other, but to explore in this chapter and the next the benefits of these backgrounds, and more particularly their gaps or even their blind spots.

To do this, I will analyse in detail two particular true stories: *In Cold Blood* by Truman Capote and *The Final Days* by Bob Woodward and Carl Bernstein. These were published decades ago—1966 and 1976 respectively—but I have chosen them because for several reasons they are especially illuminating. They are both landmark works that were runaway bestsellers and prompted both lavish praise and sharp criticism on publication. Both works have had a significant impact on succeeding generations of writers. Capote and Woodward and Bernstein's works were both recognised in the New York University Journalism department's list of the best American journalism of the twentieth century. But their works raise important issues and, especially in Capote's case, do so in dramatic ways that offer bracing lessons for later generations of writers. It may be necessary to keep in mind that Capote, Woodward and Bernstein were working within the standards of their time, but it is equally necessary to peel back the mythology that has grown up around their works. Importantly for my purposes here, where Capote came to his project from a novelist background with openly literary aims, Woodward and Bernstein were journalists who came to writing books from their newspaper work. Woodward, Bernstein and Capote faced similar issues in researching and writing their true stories despite differing subject matter and their differing approaches; where Woodward and Bernstein were dealing with events of historic importance, Capote was writing about a multiple murder that, while shocking, is depicted as an example of life in America. Their differing backgrounds helped them resolve some difficulties that stymied the other(s) but, crucially, some issues arose that none of them was able to solve. Finally, there is a sizeable literature about Woodward and Bernstein and Capote's work, but most of it squats in adjacent academic fields—journalism and literary studies—and their work is rarely compared, which is a real pity, as what I found is that a comparison of their work cracks open crucial issues for anyone wanting to write or understand true stories.

I will spend more time on Woodward's work rather than his collaboration with Bernstein, because Bernstein was less involved in *The Final Days* than he had been in *All the President's Men* (Havill 1993, p. 110; Shepard 2007, pp. 124–30) and because the main ethical issues arising in their book-length true stories have become characteristic of Woodward's approach, which has extended over a further sixteen books. Woodward and Bernstein won a place in history through their disclosures in *The Washington Post* about the break-in during the early hours of 17 June 1972 of the Democratic Party's National Committee headquarters, at the Watergate Hotel complex, by five men carrying equipment to copy documents and plant electronic listening devices. Their reporting led the way in revealing how the break-in was not a 'third-rate burglary', but part of a long-running campaign of political dirty tricks that was covered up by President Richard Nixon. Facing impeachment, Nixon was forced to resign in 1974—the first president to do so in American history. State investigative agencies and televised senate committees were important in forcing Nixon's hand, but the first impetus came from Woodward and Bernstein's newspaper disclosures.

Historically important though these original disclosures are, they are largely incomprehensible to modern readers because they are incremental news articles that provide little context to help us understand their import. It is because Woodward and Bernstein extended their reporting to book length that they became famous. Initially, they planned a book about the burglars and those associated with them; the working title was *Reporting Watergate*. Then Robert Redford called. He had recently finished making a film about politics, *The Candidate*, and had been following Watergate closely. He had noted the joint by-lines in *The Washington Post* and was intrigued by what seemed an odd pairing. As a biographer of Woodward and Bernstein, Adrian Havill, put it: 'The coupling of the classic Ivy League WASP and the dead-end, dropout Jewish kid was, to Redford, as if [Dean] Martin and [Jerry] Lewis had gone into journalism instead of comedy' (1993, p. 80). He checked, and the contrast sharpened into 'Bob's iceberg-lettuce crispness and Carl's seething volatility'. He contacted Woodward and, before the book was written, it had been optioned for adaptation into a film.

It is impossible to know for certain what effect Redford had on the writing of *All the President's Men*, but it is fair to deduce he had at least some, and possibly a major, influence. Woodward and Bernstein were twenty-nine and twenty-eight respectively when the Watergate burglary occurred; Woodward was just beginning to establish himself in the newsroom while Bernstein was widely regarded as highly talented, but also the 'prize office screw-up' (Halberstam 1979, p. 619). As newspaper journalists covering a breaking news story, their inclination was to write a chronological narrative focused on the burglars and the White House, but both journalists also had a modicum of literary ambition. A few years earlier Woodward had written a novel about his youth that was rejected by publishers Charles Scribner, while Bernstein enjoyed writing lengthy feature articles, some of them in the style of the New Journalism. He chafed against the strictures of daily newspaper journalism, and wanted to work for Jann Wenner's then recently established counter-culture magazine, *Rolling Stone* (Havill 1993, pp. 25–6, 57; Halberstam 1979, p. 626). Redford's suggestions still seem influential, though, especially when it is recalled that at the time of writing the book the issue of Watergate and Richard Nixon remained unresolved.

Focussing the narrative on their reporting of Watergate proved an inspired choice, plugging the book into two master plots—the quest and David versus Goliath. The two journalists' account of how they covered the burglary and tried to find out what, if any, links there were to the White House reads like a detective story. *All the President's Men* was actually described on the dust jacket of its first edition as 'the most devastating political detective story of the century'. The average reader would have known about Watergate before picking up the book, but with Nixon still president the mystery, as it were, remained unsolved. The book became hugely popular, selling 2.3 million copies in its first year (Hackett & Burke 1977, p. 17). *The Washington Post* was a powerful institution in its own right, but Woodward and Bernstein were not big-name political correspondents-cum-authors like Theodore White, but junior journalists. At the time, the idea that a series of newspaper articles had a power that would eventually lead to forcing a president's resignation was unheard of.

All the President's Men was written at the height of the New Journalism, and so the idea of using a chronological narrative with the two journalists as central characters was not as innovative as it might have seemed even a decade beforehand, but the majority of New Journalists worked for magazines or newspapers' magazine supplements rather than newspapers, and the majority of them did not work on breaking political news (Pauly, cited in ed. Sims 1990, pp. 110–29). *All the President's Men* is tightly focused on the Watergate burglary and the events that flowed from it. People are introduced only as they relate to Watergate and descriptions are primarily confined to their professional identity. The narrative is presented in a spare style, in which people's actions are left to speak for themselves, and the journalists only infrequently comment directly on events or people. The energy of the narrative derives, then, not from a Sherlock Holmes-style speculation on a criminal's state of mind or motives, but from the two journalists' ceaseless gathering of information and dogged piecing together of clues.

All the President's Men remains compelling to read even though questions have been raised about whether some material had been invented. According to one biographer, Woodward and Bernstein invented details to add drama and atmosphere to the narrative. In four passages in *All the President's Men* the weather became 'conveniently metaphoric'. When the journalists were stuck or stymied in their digging it rained; when Woodward had an important appointment at the White House the weather was warm and sunny. Havill checked the weather records with the National Oceanic and Atmospheric Administration and found that the recorded weather differed from the book's description. On another occasion, in February 1973, *The Washington Post* executive editor, Ben Bradlee, told Bernstein not to return to the newsroom because legal officers were trying to serve him a subpoena, and to go and see a film and come back at 5 p.m. In *All the President's Men*, Bernstein went to see *Deep Throat*. It was a nice touch but impossible, according to Havill, because the film was no longer showing in Washington at that time. Havill concludes that the pair's initial newspaper reporting had been sound but extending it to book length induced some 'fictionalising', which went even further in the film adaptation (1993, pp. 80–103).

Deep Throat was the name not only of an infamous pornographic film starring Linda Lovelace (that Bradlee sent Bernstein to see) but was the alias given to Woodward's most important anonymous source, who provided crucial information for his reporting about Watergate. Anonymous sources are central to Woodward's journalistic approach, whether in his original newspaper reporting or his book-length work. His reliance on them becomes both a core strength and a core weakness in his work. Where Woodward and Bernstein used anonymous sources in *All the President's Men*, there is an important difference between their first book and Woodward's later work, beginning with *The Final Days*. The former book rarely goes beyond the two young reporters' field of vision, and they also show a willingness to write about and, to a limited degree, reflect on how they went about their work. Woodward and Bernstein resolve the question of co-authorship by presenting themselves in the third person, an approach Bernstein had picked up from reading Norman Mailer's *The Armies of the Night* published a few years earlier (Shepard 2007, p. 76). They also use only their surnames and allow some self-deprecating humour. Bernstein, for instance, relayed the office rumour that 'English was not Woodward's native language'.

Originally referred to in *The Washington Post* newsroom by Woodward as 'my friend', Deep Throat's existence became known only because he was included in *All the President's Men*. His real identity (he was identified as male in the book) became the subject of intense speculation and mystique because of the importance of his information, because of Hollywood star Robert Redford's film adaptation of the book and because Woodward steadfastly refused to divulge the identity of his source. Deep Throat remained anonymous despite the best efforts of numerous journalists and scholars until 2005 when he outed himself, not via Woodward and *The Washington Post*, but through his family's lawyer in an article for *Vanity Fair* magazine. He was W. Mark Felt, deputy head of the Federal Bureau of Investigation during the Watergate period. Scooped but not outdone, Woodward soon released a book entitled *The Secret Man* about his relationship with Felt.

Woodward recounts how he first met Felt by chance, in 1970, at the West Wing of the White House, when he was a navy lieutenant and Felt was an assistant director in the FBI. Woodward was anxious and unhappy in his job while Felt was brimful of confidence and authority. Felt was the same age as Woodward's father, and Woodward looked to Felt as a mentor, almost a surrogate father figure, in fact. What emerges in reading *The Secret Man* and Felt's memoir, reissued and expanded after his identity as Deep Throat was made public, is not how close the two men were during Watergate but how little Woodward knew about Felt (Felt & O'Connor 2006, pp. 199–226). Some distance can be attributed to the difference in age and status, to Felt's general distrust of journalists and to his enjoyment of intrigue; but the two men placed great trust in each other and the stakes could hardly have been higher.

The basis of their relationship, Woodward writes in *The Secret Man*, was that 'He knew and I didn't. I would flounder, fall dangerously off course, and he would right the ship of knowledge' (2005, p. 111). After Nixon resigned as president, Woodward and Felt had little to do with each other; Woodward was unable to learn how Felt saw their role in Watergate. In 2000, Woodward tried to re-establish his relationship with Felt, who was by this time frail and forgetful. Woodward believed Felt's role in bringing to light political corruption was honourable and should be recorded for posterity. He describes an occasion when Felt's daughter Joan drove him and Felt to a restaurant near Felt's home. As Felt's memory of the Watergate days fades in and out like an errant radio signal, Woodward oscillates between frustration and elation. When, for a moment, Felt remembers forming 'a very favorable impression of Bob Woodward and his work at the *Post*', Woodward starts bouncing with joy. 'I wanted to jump in the front seat and hug him.' The scene reverberates with Woodward's yearning for the older man's approval for his early work, but what is clear from *The Secret Man* is that, despite the intensity of their encounters during Watergate, Woodward and Felt's relationship remained bounded by the exchange of information that propels daily journalism.

Since Felt revealed himself as Deep Throat and the University of Texas bought the two reporters' Watergate materials for an astounding US$5 million in 2003, researchers have been retracing the steps of earlier work, most notably Max Holland, whose 2012 book *Leak: Why Mark Felt Became Deep Throat* made a convincing argument, grounded in documentary evidence, that Felt's leaking was not the act of a noble public servant blowing the whistle on a corrupt presidency, but of a ruthlessly ambitious careerist. It is often forgotten that a matter of weeks before the Watergate burglary, J. Edgar Hoover died. The bureau's director for a staggering forty-eight years, Hoover's decline and eventual death set off an almighty internal struggle for succession. As deputy director Felt believed the job should have been his and was aggrieved when Nixon appointed L. Patrick Gray over him. Holland argues Felt leaked to undermine Gray's leadership so that he would be sacked and replaced by Felt. As much as anything, Holland argues, Felt's motive can be gleaned from how, to serve his purposes, he sometimes leaked misinformation to Woodward and at other times refused to divulge the kind of information about the White House that would have prompted others to become whistle-blowers. Woodward was an extremely tenacious journalist, but he was also inexperienced and vulnerable to being manipulated by Felt. It comes as a surprise, given the lengths to which Woodward went to protect the identity of his famous source, to learn from *Leak* that Felt provided background information to other journalists covering Watergate, notably Sandy Smith from *Time*, who had written about the FBI for years.

As much as anyone, though, Woodward has benefited from the mythology surrounding Deep Throat. He has strategically used what we now see as a relatively contingent relationship with Felt to gain access to powerful people in government, the military and intelligence agencies, as he recalls in *The Secret Man*:

> I would even say at times that this was a 'Deep Throat' conversation, and some of those in the most sensitive positions or best-placed crossroads of the American government would nod and then talk in remarkable detail, plowing through security classifications and other barriers as if they did not exist, including private conversations with a president (2005, p. 184).

There is continuing debate in the literature about the worth and the difficulties of anonymous sources (Karen Sanders 2003, pp. 107–19; Shepard 2007, pp. 101–13; Chadwick 2008). The problem was well summarised by Hugh Culbertson: 'The unnamed news source has been called a safety valve for democracy and a refuge for conscience, but also a crutch for lazy, careless reporters' (cited in Christians et al. 1995, p. 72). In the case of Woodward, few deny that his use of anonymous sources has enabled him to make important journalistic disclosures. What concerns many is the absence of any transparency about the terms of engagement between Woodward and his anonymous sources and, consequently, the high degree of trust he asks of readers. The paradox is that Woodward has built his career on the premise that everyone has secrets, and when those in positions of power and authority ask us to trust them we should be sceptical, because almost invariably they are hiding something. By Woodward's own reasoning, then, why should we trust him, a powerful, wealthy senior journalist whose books have made him a 'human brand', as one of his biographers, Alicia Shepard, puts it?

Woodward defends his use of anonymous sources on the ground that it has enabled him to publish information that otherwise would have been kept hidden for fifty years, and that he fills a gap between daily journalism and history. Several question this approach, including Steve Weinberg, a fellow investigative journalist and a former director of the organisation Investigative Reporters and Editors. In an article written in 1992 he points to several journalists who have made important disclosures and quoted sources on the record, as Seymour Hersh did with Ari Ben-Menashe for his book, *The Samson Option: Israel's Nuclear Arsenal and American Foreign Policy*, or made valuable use of documentary evidence, as James Bamford did in writing about the secretive National Security Agency in *The Puzzle Palace*. Interviewed by Weinberg, Woodward said a careful examination of such books would show the most revelatory passages were based on anonymous sources, but when Weinberg did so he found Woodward's generalisation unjustified (1992b, pp. 52–9). In a more recent article on book-length journalism about the war in Iraq, Weinberg (2007) found several more examples of important disclosures in books that rely far less on anonymous sources than does Woodward.

Woodward often avows, in his flat Midwestern accent, 'I am just a ra-por-ter' trying to find out what happened rather than be an analyst of the events he writes about, as if facts and their interpretation are always, irrevocably separate. But in trying somehow to hold them apart, Woodward has left himself open to manipulation by his anonymous sources, an argument Shepard makes, ironically, by citing an anonymous source:

> I think there are a number of cases where smart, smooth operators have fooled him and have figured out his appetite for the detail that he loves—the quotations, the atmosphere, the color, the dress, and so on, and they get the best of him … People learn that if 'I give him that stuff, then I can give him my personal spin' (2007, p. 235).

Asking sources for material to help reconstruct a scene is not automatically a problem, as will be discussed in Chapter 8, but it is for Woodward because he needs a lot of such assistance due to not witnessing most of the events he writes about, because he is reliant on people practised in the dark arts of manipulation and because his goal is to write about politics in a narrative style.

Woodward does use the time granted him in writing a book as distinct from a newspaper article to gather many documents, whether minutes of meetings, participants' private diaries or classified government documents, but he does not use it for firsthand observation, which is rarely open to him because the subject of most of his books is what happens behind government's closed doors. Instead, it appears that Woodward grants anonymity to political leaders, military officers and government officials in exchange for their version of events buttressed by access to government documents that otherwise would remain secret. The core problem at this point, then, is that Woodward transplants what is a difficult, easily abused practice in daily journalism—the use of anonymous sources—into book-length narrative non-fiction where he makes it, almost literally, his trademark. In doing this, he resolves none of the problems of anonymous sourcing. He actually disregards the time available to writers of this form to build relationships and persuade his highly placed sources to speak on the record.

If Woodward became one of the most famous print journalists in the world, his working conditions are also a rarity. More than four decades after he began as one of the lowest paid reporters on *The Washington Post*, Woodward is still on the newspaper's staff, apart from an agreed number of weekends when he edits the Sunday edition; however, he works primarily from a home office (Havill 1993, p. 69; Shepard 2007, p. 204). Woodward does give his newspaper first right to publish anything from a coming book, for the token amount of US$1, and he does contribute articles, but he retains the title of associate editor and is paid a stipend while he researches and writes book-length journalism, an arrangement that is rare, perhaps unique (Shepard 2007, pp. 243–5).

Where *All the President's Men* is narrated through the journalists' eyes, in *The Final Days* they absented themselves as an overt narrative presence. Newspaper journalists such as Woodward were, and to a large degree still are, trained in a writing style that emphasises the importance of the subject matter, not the journalist's subjectivity. It is common for textbooks to advise journalists to keep themselves out of their articles unless they believe their overt presence will add something useful.

In *The Final Days* Woodward blends the plain style with a seemingly omniscient narrative voice, which appears to have been influenced by the success of Theodore White's series of works of book-length journalism about presidential election campaigns, beginning in 1960. Before White, campaign coverage was perfunctory and superficial, but he decided to present it 'in novelistic terms, with generous helpings of colorful detail to sugar the political analysis', as Timothy Crouse writes in his journalistic book about coverage of the 1972 campaign, *The Boys on the Bus*, that is also a pathfinding piece of media criticism. White said that for a book about politics to succeed it 'must have a unity, a dramatic unfolding from a single central theme so that the reader comes away from the book as if he had participated himself in the development of a wonder' (cited in Hoffman 1995, p. 110). Through White, readers saw their candidates afresh, which catapulted *The Making of the President* series to the annual national non-fiction bestseller lists. *The Final Days* was even more successful commercially, becoming the number one bestselling non-fiction book of 1976, according to *Publishers Weekly*. By the 1970s, however, White's innovation had curdled into mythologising candidates and downplaying events that were anything but 'the development of a wonder', such as the Watergate cover-up. As the radical journalist I.F. Stone comments in a review of one of White's books: 'A writer who can be so universally admiring need never lunch alone' (1968, p. 63).

The use of an omniscient narrative voice in *The Final Days* has troubling results, as it had in White's books. The book opens with a reconstructed scene of two presidential aides, Fred Buzhardt and Len Garment, travelling by air to Miami on 3 November 1973 to advise Nixon to resign, and ends on 9 August 1974 when it actually happens. The reader is positioned in the book as if they are on board the aeroplane watching Buzhardt tap his hand on the armrest and as if they are inside the White House watching as aides and politicians, including the president, discuss how to deal with the enveloping crisis. Much of the narrative's impact derives from the events it describes rather than any particular skill in the writing. Think of it this way: if *The Final Days* concerned the demise of the state manager of a life insurance firm, it is hard to imagine it winning many readers. This is not a trite point, for two reasons: first, several successful works of narrative non-fiction have been written about apparently mundane subjects, such as Tracy Kidder's book-length accounts of building a house in *House* and a year spent sitting in a primary school classroom in *Among Schoolchildren*. Second, the issues here stem from Woodward's decision to adopt a narrative approach. *The Final Days* is written in a doggedly single-paced, monotonal narrative style. For instance, when Nixon needs to review conversations taped by the White House recording system, his aide-de-camp, Steve Bull, provides detailed instructions—'Push the play button when you are ready to listen, sir. Depress the stop button when you are done or want to stop the machine, sir.' There is more, after which the narrative offers some background:

> The president was almost totally lacking in mechanical ability and was not well coordinated physically. After four years of handing out souvenir presidential favors of cufflinks, tie clasps, pens and golf balls, Nixon still required assistance to open the cardboard boxes. Bull was accustomed to providing such help.

Once, the president had called him in to open an allergy-pill bottle, which Nixon had been struggling with for some time—the childproof type of bottle, with instructions saying 'Press down while turning'. The cap had teeth marks on it where Nixon had apparently tried to gnaw it open (1976, p. 44).

Perhaps these details were intended to humanise Nixon, but the wooden language and flat declarative sentences read like an unintentional parody of the 1950s television police procedural *Dragnet*. Perhaps they were meant to be humorous, but I doubt it. 'The problem with Woodward is that he cannot write to save himself', comments David Marr, 'and his achievement in the light of that is heroic'.

The quality of Woodward's prose sometimes goes unremarked because the people in *The Final Days*, and most of his other books, occupy important national positions; any representation of them beyond their public roles immediately takes on an intensified level of intimacy for the reader. Some material shocked readers and reviewers when the book was published in 1976 (Havill 1993, pp. 110–12; Shepard 2007, pp. 142–9). The incidents most commented upon were the contention that Nixon and his wife Pat no longer shared a bed, having 'rejected his advances' since the early 1960s, and Nixon's deterioration; he is often shown drinking heavily, wondering aloud to his chief of staff, Alexander Haig, whether he should follow military protocol and kill himself and, finally, his tumultuous three-hour meeting with Secretary of State Henry Kissinger the night before his resignation, where the two men are reported to have prayed together in the Lincoln Sitting Room. Nixon broke down and began thumping the carpet with his fist, saying 'What have I done? What has happened?'. He lay 'curled on the carpet like a child' while Kissinger tried to reassure him about his accomplishments as president. Woodward and Bernstein had not observed these dramatic moments for themselves, but relied on anonymous sources to reconstruct the scenes. In a foreword they write that they interviewed one or more participants in meetings they describe, and resolved differences in various people's accounts by re-interviewing. Where they were unable to talk to any of the people who participated in particular meetings, they relied on accounts from those who spoke to the participants immediately afterward. 'Nothing in this book has been reconstructed without accounts from at least two people' they write, but acknowledge that they were unable to interview the president. That is hardly surprising considering the anguish their disclosures had caused him, but what is alarming is the gulf between the narrative tone, which through 435 pages implicitly tells the reader this is *exactly* how events unfolded, and the reliance not just on anonymous sources but on second-hand accounts of volatile meetings.

Only Kissinger and Nixon were present in the Lincoln Sitting Room, and the journalists admit Nixon did not speak to them. The source, then, had to be Kissinger or those he spoke to immediately afterward. Even if the journalists heard accounts from Lawrence Eagleburger and Brent Scowcroft, two members of Kissinger's staff, as is suggested in the book, they are two accounts of one person's recollection of a meeting. They are also second-hand accounts, meaning they do not know what Kissinger may have omitted, exaggerated or misrepresented.

Shepard quotes Woodward and Bernstein, saying their account was confirmed later when Kissinger and Nixon published their memoirs. She also quotes Kissinger from a contemporaneous television interview, saying he believed the book was 'essentially accurate' even if their reporting of Nixon's breakdown showed 'an indecent lack of compassion'. Havill writes that Nixon and Kissinger may have included their praying together in their respective memoirs, but both denied Nixon pounding the carpet and quotations attributed to him. Kissinger's two staff members also denied that Kissinger had described the scene to them (1993, p. 201; Emery 1994, p. 474). In his memoirs Nixon describes himself inviting Kissinger to kneel and pray with him and acknowledges that he 'found himself more emotional than I had been at any time since the decision [to resign] had been put in train' (p. 1076). In his memoir, *Years of Upheaval*, Kissinger confirms the gist of the account, but describes it as 'unfeeling' and denies that Nixon beat the carpet. A later biography of Kissinger that drew on interviews with Nixon, Kissinger, Eagleburger and Scowcroft confirmed the essence of the journalists' version but rejected the detail of Nixon pounding the carpet (Isaacson 1992, pp. 597–600, note 8 p. 816).

Where a newspaper editor might be satisfied with that level of accuracy, a work of book-length journalism that has been researched for six months with the aid of two full-time researchers aspires to a higher level of accuracy, especially when it is presented in a narrative style that invites readers to believe they are being taken into high-level private meetings. By comparison, another practitioner of book-length journalism, J. Anthony Lukas, published a book entitled *Nightmare* in the same year on the same subject that included a briefer and less dramatic account of the Nixon–Kissinger meeting: 'they talked of their past triumphs and diverging futures' (1976, p. 565). Lukas, who later won a Pulitzer Prize for general non-fiction for another book, *Common Ground*, reports stories of Nixon's erratic, disconnected behaviour as his presidency unravelled, but writes: 'There were other stories, stranger yet, which one is reluctant to report because they are so difficult to confirm' (*Nightmare* 1976, p. 562). These may well be the same stories Woodward and his researchers were hearing; the difference is that Woodward chose to publish them.

Practitioners writing in a narrative style commonly gather material about how people look, feel and behave, especially at critical moments in their lives, so that is not the prime concern with Woodward's practice. Rather, four ethical issues arise in Woodward's representation of people and events: first, as mentioned earlier, he relies, for these intimate details, on anonymous sources who may well be trying to manipulate him. Second, there is a persistent stream of criticism in the literature about Woodward that he embellishes or even invents details to enliven his narrative. Steven Brill, publisher of the now defunct media watchdog magazine *Brill's Content*, raised questions about *Shadow: Five Presidents and the Legacy of Watergate* that he and Woodward trenchantly debated over eleven pages of the magazine's September and November 1999 issues. Woodward was widely accused—and vehemently denied—inventing a hospital visit he made to a seriously ill William Casey, director of the Central Intelligence Agency, for his book *Veil* (Havill 1993, pp. 182–95; Shepard 2007, p. 232–5). Woodward also has strong defenders, including Shepard and David Greenberg, who worked as a research assistant to Woodward on *The Agenda: Inside the Clinton White House* and who has written an original, thoughtful book entitled *Nixon's*

Shadow: The History of an Image. Greenberg argues *The Final Days* is grounded in careful research, drawing on a much wider range of sources than Woodward's oft-noted reliance on Deep Throat suggests. Greenberg looked at some of Woodward and Bernstein's original notes in the Harry Ransom Center and found they 'hewed strictly to what the sources recalled' (2005, p. 52).

Max Holland, by contrast, found discrepancies between what was published inside quotation marks in *All the President's Men* and Woodward's contemporaneous notes, stored at the University of Texas. On at least one occasion he found a quotation attributed to Deep Throat that was not in Woodward's notes at all. In one of their notorious late-night underground car park meetings, Woodward asks Deep Throat about the 'Canuck letter', a letter to a newspaper planted to smear a prominent prospective Democrat candidate, Edmund Muskie, for the election. 'Deep Throat stopped and turned around. "It was a White House operation—done inside the gates surrounding the White House and the Executive Office Building"'. Asked by Holland about the discrepancy, Woodward replied: 'It's just like when you testify under oath in a courtroom. You may have some notes, and you may say, "the notes say this, but I recall *that* in addition"' (Holland 2012, note 10 pp. 232–3). Given that Woodward made his notes soon after his meetings with Deep Throat, it is conceivable the words were said and not noted, but the solution for him was to paraphrase rather than quote directly, especially as the allegation was serious and was eventually disproved (Holland 2012, note 18 p. 234). The debate about whether Woodward embellishes or invents details has not been settled, but Max Holland's comprehensively documented work—*Leak*'s endnotes and sources occupy a quarter of the entire book—coupled with Woodward's generally unconvincing responses, tips the scales against him.

The third issue is that Woodward writes about events and people of national importance engaged in controversial events where every action and word is contested. Fourth, and perhaps most importantly, Woodward presents his findings through the prism of an omniscient narrative voice, which makes me, at least, feel uncomfortable. You are positioned inside the Lincoln Sitting Room as if you can watch events unfold on a critical night in American history. That is the source of the passage's power; it is also its transgression. Even if Nixon and Kissinger did say the words attributed to them in *The Final Days*—and that is contested—the scene is presented as if it is the only possible version of events. Lukas's *Nightmare* again offers a useful counterpoint. When he recounts recalled dialogue between, for instance, Alexander Haig and Caspar Weinberger, he writes that it 'went something like this', gently reminding the reader that they are being offered one person's reconstruction. It is not clear whether Woodward initiated the omniscient narrative voice, but there is evidence the book's editor, Alice Mayhew, encouraged and enforced it. She comments on one draft that events were being narrated through the journalists' eyes. 'We should never see that. Always must be through somebody else: Eagleburger, Scowcroft, Haig, Garment, etc.' (Shepard 2007, p. 129). Regardless of its origins and despite the ethical problem it creates, omniscient narration has remained a staple of Woodward's book-length journalism.

The lack of public accountability for Woodward's anonymous sources has masked a shift in the nature and range of his sources over his career. Where *All the President's Men* and *The Final Days* are the work of young outsiders, in later books Woodward has become a Washington insider. Nixon did not talk to Woodward and Bernstein for their books, but later presidents have been interviewed, including Gerald Ford and Jimmy Carter for *Shadow: Five Presidents and the Legacy of Watergate*, George W. Bush for *Bush at War* and *Plan of Attack*, and Barack Obama for *Obama's Wars* and *The Price of Politics*. Where the first two Woodward books provide deeply unflattering portrayals of those in power, in later books Woodward persuades political leaders to talk because, he says, 'essentially, I write self-portraits'. Mark Danner, an American journalist and author of *Torture and Truth: America, Abu Ghraib and the War on Terror*, has compared Woodward with another veteran investigative reporter and practitioner of book-length journalism, Seymour Hersh. Where Woodward relies for his disclosures on officials at the highest levels of government, Hersh's sources come from lower levels of the government and intelligence bureaucracy. Where Woodward provides the 'deeper' version of what is, essentially, 'the official story', Hersh unearths a version of events that 'the government does *not* want public—which is to say, a version that contradicts the official story of what went on' (Sherman 2003, p. 42).

Danner implies the public interest value of disclosures by Woodward is less than those by Hersh, but Joan Didion has gone further, provocatively arguing that Woodward writes 'political pornography'. A long-time political essayist as well as a novelist and author of several works of narrative non-fiction, Didion argues that Woodward writes books 'in which measurable cerebral activity is virtually absent' (2001, p. 194). That is, Woodward relentlessly accumulates quotidian details—what people eat, what they wear—but refuses to question the meaning of events or discuss the issues he is reporting. People within various administrations talk to Woodward not only because he grants them anonymity but because:

> What they have in Mr Woodward is a widely trusted reporter, even an American icon, who can be relied upon to present a Washington in which problematic or questionable matters will be definitively resolved by the discovery, or by the demonstration that there can be no discovery, of 'the smoking gun,' 'the evidence.' Should such narrowly defined 'evidence' be found, he can then be relied upon to demonstrate, 'fairly,' that the only fingerprints on the smoking gun are those of the one bad apple in the barrel, the single rogue agent in the tapestry of good intentions (Didion 2001, p. 214).

Didion's essay was written during the Clinton presidency and reprinted in a book early in Bush's presidency. Hersh, a staff writer at *The New Yorker*, was the first print journalist to report on abuse of prisoners at the Abu Ghraib prison in Baghdad, in mid–2004; the revelation shocked people around the world and was denounced by the White House. By late 2006 Woodward had written three books about the Bush government that tacked closely to public perception of the presidency (Rich 2006, pp. 125–7). The first two books, *Bush at War*, published in 2002, and *Plan of Attack*, published two years later, were broadly favourable portraits of the administration; it was only in the third book, *State of Denial*, published in late 2006 after it had become clear to even the least interested citizens that the

'War on Terror' had been poorly conceived and was being poorly executed, that Woodward meted out strong criticism. The giveaway, according to Jacob Weisberg, editor of online journal *Slate*, could be discerned in Woodward's treatment of key administration figures, such as Secretary of Defense, Donald Rumsfeld, who was shown as commanding, intense and incisive in the first two books but in the third as an arrogant micromanager loathed by staff and refusing to acknowledge the growing Iraqi insurgency. But Woodward, too, never acknowledges his changed perspective, writes Weisberg (2006). 'He can't say he's revising his judgments because he claims never to have made any. But, of course, Woodward does have a consistent worldview—the conventional wisdom of any given moment.' To Weisberg, the state of denial applied as much to Woodward as it did to the Bush administration.

Didion and Weisberg are acute and experienced observers of politics—what about everyday readers? How much help does Woodward give them in disentangling political rhetoric from reality? To what extent does he pander to their voyeuristic inclinations, as Didion argues? Just as there is a gap between the sharply contested events and Woodward's Olympian tone, so there is a parallel gap between the sweeping promises made to the reader and the thinness of the material assuring them of the book's veracity. The dust jacket of the first hardback edition of *The Final Days* describes the book as follows:

> In an enthralling narrative that flashes from one private discussion to the next, Bob Woodward and Carl Bernstein chronicle the previously unknown events leading to the resignation of President Richard Nixon. This is a story you have not read in the newspapers ...
>
> The authors accomplish what no other reporters have: they take us inside the rooms where Nixon's tapes were made and edited; where the President, his lawyers and staff committed themselves to increasingly desperate tactics to save the Nixon presidency ...
>
> Here is the moment-by-moment account of Richard Nixon's last days in public office—brought vividly alive with the *same*

novelistic detail and dialogue that made *All the President's Men* a number one national best seller [emphasis added].

The promotional copy offers a heady brew: the book is true, it is about important events and people, it will give the reader the 'inside' story and it reads like a novel. The supporting material consists of a half-page of acknowledgements, a dedication to partners and to sources, a one-paragraph authors' note acknowledging the contribution of two researcher–writers, a 'cast of characters', a four-page chronology, an index and a three-page foreword. The last named item is the journalists' explanation of their method and justification for their reliance on anonymous sources. They write that they interviewed 394 people, some of them for dozens of hours; many interviewees supplied contemporaneous notes, memoranda, correspondence, logs, calendars and diaries. In exchange for granting anonymity, sources 'were willing to give us information we would never otherwise have been able to obtain'. As mentioned above, they write that they interviewed one or more participants in meetings they describe and resolved differences in various people's accounts by re-interviewing.

The three-page foreword is asked to bear the burden of establishing the journalists' veracity, though it should be recalled that at the time Woodward and Bernstein's reputation was at its highest, on the strength of their Watergate reporting. There is some confusion about the number of interviewees. In the Woodward and Bernstein archives at the University of Texas, Woodward wrote in an undated draft of the foreword that more than 700 interviews were conducted, but that 'the bulk of the information came from 65 people' (Shepard 2007, p. 126). These discrepancies could be explicable—perhaps the figure of 700 refers to the total number of interviews regardless of person—but they weaken the confidence a reader today has in the book. There is a very big distance between 65 people and 394 and, of course, at the time readers were given only one figure. By comparison, Lukas's *Nightmares* carries an eleven-page note on sources, broken down chapter by chapter, that includes reference to specific documents and books, comments on the veracity of source material and, importantly, lists and names of interviewees. The note on sources is more expansive, then, than Woodward and Bernstein's, and explicitly states the difficulty in writing about Nixon's demise was 'in sifting truth from this surfeit of incomplete, self-serving and conflicting data' (1976).

Despite the suggestion on the dust jacket that *The Final Days* adopted the same narrative approach as *All the President's Men*, there was a marked difference in reception to the books. The two journalists' first book was almost universally praised by critics and generated hundreds of letters, according to Shepard, most of which read like 'love letters' to the nation's two new heroes. By contrast, *The Final Days* was vehemently attacked by numerous critics on three main grounds—that the book was disrespectful of the Nixon family's private life, that it was written as an 'omniscient narrative' and that the sources were anonymous. Readers who had applauded the 'investigative efforts of Messrs Woodward & Bernstein' now saw them as a 'pair of gossipy little men' (Shepard 2007, pp. 145—6). A number of those included in *The Final Days* came forward to contest the book's veracity; some complaints could be dismissed as self-serving, but others could not. Three Nixon aides disputed Republican senator Barry Goldwater's anecdote about Nixon being incoherently drunk at a dinner at the White House. One of the aides, speechwriter Ray Price, said he and his two colleagues all told Woodward and Bernstein that the anecdote was incorrect but 'they used it anyway' (Havill 1993, p. 113). Kissinger complained to Woodward and Bernstein's editor at *The Washington Post*, Ben Bradlee: 'Just how did they know what I was thinking?' (Havill 1993, p. 116). More seriously, perhaps, Mrs Pat Nixon suffered a stroke reportedly just after reading the book; this prompted her husband to seriously consider suing, but he was dissuaded on the grounds of cost and difficulty and, perversely, increasing sales of the already bestselling book (Havill 1993, p. 112).

The key elements of the supporting and promotional material in Woodward's later books have remained largely unchanged: a note on the use of anonymous sources, fulsome acknowledgement of his current research assistant/s and an index, but not endnotes or a bibliography. But where he defended (albeit briefly) the use of anonymous sources in *The Final Days*, in later books he simply states that he draws on them. Later books, though, do explicitly say that, where thoughts and feelings are attributed to people, he has obtained accounts of them 'from that person directly, from the written record, or from a colleague whom the person told' (*State of Denial* 2006, p. 493; see also *Veil: The Secret Wars of the CIA 1981–1987*, 1987, p. 13; *Plan of Attack* 2004, p. x). *State of Denial*, Woodward's third book about the Bush presidency, does contain twenty-nine pages of endnotes, which improves its level of transparency for readers. Some interviewees, such as Secretary of Defense Donald Rumsfeld, are named, but most are still not and by the time Woodward wrote *State of Denial* Rumsfeld was embattled and would soon be forced to resign; that is, as Rumsfeld's power declined Woodward had less need to protect him as a source.

What, then, can be drawn from this analysis of Woodward's book-length journalism? His books continue to sell in large numbers. On publication, they continue to generate widespread news coverage. They continue to draw scorn for his clunky prose style. They continue to win praise from reviewers for disclosures he makes about the inner workings of government, though there is some recognition that they do not discomfort governments in the way that Watergate did. The unseen trading of information about what goes on behind closed doors in government and other agencies discomforts a number of reviewers, however. There is also, as I have laid out, a clear through-line in the ethical issues arising in Woodward's book-length journalism that begins in his research where he has made anonymous sources his touchstone, but has resolved none of the tensions inherent in the practice. The issue is magnified by his writing in an omniscient narrative voice, where he could have signposted the difficulties of reporting and interpreting major political events. The problem is cemented in the relationship he establishes with readers, which amounts to: trust me, I'm Bob Woodward. 'Well, I don't', is the response of Ken Fuson, a journalist with the *Des Moines Register*, and he is by no means a lone voice (Lorenz 2005, p. 491).

Chapter 4

Learning from the novelist's sensibility

The difference between fiction and non-fiction is that you have to make things up for fiction, which is surprisingly hard work. You can't do that for non-fiction, although sometimes you might wish you could. Fiction and non-fiction are different activities. That sounds obvious, but it is very important. In non-fiction you are asking the reader to allow you to lead them on a journey, and if you mislead them about what they are reading then, like all lying, it is an abuse of power. It's not as bad as police corruption, of course, but it is an abuse of power, and wrong for that reason.

Margaret Simons, journalist and novelist

We have seen that whatever the many strengths Bob Woodward brings to book-length narrative non-fiction, his limitations weaken his work in important ways. Woodward works on a vast canvas—presidential intrigues, wars, international terrorism—but carries few colours in his palette and paints in only one corner. What happens, then, when a novelist decides to take on a major non-fiction project? Truman Capote's creation of *In Cold Blood* presents itself as a particularly good case study, for the reasons outlined in the previous chapter. By the end of the 1950s Capote was a well-regarded novelist, best known for *Breakfast at Tiffany's*, which would become a 'small classic', according to Norman Mailer, who in *Advertisements for Myself*, described Capote as 'the most perfect writer of my generation, he writes the best sentences word for word, rhythm upon rhythm'. Capote had also written some journalism, notably what for the 1950s was an extraordinarily intimate profile of actor Marlon Brando, 'The Duke in his Domain'. Capote believed journalism was 'the most underestimated, the least explored of literary mediums' (Plimpton cited in ed. Inge 1987, p. 47), and he aimed to create a work of art by reporting actual events in what he termed in an interview a 'Nonfiction Novel'.

In many ways Capote exceeded even his grand ambitions. Today, *In Cold Blood* is an icon of modern popular culture. First published over four consecutive weeks in 1965 in *The New Yorker* and then by Random House on 1 January 1966, the book became an instant bestseller, swiftly garnering for Capote the then—and even now—astounding sum of US$2 million for paperback, foreign and movie rights. The book won an Edgar Award for best factual crime book, but unlike any of the award's previous seventeen winners, it legitimised a sub-genre—true crime, as it is now called. Since 1966, *In Cold Blood* has been released in 250 editions, translated into 30 languages and remains easily available today in the Penguin Modern Classics edition.

The book is an account of the apparently senseless murders in 1959 of four members of a farming family, the Clutters, in Holcomb, Kansas, by two drifters, Perry Smith and Richard Hickock, and of their subsequent capture, conviction and execution. The account of the murders is shocking to read, but the book depicts them as an example of life in America rather than as extraordinary for the nature of the crime as in, say, the Jack the Ripper case, or the notoriety of those involved as in the O.J. Simpson trial. *In Cold Blood* has been adapted for film twice, and the writing of the book has been picked over in two films, *Capote* (2005) and *Infamous* (2006). Among literary critics, *In Cold Blood* is generally seen as Capote's most important work, and in journalism it has been canonised. It sits twenty-second on New York University's list of the top 100 works of twentieth century American journalism, and is reverently passed around in newsrooms from one generation of hacks to the next as the exemplar of gritty, on-the-ground reporting and words that sing on the page. Jonathan Harr, author of a fine 1996 true story later adapted for film, *A Civil Action*, has said he tried to imitate Capote's opening description of Holcomb that is 'so vivid and clean, with no characters other than the town itself', but despite rereading the scene a dozen times, 'I didn't come close to him'. Another leading American writer, Alex Kotlowitz, says: 'You read that book and have to remind yourself constantly that this is all true. What better, more gripping way to write non-fiction?'

And here we come to the nub of the problem: first, it is *not* all true, and, second, how does a practitioner of Kotlowitz's calibre turn a blind eye to the problems with *In Cold Blood* that were documented as early as the year of its release? These issues, and others connected to them, need to be examined in detail because, while questions about the book's accuracy were raised early, for some, especially certain literary critics, such matters are less important than the book's artistic merit. Questions about accuracy, invention and accountability to readers arise in the work of both Woodward and Capote, but where most reviewers critique Woodward's work on these grounds, fewer literary scholars take up the same issues in Capote's work, and a good number of them read *In Cold Blood* as if it is entirely a novel (Heyne 1987, p. 481).

Certainly, Capote opens the door to misreadings by describing his book as a 'nonfiction novel', but the subtitle, *A True Account of a Multiple Murder and Its Consequences*, and the numerous media interviews he gave attesting to the book's factual accuracy, show he was not echoing the approach of early eighteenth century writers such as Daniel Defoe and Henry Fielding, who described their novels *Robinson Crusoe* and *Joseph Andrews* as a 'just history of fact' and 'copied from the book of nature' respectively, nor was his subtitle playful, as is novelist Peter Carey's title of his reimagining of the story of Australian bushranger Ned Kelly, *True History of the Kelly Gang*, published in 2000. Phillip K. Tompkins challenged the factual accuracy of *In Cold Blood* in an article written for *Esquire* magazine after he visited Kansas to reinterview several of Capote's sources and examine the court record of the case central to the book. Published six months after the release of *In Cold Blood*, Tompkins's most serious charge is that Capote altered facts and quotations to substantially skew his portrait of one of the killers, Perry Smith, making him look less like a cold-blooded murderer than a victim whose considerable potential had been crippled by a miserable childhood. A number of literary critics have cited Tompkins's article and, to my knowledge, none has seriously contested its factual grounding, but that does not necessarily diminish Capote's book in their eyes. Melvin Friedman writes that he believes Capote 'cheated', but the consequences are unimportant. 'Despite the convincing claims of unreliability ... we must still believe in the essential authenticity and integrity of Capote's account', but Friedman does not say why he or we should (cited in Heyne 1987, p. 482).

Discussing arguments that Capote had made factual errors about the basketball skills of one person portrayed in the book and the buyer of the beloved horse of one of the four murder victims, Chris Anderson writes: 'Even fact is finally beyond certainty when the author is not inventing the story. Experience is too various and complex, too fine, to be represented completely in words' (1987, p. 66). That may be right in the abstract, but does it mean the author of a true story need make no effort to verify the accuracy of their account? The scale of error is also important; the basketball skills of a peripheral person in the book is not a crucial fact, but the sale of the horse is significant because Capote mentions it in three separate passages, showing Nancy Clutter's fondness for her horse and how poignant it is that 'Babe' was sold to a farmer from outside the county who 'said he might use her for ploughing'. The horse was sold to a local man who treasured her, however, according to Tompkins.

Tentativeness about looking beyond the text to the actual people and events it concerns extends even to those like Ronald Weber, author of three books about literary non-fiction, for whom the core 'critical problem with literary nonfiction cast in the form of fiction is always credibility' and 'the writer's commitment to fact' (1974, p. 53). Weber walks up to the abyss but then turns back:

Such inaccuracy, if it exists, is of course devastating. If Capote has distorted Perry's character, the book is fatally weakened as a 'true account.' But most readers know nothing of the Clutter murders beyond what Capote relates and so are in no position to measure the book as Tompkins does. Even if they could, such detective work might seem of small importance for the book patently reaches beyond its factual grounding to grasp the reader in the manner of the novel. It seeks to be, finally, a work of the literary imagination, and it is on this level that the reader can best measure it (1974, pp. 74–5).

It is not at all clear why Weber prefers Capote's account over that of Tompkins, which quotes extensively from official documents and from his interviews. Despite Weber's assertions of the importance of credibility and a writer's commitment to fact, he lets Capote off the hook by invoking his artistry, even though it is his artistry that appears to have caused the problem in the first place. Just because someone is an artist, or aspires to be, does that absolve them of all responsibility to the actual people they write about?

Some critics are hostile to weighing the relationship between fact and fiction, even in works that make crystal clear they are to be read as non-fiction rather than as a novel. Discussing Janet Malcolm's *The Journalist and the Murderer*, Phyllis Frus questions the grounds on which Daniel Kornstein, the lawyer who defended journalist Joe McGinniss in the civil suit brought by the convicted murderer Jeffrey MacDonald, contests the factual validity of Malcolm's book. She writes:

This tradition of tedious recital of error has a long and dreary history … There are numerous articles detailing what both Capote and Mailer invented surrounding their subjects [in *In Cold Blood* and *The Executioner's Song*]; indeed at least one reviewer of true-crime nonfiction novels invariably feels obligated to set the record straight by pointing out false facts rather than reading carefully to note how the writer has made the material speak. As Malcolm says, "The material does not 'speak for itself'" (1994, pp. 257–8).

If Frus is referring to an unblinking belief in objective truth, then treating facts as so many sliding balls on an abacus is simplistic and probably tedious, but there are many shades of meaning between that and Frus's argument that 'unless the reader has firsthand knowledge of the subjects she has no way of knowing what is actual, unless it is verified by other narratives' (1994, p. 7). The material may not speak for itself, as she approvingly quotes Malcolm, but even careful readers can be flummoxed by omissions and errors in a work of literary non-fiction. Frus inadvertently impales her argument by drawing a conclusion about the murderer, MacDonald, from information in Malcolm's book that Kornstein has contested, with evidence, in his 'tedious recital of error' (Frus 1994, p. 194; Kornstein 1989, pp. 132–3).

Assessing which of Kornstein's or Malcolm's evidence and argument is more persuasive requires further checking and verification. Frus may well be right to argue that the average reader has neither the time nor the direct experience to verify most of what is printed in narrative non-fiction works, but that prompts an important question that is examined in this book—what obligations do practitioners owe their readers? What is puzzling about Frus, Friedman, Anderson, Weber and other scholars (see, for instance, Booth 1988, p. 210 or Lounsberry 1990, p. 192) is the disparity between the rigour and precision they apply to even the smallest details of their scholarship (and that of others), while appearing to have little interest or understanding of the importance of parallel practices of verification in true stories or, to use their term, literary non-fiction. Daniel Lehman is rare among literary studies scholars for commenting on this disparity in his study, *Matters of Fact*. In no way am I suggesting precision in scholarship is unimportant, but I am asking: if you believe it is important in your work, why would you take a different attitude towards representing people and events in narrative non-fiction? Anthropologists and sociologists understand well the ethical issues inherent in their study of people, not least through the exhaustive procedures required by university ethics committees for researching 'human subjects'. Scholars in literary studies usually deal with texts rather than people, which may go some way towards explaining this peculiar blind spot.

It is certainly understandable if later generations of readers—and scholars—feel little connection to the actual people portrayed in Capote's book, but in 2004 Capote's biographer, Gerald Clarke, published a generous selection of his letters, *Too Brief a Treat*, which shed new and harsh light on how Capote went about his task. These have generated surprisingly little attention among scholars, even though the director of *Infamous*, Douglas McGrath, drew on them for his film about the making of *In Cold Blood* (Ricketson 2007). For many critics it seems a case of 'move along folks; nothing to see here'. I have been through both the primary and the secondary source material about *In Cold Blood*, and when it is all laid out there *is* something to see: the extent to which Capote deceived both his readers and his principal sources, the two convicted murderers.

To begin with, let's look at how Capote approached the research work. When he read a news article published on 16 November 1959 in *The New York Times* about the murder of four members of a farming family in Kansas, the Clutters, he immediately felt he had found an event that offered an opportunity to create a work of art (Plimpton 1998, pp. 196–211). From the beginning, then, Capote saw the murder of four innocent people as an opportunity to make a reputation for himself as a major artist; when he told the detective in charge of the investigation, Alvin Dewey, that he had little interest in whether the crime was solved, Dewey rebuked him. It took time; payment to some interviewees; the calm manner of his childhood friend, author and research assistant, Nelle Harper Lee; and persistence for Capote to gain the trust of people he wanted to interview, but eventually he developed a close relationship with both Dewey and the two convicted murderers, Dick Hickock and, especially, Perry Smith (Clarke 1988, pp. 321–4; Shields 2006, pp. 140–1).

From Dewey, Capote gained a rare level of access to key documents, such as the diary of the Clutters' teenage daughter Nancy and the murderers' signed confessions, as well as an insight into how the investigation was conducted, and was able to check countless details with him over the years Capote took to write *In Cold Blood* (ed. Clarke 2004, pp. 273–367). Dewey persuaded some reluctant locals to be interviewed by Capote, including Nancy Clutter's boyfriend, Bobby Rupp (Helliker 2013). Dewey even provided stage directions for the transcripts of the police interviews: when the detectives confronted Smith with their belief he had been at the Clutter farmhouse the night they were killed there was 'a full minute of silence. Perry turns white. Looked at the ceiling. Swallows'

(New York Public Library, Capote papers, Box 7, Folder 9). Capote became close to Dewey and his wife, Marie, and children; there are more letters to the Deweys in *Too Brief a Treat* than to anyone else, many of which testify to how fond Capote was of Alvin and Marie Dewey and they of him, to the point where they holidayed together in 1963. The following year Capote took them to Beverly Hills to socialise with a raft of his actor friends, including Frank Sinatra, Jack Lemmon, Natalie Wood and producer David Selznick (Capote papers, Box 23, Folders 7 and 11). When *In Cold Blood* was adapted for film, Capote persuaded Columbia Pictures to hire Marie Dewey as a consultant for the handsome sum of US$10,000, according to a report by Kevin Helliker in *The Wall Street Journal*. From Smith and Hickock he gained not only their accounts of what they did at the Clutter family's farm house, but the full background of their lives and the period they were on the run after committing the murders (Clarke 1988, pp. 343–4). What makes the creation of *In Cold Blood* such a compelling example of the problems writers face when becoming close to their principal sources is the length of time between Smith and Hickock's conviction—29 March 1960—and the eventual date of their execution after numerous appeals and stays—14 April 1965. Capote was forced again and again to choose between his allegiance to his project and to his principal sources; his obligations to his readers appeared to be swallowed by his ambitions for the book, on the grounds that whatever was good for his book would be good for his readers too.

Capote's dilemma is captured in the many letters he sent and received from his principal sources and his friends. Capote conducted his primary research in Kansas over a month between 16 December 1959 and 20 January 1960 and then when he returned for the trial in March 1960. Between then and 1963 he lived overseas and worked on his manuscript before returning to the United States to finish writing it, which he did in February 1965. As early as April 1961 he told Dewey in a letter that he could not finish the book until he knew how the matter ended (ed. Clarke 2004, p. 314). In November the same year he was told by the editor of *The New Yorker*, William Shawn, who had read 60,000 words of the manuscript that it was 'much the best work' he had done (ed. Clarke 2004, p. 328). By the time Capote had finished the third of the book's projected four parts, Shawn was describing it to him in a telegram as a masterpiece and a 'work of art people will be reading two hundred years from today' (ed. Clarke, p. 382). Capote knew, then, that he had every chance of realising his artistic ambition, but that it would be achieved at the expense of a further two lives, those of Hickock and Smith. There was little doubt that the two men had committed murder in cold blood, as the book's title suggests. It is possible to read a second meaning into the title, namely that capital punishment is also a cold-blooded killing, but Capote's letters reveal that he was less concerned about the morality of capital punishment than with how the seemingly endless opportunities for appeals and stays of execution made justice a cruelly slow business, for those convicted as well as for the victims' surviving family members (ed. Clarke 2004, pp. 386, 415). But the party he seemed most concerned about was himself.

There are at least fifteen letters in *Too Brief a Treat*, and several more in the Capote papers held by the New York Public Library that Clarke did not select, in which Capote laments the delay in carrying out the executions, beginning with one he sent to Dewey in February 1961: 'Am most anxious to hear at once the outcome of D.H [Dick Hickock] and P.S [Perry Smith] appeal' (Capote papers, Box 23, Folder 4; other similar letters in Folders 8 and 12). In September 1962 he was sarcastic about the setting of a date for the execution. 'Will H & S [Hickock and Smith] live to a ripe and happy old age?—or will they swing and make a lot of other folks very happy indeed? For the answer to these and other suspenseful questions tune in tomorrow to your favorite radio program, "Western Justice", sponsored by the Slow Motion Molasses Company, a Kansas Product' (ed. Clarke 2004, p. 363). By 1964, after more delays, Capote was exasperated, telling Dewey, 'My God! Why don't they just turn them loose and be done with it?'. Early the following year, when yet another execution date was set, Capote told a friend 'Now let's keep everything crossed—knees, eyes, hands, fingers!', but when that date, too, was postponed, he told another friend 'I hardly give a fuck anymore what happens. My sanity is at stake'. Sandwiched between these last two letters is one he sent to Perry Smith: 'I've only just heard about the court's denial. I'm very sorry about it. But remember, this isn't the first setback.' It is clear from Capote's letters and from Clarke's comprehensive biography published in 1988 that he enacted Janet Malcolm's famous pattern of seduction and betrayal (discussed in detail in the next chapter) by appealing to Smith's own unrealised artistic ambition through name-dropping of Hollywood stars he knew, such as Humphrey Bogart, and discussing art and literature with him to persuade Smith to reveal everything he could (Capote papers, Box 11, Folder 1). As the years dragged on, Smith and Hickock continually asked Capote how they would be portrayed in his book, but Capote 'danced round the subject, pretending, until the day they were executed, that he was barely half-done and, in fact, might never finish' (Clarke 1988, p. 346). When they independently discovered the title Capote lied, telling them they were wrong, even though he had known what the title would be since June 1960, just three months after Smith and Hickock were convicted (Clarke 1988, p. 346; ed. Clarke 2004, p. 287).

It must be kept in mind that Capote was dealing with two convicted murderers, but their crimes did not exonerate him from all care towards them. And it is clear from Capote's letters, the biographies by Clarke and a 1998 oral biography edited by George Plimpton that Capote was deeply torn. His ambition for his project impelled him to manipulate Smith, but he also became close to him and did care for him. A number of Capote's friends noticed that he was obsessed with Smith, and he himself in several letters wrote about how difficult he found composing the book because he was 'too emotionally involved with the material'. In one letter he describes himself, without any apparent irony, as 'imprisoned by *In Cold Blood*'. When Capote had first arrived in Kansas his assignment for *The New Yorker* was to portray the impact on a small rural community of the multiple murders, but that altered when Capote saw Smith and Hickock sitting in court for the arraignment. 'Look, his feet don't touch the floor', he told Harper Lee. 'Oh, oh! This is the beginning of a great love affair', she recalled to Clarke. Each man looked at the other and saw what he could have been. Both were short and physically odd; a motorcycle accident had left Smith with a limp and Capote had a voice so high only a dog could hear it, as was bitchily remarked in New York literary circles, and even in conservative post-war America Capote never hid his homosexuality. As Todd Schultz writes in his 2011 psychobiography of Capote, *Tiny Terror*, both had been abandoned as children and their mothers were alcoholics. Their fathers were mainly absent and there had been suicides in both families. It was as if the two of them grew up in the same house and that, where Capote had left by the front door, Smith had taken the back, as Philip Seymour Hoffman said in his role as Capote in the eponymous 2005 film.

In his letters to Smith, Capote's tone was generally formal, whereas his letters to friends were colloquial, often gossipy; when Smith asked Capote whether he was homosexual, though, Capote said he was. One detective in the Clutter case, Harold Nye, went so far as to say the two men became lovers while Smith was in jail (Plimpton 1988, pp. 188–9). Sex between a journalist and their principal source is clearly outside the code of ethics, but Nye's unsubstantiated claim is flatly denied by Clarke, who spent thirteen years researching and writing his Capote biography. 'Harold Nye hated Truman and he would say anything to denigrate him. I could give you several reasons why they *couldn't* have had sex on death row, but it would require a longer explanation than I can give now,' he told me. What transpired between Capote and Smith during his years in prison may never be known; what looks clear is that Capote crossed a boundary between developing a trusting professional relationship with a principal source and becoming psychologically enmeshed with him, to the point where it appears to have substantially affected his representation of Smith and the overall case.

This is one of the five main issues that arise in the writing of *In Cold Blood*: Capote's avowedly omniscient narrative voice, the extent to which Capote relies on reconstruction of scenes, the paucity of attribution of information, Capote's willingness to invent details and even scenes, and his distorting of evidence to match his artistic vision.

In Cold Blood is a considerably more sophisticated book than *The Final Days*. Other practitioners before Capote, notably John Hersey with *Hiroshima* in 1946 and Lillian Ross with *Picture* in 1952, had taken a narrative approach to reporting and writing about, respectively, the dropping of the atomic bomb and the making of a film, but *In Cold Blood* significantly enlarged the scope of narrative non-fiction by exploring the extent to which such works could be developed so they read like a full-length, socially realistic novel. Capote skilfully builds tension by using sequential narration, alternating scenes of the Clutter family with scenes of their two killers that overlap and propel the action of the book (eds Talese & Lounsberry 1996). In the middle section, Capote not only alternates between the killers and their pursuing detectives, but makes the scenes progressively shorter to develop suspense (eds Kerrane & Yagoda 1997).

Capote's literary talent is unquestioned, but does that enable him to solve the problem of an omniscient narrative voice in narrative non-fiction? How does Capote present the Clutters' final days when it was their deaths that sparked his interest in the case, and how can he report Smith and Hickock's time on the run when he had not yet met them? Capote's answer was that he interviewed numerous people in Holcomb about the Clutters and interviewed the murderers extensively and separately, cross-referencing their answers and only using material that they agreed on (Plimpton 1987). Sometimes Capote shows the source of his material indirectly, as when the Clutters' home telephone rings and the daughter who was killed, Nancy, answers it and speaks to a Mrs Katz, who Capote had interviewed (Nance 1970, p. 183). Sometimes he draws inferences from his material, as when the father, Herb Clutter, was showering and dressing in his own bedroom, and Capote writes 'he had no fear of disturbing' his wife, Bonny. The point of view is that of a dead man, but the inference Capote draws from his interviews is modest, and evidence provided in the passage supports it. That is, argues Jack Fuller (1996), himself both a journalist and a novelist, the Clutters are reported to sleep in separate bedrooms, and describing Clutter's state of mind here—'he had no fear of disturbing her'—is unremarkable. Ben Yagoda offers qualified support for Capote's reconstruction of Smith and Hickock's flight from the farmhouse, acknowledging Capote's extensive interviews, but questioning any person's ability to recall exactly what they said years, months or even days beforehand. In the end, though, 'it is indisputable that Capote, with his novelist's ear, heard what his characters *could* have said and transcribed it more faithfully than any journalist before or since' (eds Kerrane & Yagoda 1997, p. 161).

The problem, though, as with *The Final Days*, is that *In Cold Blood* is presented as a seamless account of events, admitting of no alternative versions. Capote explicitly described his narrative persona as omniscient. 'My narrator is always an observer. He's better the less he participates in the action. He is the omniscient eye. I always try to make him the object sitting there vibrating—seeing, observing' (Nance 1970, p. 184). Capote believed the success of a non-fiction novel depended on the author withdrawing his overt presence. 'The I-I-I intrudes when it really shouldn't.' (Nance, 1970, p. 182–3) On a few occasions Capote represents himself in the book as 'an acquaintance' (1966, p. 50) or an anonymous 'journalist' (1966, p. 274) but said he did this only because he could not find another way of relating the material (Nance 1970, p. 184). Lawrence Weschler, author of eight works of narrative non-fiction, says he uses 'I' in his work out of modesty, and believes its absence signals the opposite. '*The New York Times* is megalomaniacal. They use the voice that says, "This is how it *is*" ... The "I" doesn't have to show up every five sentences ... But there had better be an individual voice that says, "This is just one person's view, based on one series of experiences"'. His comment is apt for both Woodward and Capote. The latter, despite his recognised literary talent, does not appear to have given much thought to the ethical problems of omniscient narration in non-fiction, or to alternative narrative approaches. There is little doubt Capote spent a lot of time and energy researching his subject. His and Harper Lee's research notes from their initial visit to Holcomb fill fourteen folders in a box in the Capote papers at the New York Public Library, which include, among other things, an eighteen-page chronology of events for the day of the murder and Capote's hand-drawn maps of Smith and Hickock's time on the run. There are at least seven letters in Clarke's selection where Capote checks information with his sources, especially the detective leading the investigation, Alvin Dewey (ed. Clarke 2004), and a longstanding fact checker assigned by *The New Yorker*, Sandy Campbell, described Capote as the most accurate writer he had worked with (Clarke 1988, p. 350).

This is not to say Capote's research is beyond questioning, as should already be apparent. The editor of *The New Yorker*, William Shawn, wrote in the margin of the galley proofs of the first part to be serialised: 'How know? No witnesses? General problem', and later, 'A device needed for author to account for his knowing what was said in private conversations' (Yagoda 2000, p. 347). In his comprehensive history of the magazine, Ben Yagoda writes that Shawn did not act on his qualms, and suggests his hands may have been tied because Capote had already signed a book contract with Random House, which was determined to release the long-awaited work less than three months after it appeared in his magazine. Many years later, Shawn told his deputy editor, Charles McGrath, that he wished he had not published 'Annals of Crime: In Cold Blood', but did not elaborate. Lillian Ross, a writer for the magazine who for many years lived with Shawn even as he remained married to his wife, later wrote that neither she nor Shawn believed in journalists reconstructing scenes or writing interior monologues. When she listed her favourite writers for the magazine Capote was not included (Roberts in ed. Connery 1992, pp. 232–4; Ross 2002).

A friend of Capote's, Donald Windham, writes in his memoir *Lost Friends* that '*In Cold Blood* couldn't be and wasn't published until Dick [Hickock] and Perry [Smith] were dead. When the book came out, the only living authority for the factualness of much of the narrative was Truman himself. It was the perfect set up for this kind of invention' (1987, p. 79). Smith and Hickock sent hundreds of letters to Capote between 1960 and 1965, some of which were used in Clarke's biography, and a small number (three) were reprinted in Clarke's selection of Capote's letters. Smith and Hickock were concerned that they would be presented in Capote's book as 'psychopathic killers', but this was largely special pleading on their part and it is legitimate, even necessary, for a writer to go beyond a single source's version and present an event in its complexity. However, Capote oscillated between gaining the trust of his principal sources and treating them as if they were characters in a fictional universe of his own making. Capote did exhaustive research, then, but he did not always follow where his research led, and it is in deviating from his research that Capote invented details and distorted material in ways that seriously undermine the credibility of his work as narrative non-fiction.

Capote had difficulty expunging his overt presence from his book when he had interviewed so extensively and observed numerous events firsthand. In June 1960 he discussed this problem, which he described as 'a technical one', in a letter to Donald Cullivan, a former army acquaintance of Smith to whom Smith had confessed the murders. Capote writes that he wanted to move conversations he and Smith had had about the murders to a scene between Smith and Cullivan (ed. Clarke 2004, p. 286). Cullivan apparently agreed, because such a scene is included in the book (Capote 1966, pp. 237–40). Capote's problem was ethical rather than technical, as he gave readers no clues as to what he had done, but at least he was transposing the substance of statements he too had been told. In another letter, dated 16 August 1961, to Alvin and Marie Dewey, Capote asked if Marie could recall for him when and how Dewey had first mentioned Smith and Hickock. 'I want to do this as a "scene" between you and Alvin. Can you remember anything more about it (not that I mind inventing details, as you will see!)' (ed. Clarke 2004, p. 326). At this point Capote's habitual impulse to write fiction irretrievably begins to muddy his stated purpose of writing a factually accurate account of the Kansas murders. His letters do not reveal which details he invented; perhaps he was referring to the Smith–Cullivan transposed scene or perhaps he was referring to two scenes that were invented.

At the beginning of the book's third section, 'Answers', Capote relates how local detectives acted quickly on an important clue and an agent interviewed Dick Hickock's parents late that evening. Harold Nye gained vital information by pretending to be checking on a parole violation rather than pursuing their son about the murders. It is a dramatic scene that over six pages describes in intimate detail the parents (Walter Hickock is a 'man with faded, defeated eyes and rough hands; when he spoke, his voice sounded as if it were seldom used'), the dialogue between them and Nye's barely contained excitement ('Nye shut his notebook and put his pen in his pocket, and both his hands as well, for his hands were shaking with excitement'). According to a cache of Kansas Bureau of Investigation documents found among Nye's papers after he died in 2003, the bureau did not act on the clue immediately but five days later, and it was not a sole agent who interviewed the Hickocks late at night but four agents who arrived in the middle of the day and executed a search warrant. Journalist Kevin Helliker writes that there was no pretence about a parole violation and Walter Hickock was not even there at the time. Nye first visited the Hickocks a few days afterward.

It is possible some details in the scene have been transposed from Nye's later meeting with the Hickocks, but the ending of *In Cold Blood* is entirely invented, according to Clarke, who writes that Capote felt uneasy ending with the killers' executions and opted for a happier scene showing Dewey meeting one of Nancy Clutter's girl-friends in the local cemetery and conveying the message: life continues even amid death. It almost replicated the ending of *The Grass Harp*, a Capote novel published in 1951. 'But what works in *The Grass Harp*, which is a kind of fantasy, works less well in a book of uncompromising realism like *In Cold Blood*, and that nostalgic meeting in the graveyard verges on the trite and sentimental' (Clarke 1988, p. 359).

A number of contemporary critics noted similarities between Capote's fiction and his non-fiction, especially in the portrayal of Smith, who was 'a dreamer, an androgynous father-seeker' like Joel Knox in *Other Voices, Other Rooms*, Capote's first published novel and, like Holly Golightly in *Breakfast at Tiffany's*, the maker of his own morality (De Bellis 1979, p. 533). Many characters in Capote's fiction are victims and Smith becomes, according to another critic, Robert Morris, 'the total symbol for the exile, the alienated human being, the grotesque, the outsider, the quester after love, the some-times sapient, sometimes innocent, sometimes evil child'. These critics may want to read *In Cold Blood* in the context of Capote's fictional oeuvre, but if you want to write or understand true stories, the relevant question is: how does Capote's representation of Smith correspond to the person? It is conceivable, and perhaps inevitable, that there are patterns in how novelists create their fictional worlds and that these patterns may translate to their non-fiction. A writer of narrative non-fiction, though, like an historian or biographer, needs to honestly report what they have found in their research. Smith is more vividly presented than any other person in the book. Mailer went so far as to describe Smith as one of the 'great characters in American literature'. It does not appear he was being ironic, as there was much he admired about *In Cold Blood* and used it partly as a model for his 'true life story', *The Executioner's Song*.

Phillip Tompkins's comparison of the book with the court record and his interviews with people involved in the case show how Capote distorted his portrait of Smith to make him look more like a victim whose considerable potential was crippled by a miserable childhood. The undersheriff and his wife, Mr and Mrs Wendle Meier, told Tompkins that they had never heard Smith crying in his cell, as Capote describes, nor did Smith ever say to Mrs Meier 'I'm embraced by shame'. Capote reported Smith apologising at the gallows for his crime, but two newspaper reporters who attended the executions told Tompkins he did not apologise. Nor is it clear Capote even stayed to witness Smith's execution, according to Tompkins and Harold Nye. Most damaging for Capote, though, is Tompkins's comparison between the transcript of Smith's confession, the police testimony in court about the confession and Capote's reporting of Smith's confession as narrated to detectives at the end of the 'Answer' section. Capote's account is contradicted on a number of factual details, such as which question prompted Smith to begin confessing and whether Smith and the detectives were travelling in a car ahead or behind the car in which Hickock was being driven. More importantly, Capote's account is contradicted on the extent to which Smith could be held personally responsible for his actions. Capote has Smith saying, when he began killing Mr Clutter, 'But I didn't realize what I'd done till I heard the sound. Like somebody drowning. Screaming under water.' Conversely, Dewey testified that Smith and Hickock told him they debated who was going to kill Herb Clutter and finally Smith said he would do it. Smith said he hid a knife along his arm away from Clutter's line of sight and told Clutter he was going to tighten the cords on his hand and then he cut Clutter's throat. In Dewey's testimony, Smith commits murder 'with full consciousness and intent', while in Smith's version, as rendered by Capote, his responsibility is diminished because he suffers what Capote later termed in interviews a 'brain explosion' or a 'mental eclipse'.

The accuracy of Tompkins's most serious charge—that Capote's book distorted the real Smith—was not contested by Capote in any letter to *Esquire* over the year following Tompkins's article, even though he had replied vigorously and at length to an earlier attack by the English critic Kenneth Tynan. Nor is the article mentioned in Capote's letters. But Capote was supported by William Nance, who noted that, in the scene with Cullivan mentioned earlier, Smith explicitly says he is not sorry for what he did and that Tompkins's depiction of Smith as an 'obscene, semiliterate and cold-blooded killer' is a cliché. It is possible, though, to read Smith's gallows' step apology as repudiating his earlier callousness and gaining redemption. That, along with the potential to read Capote's portrait of Smith as a killer whose talents were blighted by a miserable childhood, also teeters on cliché. More usefully, Nance contributes the insight that in the five years between Capote and Smith's first meeting and the execution, each affected the other. Smith aspired to be an artist and was entranced with Capote from the moment the writer dropped Bogart's name during their first interview (Bogart had starred in a film for which Capote wrote the screenplay). Capote looked at Smith and saw his 'shadow', as Clarke puts it. Harper Lee, who worked with Capote on the book's research, says: 'Perry was a killer, but there was something touching about him. I think every time Truman looked at Perry he saw his own childhood' (Nance 1970, p. 211).

If, from this, you conclude that the vividness of Capote's portrayal of Perry Smith stems partly from it being a self-portrait, that does not quite do justice to the impact Capote's book appears to still have on many readers, including me when I first read it. Nor, though, does the book's continuing influence absolve its creator of the very real ethical issues he faced and, in significant ways, failed to overcome. Capote's talent as a writer, then, enables him to draw readers deeper into the world of his book than does Woodward, but that alone does not help him resolve the issues. If anything, it magnifies them. Madeleine Blais, a writing teacher and author of *In These Girls, Hope is a Muscle*, infers from Capote's stated intention to use the Clutter murders for a literary experiment: 'There is something creepy about the prettiness of the prose in contrast to the grotesquerie of the killings. In the end, the author may have driven himself nearly insane with the question: what purpose is served by making art out of something so vile?' (cited in Sims 2007, p. 241).

To date, it is the response of critics to *In Cold Blood* that I have discussed, but what about everyday readers? The book's massive sales—it was the third highest selling non-fiction book in the United States in 1966—attest to its popularity, but also to Capote's adroit marketing of the book, which at the time was almost unprecedented among writers with literary aspirations, according to Clarke. If the

five years between Smith and Hickock's conviction and their execution frustrated Capote, it also served to build prospective readers'
anticipation to fever pitch. The promotional copy on the dust jacket of
the first edition published in the United States and in England could
confidently announce the book 'has already been hailed as a masterpiece'. In 1966 Capote was the subject of twelve articles in national
magazines, several of which featured his picture on the cover, two
half-hour television programs and numerous radio and newspaper
interviews. He was also the first writer to be asked to appear on television's *Meet the Press*, a program usually reserved for politicians and
statesmen. *Life* magazine ran eighteen pages about *In Cold Blood*, the
most space it had ever devoted to a professional writer. 'Such a deluge
of words and picture has never before been poured out over a book',
The New York Times reported.

Capote, the spinner of stories since boyhood, transfixed interviewer after interviewer with his story of the making of *In Cold
Blood*. There were three main threads to his public pitch: first, the
immense labour of his research; second, what he endured to write the
book; and third, that he had created a new art form (ed. Inge 1987;
Stanton 1980). Partly, this was strategic on his part; the events of the
book were, sadly, relatively common in America and their outcome
well known, but Capote's elaborate campaign also illustrated the scale
of his ambition and his egocentricity. As Clarke remarks: 'He told the
tale of his nearly six-year ordeal so often that it almost became part of
the national lore, like Washington's chopping down the cherry tree'
(Clarke 1988, p. 363). Capote's story-behind-the-story was not, like
Washington's cherry tree lopping, apocryphal, but he certainly exaggerated and, in parts, to put it bluntly, lied. In numerous interviews
Capote trumpeted the accuracy of his work and the near infallibility
of his memory that had enabled him to interview people without
taking notes. 'One doesn't spend almost six years on a book, the point
of which is factual accuracy, and then give way to minor distortions',
he sniffed to Plimpton, himself a practitioner of narrative non-fiction
as well as founding editor of *The Paris Review*.

You might argue Capote's emphasis on his accuracy was a way
of reassuring prospective readers, as *In Cold Blood* contained no
endnotes, index or notes on sources, even though the book's subtitle

is *A True Account of a Multiple Murder and Its Consequences*. There is a half-page of acknowledgements before the body of the book that reads: 'All the material in this book not derived from my own observation is either taken from official records or is the result of interviews with the persons directly concerned, more often than not numerous interviews conducted over a considerable period of time'. This is slightly more than readers of the original four-part series in *The New Yorker* were given. At the top of each part, under the headline and before the opening paragraph, is the following: 'Editor's note: all quotations in this article are taken either from official records or from conversations, transcribed verbatim, between the author and the principals'. By saying the conversations were transcribed verbatim, the editor's note promises a level of precision that Shawn, as the editor, could not have, and actually doubted Capote had.

Some of the inaccuracies and distortions of *In Cold Blood* have already been discussed; what needs to be highlighted here is the discrepancy between Capote's repeated claims in promotional interviews and documented sources. In one interview he said he had spent seven months in Kansas after the murders, but it was actually just one month. In several interviews Capote played up the thousands of pages of research notes he had taken before sitting down to write, but though 6000 pages was the figure commonly mentioned, his biographer lists it as 4000 pages, and in his letters Capote refers to 4000 pages in July 1960 but early the following year that figure had shrunk to 2000. In another interview Capote misremembered the headline of *The New York Times* article that had prompted his interest in the Clutter murders. It was 'Wealthy Farmer, 3 of Family Slain' but Capote recalled it as 'Eisenhower Appointee Murdered'. Herb Clutter had been appointed to the Federal Farm Credit Board by President Eisenhower, but that information was contained not in the headline but in the fifth paragraph of the news report (*The New York Times* 1959). It is not a substantial error but the *Times* article was a key part of the backstory of *In Cold Blood* and, as the English critic Kenneth Tynan tartly notes, Capote repeatedly claimed in interviews that he had trained himself to remember long conversations, but the percentage figure he gave for this near perfect accuracy wandered between 92, 95 and 97 per cent.

What is a more substantive matter is the discrepancy between what Capote said publicly and privately about waiting until the execution of Smith and Hickock to finish his book. Soon after the book's publication, Tynan, writing in *The Observer* in London, questioned Capote's morality on the ground that, 'For the first time, an influential writer of the front rank has been placed in a position of privileged intimacy with criminals about to die, and—in my view—done less than he might have to save them' (Tynan, 1967, p. 445). He also suggested a third meaning for the book's title—the cold-bloodedness of the author (1967, p. 445). Capote defended himself vigorously, saying Tynan's argument was not only incorrect, but that Tynan had 'the morals of a baboon and the guts of a butterfly' (Tynan, 1967, p. 451). Capote was probably right that it was not in his power to do anything more for Smith and Hickock, but Tynan had hit a raw nerve—Capote did not want to save them. Smith had told Capote in an interview *before* the murder trial that he had cut Herb Clutter's throat (Capote papers, Box 7, Folder 9), and as early as April 1961 Capote told the Deweys he had 'reached a point in my book where I must know how the book ends!' (ed. Clarke 2004, p. 314). But Capote did not acknowledge this publicly. Instead, he told an interviewer that 'as the years dragged on and the legal delays and complications multiplied, I still didn't know if I was going to be able to finish the book or even if there was any book there' (ed. Inge 1987, p. 123).

In 1979, Jack De Bellis analysed the production history of *In Cold Blood* and found that, between its publication in *The New Yorker* and in book form ten weeks later, Capote made more than 5000 changes. More than a third of these were matters of punctuation. Some phrases appear to have been made more colloquial, but that could be explained by the restraints imposed by the notorious prudishness of *The New Yorker*'s editor, William Shawn, who once insisted a writer change the word 'pissoir' to 'circular curbside construction'! For an author who claimed to be obsessed with accuracy, though, Capote proves surprisingly slipshod, especially considering the length of time he had worked on the manuscript and the oft-remarked status of *The New Yorker*'s fact-checking department. Late in the book Capote quotes the ninth stanza of Thomas Gray's *Elegy Written in a Country Churchyard* but introduced two changes ('boasts' became 'boast' and 'awaits' became 'await'), even though the version in *The New Yorker* agreed with the best bibliographic sources. Similarly, Capote changed the position of tattoos on Smith and Hickock's arms for the Random House edition, even though photographs taken by Richard Avedon of the convicted murderers for *The New Yorker* showed the original magazine copy was accurate. Capote even made revisions to eighteen documents mentioned in his book, including newspaper articles, a letter from Smith's sister and Hickock's police record. De Bellis comments: 'When a breach of trust is created with the reader over such confirmable matters, his doubts begin to gather about other matters of plot, characterization, symbolism, and theme of *In Cold Blood*' (1979, p. 529). Some quotations of several people change between magazine and book, notably Smith, with 187 changes. Many of these are relatively minor, but what is worrying is that they are quotations that already had been printed as such in *The New Yorker*. De Bellis says his overwhelming impression is that Capote 'could not resist re-examining his research and his style', and after comparing his findings with the evidence that Tompkins had unearthed, De Bellis concludes that a 'strain developed between Capote's intellectual strategy and the emotional reality he faced' (1979, p. 530).

This strain is evident in how Capote depicted Smith, and it is evident, too, in a closer reading of the interviews Capote gave to publicise *In Cold Blood*. This reveals a tension between the second and third threads of the yarn he spun for the public. When Capote talks about what he endured to create the book he includes the emotional strain of becoming close to the two convicted murderers (especially Smith), of corresponding with them over five years and watching as they deteriorated on death row. When Capote talks about creating a new art form, though, he reduces the two men to subjects in an experiment he is conducting. He told Haskell Frankel of *The Saturday Review* in January 1966 that he became 'very very good friends' and 'very very close intimates' of Smith and Hickock and that, if at the outset he had known what the book would cost him emotionally, he would never have started it. He told Gloria Steinem, writing for *Glamour* magazine in April 1966, that Smith had bequeathed his belongings to him and that when they arrived after the execution he 'couldn't even look at them for a long time'.

After reflecting on the inhumanity of the appeals system, Capote says he became so 'emotionally involved that it was almost a question of personal survival' and that he was now 'weary inside'. But he told Plimpton, writing for *The New York Times Book Review* in January 1966, that when Smith had asked him why he was writing a book, Capote told Smith he was pursuing a 'strictly aesthetic theory' about creating a non-fiction book that would be a work of art. In a lengthy interview with *Playboy* magazine in 1968, after *In Cold Blood* had been adapted for film and Capote had made a documentary about capital punishment, he referred to the book as an experiment at least three times:

> I'd had several dry runs that didn't work out. I was searching for a suitable subject and, like a bacteriologist, I kept putting slides under the microscope, scrutinizing them and finally reject-ing them as unsuitable. It was like trying to solve a quadratic equation with the X—in this case, the subject matter—missing (ed. Inge 1987, p. 122).

Capote's friend, Donald Windham, among others, noted that most people portrayed in the book were dead by the time *In Cold Blood* was published. Dewey was alive and presented as a diligent detective of integrity. There is no reason to think otherwise of Dewey, but Capote became a close friend of the detective and probably overemphasised the importance of his role and the unerring nature of his detective work (Helliker 2013, p. x). Capote also become close to Dewey's wife, Marie, and their son, Alvin Junior; he addressed them as 'dearhearts' in his letters, he referred to *In Cold Blood* as 'our book' and he spent considerable time reading and commenting on Alvin Junior's literary compositions. One unintended victim of the book was Hickock's son. His mother had remarried and the boy had not known the identity of his father until he read *In Cold Blood* for a school assignment, which deeply upset him. His mother feared he might commit suicide, accord-ing to Rev. James Post, chaplain at the prison where Smith and Hickock had been on death row. Post told Capote's oral biographer, Plimpton, he had immediately gone to see the boy:

I didn't minimize the horrible things that he'd done or anything like that. But I said his dad wasn't the sex fiend that Capote tried to make him out ... like trying to rape the Clutter girl before he killed her ... it didn't happen. And other things ... lies, just to make it a better story (1998, p. 195).

There is no corroborating evidence for Post's recollection, but no reason to disbelieve him either. Just as it is clear how much Capote identified with Smith from his letters and from biographies of him, it is also clear he had little interest in Hickock, regarding him as 'just a smart-aleck, small-time crook' with a 'check-bouncing mentality' (ed. Inge 1987, pp. 133, 129). In a mini-biography of Hickock that Capote compiled in his research notes, there is no mention of Hickock having sex with underage girls (Capote papers, Box 7, Folder 14). But, as we have seen, and as Capote writes in a letter, he did not mind 'inventing details'.

What are we to conclude from this catalogue of missteps, bad faith and deception? Should we simply read *In Cold Blood* as a novel and forget the non-fiction? This is certainly easy to do, nearly half a century after its publication, but the book was about actual people and events, and sought to present a 'true account'. That is certainly what Capote told interviewer after interviewer. It should be assessed on that basis. We may not lose much sleep about two convicted murderers, but what about their victims, who include (indirectly) Hickock's son as well as the Clutters? I wouldn't want to dissuade anyone from reading *In Cold Blood* because it *is* powerfully written, but you should read it with eyes open. And that means recognising its significant flaws as well as its significant achievements. Capote provides readers with even fewer means than Woodward of assessing the veracity of his work. A careful examination of public and private sources of information shows Capote manipulating and lying about his work, and distorting his representation of people and events to the point of outright invention.

It is possible to argue, as Norman Sims has in *True Stories: A Century of Literary Journalism*, that Capote was working within the standards of his time and that practices have since improved. I would agree, but for reasons that are not clear, this leads Sims to underplay

Capote's shortcomings. '*In Cold Blood* carried a model for reporting and writing that held more significance for the New Journalism than did some inaccuracies about the price paid for a horse named Babe' (2007, p. 242). Maybe, but as I have shown, the problems of *In Cold Blood* go well beyond the price of horseflesh. These problems, as well as Capote's innovations, have prompted reflective practitioners both to grapple with the issues thrown up in researching and writing true stories and to show them the exciting possibilities of the form. The fruits of those reflections are what need to be considered next.

Chapter 5

The Janet Malcolm dilemma: developing trust with principal sources *and* keeping editorial independence

There must have been occasions when U2 regretted that I was around, but they never tried to get me to bury something. They took the best attitude anyone can take with a working writer: 'I knew he was a scorpion when I put him on my back'.

Bill Flanagan, *U2 at the End of the World*

After looking at two landmark true stories, one written by a practitioner with a background in newspapers, the other in fiction, we begin to see a number of complex, interlocking questions. Is it possible to write in an omniscient narrative voice, or is omniscience incompatible with narrative non-fiction? Does it matter whether people read a work as fiction or non-fiction, as happened with *In Cold Blood*? What rules, if any, should apply to writers reconstructing scenes and dialogue that they did not witness for themselves? Should they provide endnotes or notes on sources to help readers assess the veracity of their work? There are more questions, but even listing these and thinking about how both Woodward and Capote struggled to resolve them shows why I was prompted to devise a framework in which to hold, articulate and mull over the issues thrown up by the practice of telling true stories.

The framework is built around the experience of the writer, beginning with how they research their subject, moving to how they represent in a book what they have found and on to the terms on which they offer their work to readers. The framework, then, is tripartite, taking in the research phase of the practitioner's project, the writing phase and the reception phase. Practitioners have responsibilities to those they write about as well as those they write for, and these people—the true story's subjects and its readers—are as valued in this framework as the writer. The tripartite framework sits alongside the work of Daniel Lehman, a journalist and, later, a literary academic, whose scholarship I value both because he grounds his criticism in an explicit consideration of the ethical issues arising in literary non-fiction and for the framework he developed in *Matters of Fact* for understanding the complex series of relationships that exist in non-fiction between reader, writer and subject. Lehman's framework is important for the breadth and depth of inter-relationships it envisages in literary non-fiction, but the tripartite framework I have developed revolves around the writer, mainly because it is, I think, more accessible than Lehman's framework, making it more likely to take hold, especially among practitioners, and it is at this group, as much as the academy, that this book is aimed.

The framework I have devised also begins with the knowledge that, just as ethical issues potentially arise throughout the production of daily journalism, so they can arise throughout the production of a book-length true story. Some issues are common across newspaper, magazine and book-length journalism while some, I propose, arise in a particular form or are felt more urgently in the practise of book-length or long-form journalism. As there is already a substantial scholarly and professional literature about ethical issues arising in news journalism, I am focussing on those that are distinctive to long-form journalism or narrative non-fiction. For instance, I devoted considerable space in the previous two chapters to discussing the work of Capote and Woodward, but there I focussed on the particular issues arising from them practising journalism at book length. Ethical issues that could have arisen equally if they were writing daily journalism, such as whether Capote paid bribes to get access to the two convicted murderers in gaol (Clarke 1988, p. 343) or whether

Woodward and Bernstein flouted the Federal Rules of Criminal Procedure by trying to interview members of the Watergate Grand Jury, were not discussed in the previous chapters (Bernstein & Woodward 1974, pp. 204–25; Christians et al. 1995, pp. 77–80).

The writer is the starting point and through-line for examining issues in narrative non-fiction because they generally initiate the idea for their book projects and because the subjects of their work and their readers only become involved because of their relationship with the writer or with what that person produces. Research is essential to producing true stories; accordingly, to assess a true story's success you need some sense of how the writer went about their research. If they have made significant factual errors, omitted relevant information or seriously misrepresented their subjects then their book's claims to veracity are undermined. In other words, the standards commonly applied to newspaper and magazine journalism extend to book-length projects. This does not mean two writers working on the same topic will produce identical books; as in daily journalism and in histories there is plenty of scope for conscientious writers to take differing approaches to research, to dig into the primary sources at different levels and to differ in their interpretations of documents, people and issues. But any work that is about actual people, places and events, and is presented as such, needs to be assessed in that domain, for legal reasons if for no other. The means by which novelists gather material or draw on their imagination also shapes their writing. Researching a novelist's working methods and the interplay between their imagination and events or people in their life can tell us something about the creative process, but novels can be enjoyed by readers without knowing anything of that. This is not so in narrative non-fiction, which makes claims to veracity. Or, it may be possible to enjoy a work of narrative non-fiction without knowing about the research process that shaped the book, but to do that readers either need to accept on trust the work's claims to veracity or read the book as fiction, or be unconcerned about the relationship between the two. A writer cannot control exactly how people will react to their work, but they can be held responsible for what they present readers and the terms on which they present it. The important question of how readers can assess true stories when they know little or less about the events being described will be discussed in Chapters 11 and 12. But now, investigating the research phase of narrative non-fiction has potential to illuminate issues usually not considered by literary studies scholars who historically have tended to focus more on the text than on how what is in the text came to be in it.

Practitioners working on book-length projects conduct their research by gathering and analysing documents, whether in print or online, by interviewing people and by observing events at first hand. The questions arising for practitioners as they research include: should some conventional practices of daily journalism, such as not paying sources for material (sometimes honoured in the breach, admittedly) and not showing them what has been written before publication be reconsidered in book-length projects? Should practitioners of such projects be less willing to grant sources anonymity? The time available to practitioners of book-length projects to immerse themselves in the culture of those they are writing about offers the opportunity to become closer to sources than is customary in daily journalism and to develop a trusting relationship that enables the practitioner to present such people, who I call principal sources, not in snapshots but in a more developed portrait. To do this, the practitioner needs to gather material about the principal source's appearance, their dress and their habits. They will want to know how the source felt and how they responded in situations that are highly personal or extreme, and that may have revealed them in a poor light. Practitioners will need to find a balance between maintaining their editorial independence and managing the hurt they may cause by writing honestly about their principal sources.

Before going any further, it should be emphasised that not all works of narrative non-fiction require practitioners to develop close relationships with their sources. Malcolm Gladwell's *The Tipping Point*, for instance, revolves around the exploration of an idea rather than any particular person's experience. Even in narrative non-fiction works that have principal sources, the practitioner probably will have interviewed numerous other sources briefly, or even at length, to obtain specific information. But where practitioners need a high degree of trust and cooperation from their principal sources, they encounter issues rare in daily journalism where, typically, contact with sources is either fleeting or takes place within a professional relation-ship whose terms are narrowly drawn. When daily journalists develop long-term close relationships with sources, they generally continue to draw on their information for hard news reports rather than write about their sources in a narrative style. In other words, practitioners working on long-form stories may well have little choice but to face the difficulties of the journalist–source relationship because they cannot avoid it by simply moving to their next assignment.

The most difficult issue perhaps for practitioners of this form of writing, then, is how they negotiate and manage the fine and sometimes porous boundaries between professional and personal relationships inherent in becoming close to principal sources. Few scholars and even fewer practitioners had examined this in any detail, but it was a practitioner, not a scholar—Janet Malcolm—who in 1989 shone a light of laser intensity on it. In an opening paragraph, which has been described as 'one of the most provocative in the history of American journalism' (Fakazis 2002, pp. 93–4), Malcolm wrote:

> Every journalist who is not too stupid or too full of himself to notice what is going on knows that what he does is morally inde-fensible. He is a kind of confidence man, preying on people's vanity, ignorance, or loneliness, gaining their trust and betraying them without remorse. Like the credulous widow who wakes up one day to find the charming young man and all her savings gone, so the consenting subject of a piece of nonfiction writing learns— when the article or book appears—*his* hard lesson. Journalists justify their treachery in various ways according to their tempera-ments. The more pompous talk about freedom of speech and 'the public's right to know;' the least talented talk about Art; the seemliest murmur about earning a living (1990, p. 3).

Malcolm's words, first published in a two-part article for *The New Yorker*, later published as a book, created a furore among journalists. What about sources who tried to manipulate journalists, asked some? How could Malcolm condemn an entire profession on a single case, asked others? Why did she not mention a libel suit in which her own journalistic practice was being questioned? And, finally, why did she write with such infuriating certitude? Martin Gottlieb, writing in *Columbia Journalism Review*, the American news media industry's leading trade publication, said the vehemence of many journalists' responses suggests Malcolm had hit an exposed nerve. Elizabeth Fakazis, in her PhD about a libel suit in which Malcolm was the defendant, notes that there had been little media interest in the lawsuit until after 'Reflections: The Journalist and the Murderer' was published in *The New Yorker*, and then it was overwhelmingly negative.

The journalists' objections were not entirely misdirected, however. Taking them one by one: first, Malcolm does not ignore the role of sources. She understands how sources try to persuade journalists of the validity of their perspective. She understands the still potent lure for sources of fame, or at least publicity. She also explores the source's desperate need for what Malcolm refers to as their 'story' to be found interesting by the journalist, which she compares to Scheherazade in *The Thousand and One Arabian Nights*. It is fair to say, though, that she underplays the source's role and power in their relationship with journalists. Second, of course journalism should not be condemned on the strength of one case study; nor should other groups in society, as journalists themselves might well remember before, to take one instance among many, welding the adjective 'bungling' to the noun 'bureaucrats' in newspaper headlines. Third, Malcolm did ignore in her article the lawsuit brought against her over an earlier article, headlined 'Annals of Scholarship: Trouble in the Archives' that appeared in *The New Yorker* on 5 and 12 December 1983. When 'Reflections: The Journalist and the Murderer' was published in book form she defended her decision in an afterword, but her argument was almost as thin as the original article's opening had been provocative. As one of her most perceptive, and otherwise admiring, critics, Craig Seligman, writes in *Salon* (2005): 'A more stupefying specimen of bullshit would be hard to find—though there's also something reassuring, even endearing, in this demonstration that Malcolm can be just as neurotic and self-deceiving as the rest of us'. Finally, the elegantly stinging certitude that characterises Malcolm's prose points to a paradox in her work; namely that she articulates, even delights in, the ambiguities of issues in a ringing, unambiguous tone.

The effect of Malcolm's approach has been to substantially influence a debate—for better and for worse. Her insights were soon reflected in the academic literature (Elliot & Culver 1992; Borden 1993), continue to be debated (Cowan 1998; Goldstein 2007) and have been cited approvingly by Jonathan Harr and Jon Krakauer, two of Boynton's interviewees. Malcolm's writing offers an insight into journalist–source relationships rather than a framework for analysing its range of characteristics in their complexity, and yet that is how many, including her, treat her insight. What makes her work so relevant, though, is that the case central to *The Journalist and the Murderer* involved not a newspaper or magazine journalist, but one working on a narrative non-fiction book, which means her insights, while pertinent, apply less to daily journalism where, as Wendell Rawls Sr, a newspaper executive, says, practitioners rarely spend enough time with a source to develop an emotional relationship that might later feel like betrayal to the source (Gottlieb 1989). Instead, her insights are more relevant to those working on extended projects.

A good place to begin understanding these issues is to draw on anthropology, where immersing oneself in another culture is central to the field. Anthropologists need the informed consent of their hosts before beginning; this includes making hosts aware of the potential impact of the research on their lives, and allowing them to withdraw at any time and to remain anonymous. Further, it is understood that informed consent is a process that is dynamic and continuous (eds Bromley & Carter 2001). The American Anthropological Association's code of ethics says a researcher's primary obligation is to the people they study, to the point of discontinuing projects if honouring that is jeopardised. Informed consent clearly applies to narrative non-fiction, but notions of editorial independence are central to any writing that aims to scrutinise what is going on in the world, especially in the face of opposition from those in positions of power and authority. Central, too, is a commitment to reaching the broadest possible audience. The principles underlying informed consent, though, do prod practitioners to ask whether they need to consider more deeply their principal sources' wellbeing rather than treat them simply as a conduit for information, as the word 'source' connotes.

With this in mind, it is valuable to examine Malcolm's *The Journalist and the Murderer*, which is also itself an important work of narrative non-fiction. It focuses on just one case, which originated in an approach to Malcolm by a legal team representing a journalist, Joe McGinniss, who was being sued by a convicted murderer, Jeffrey MacDonald, over his true crime book entitled *Fatal Vision*. Published in 1983, *Fatal Vision* is about MacDonald's conviction for murdering his pregnant wife and two young children. MacDonald's guilt or innocence is not the focus of my discussion, but it is important to keep in mind that despite his conviction in 1979 and several unsuccessful appeals, MacDonald still steadfastly maintains his innocence. Gaols, of course, are full of people making such protestations, but in 2012 Errol Morris published the result of his exhaustive reinvestigation of the case in *A Wilderness of Errors*, which at the least raises serious doubts about the handling of evidence that led to the original conviction. In any case, McGinniss's lawyers believed the lawsuit represented a threat to the free press protection afforded to writers under the first amendment of the American constitution.

MacDonald was not suing for defamation but for breach of contract by McGinniss. MacDonald and his legal team had originally approached McGinniss to write about the murder trial, offering unfettered access to MacDonald and the legal team's strategy in exchange for more than a quarter of the US$300,000 advance and one-third of any royalties from the book that McGinniss would write about the case. McGinniss agreed, but during the trial began doubting the innocence of his principal source. He did not share these doubts with MacDonald or his legal team. By the end, McGinniss agreed with the jury that MacDonald had murdered his family. He did not tell MacDonald his view. He had already developed a close relationship with MacDonald before the trial, staying at his home with him, drinking beer, watching sport on television, jogging together and 'classifying women according to looks', as Malcolm put it, but he still needed to gather information about MacDonald's childhood, his marriage and his military career. He was not allowed to interview MacDonald in prison, so he gathered it primarily by correspondence. The prisoner wanted to see the manuscript but McGinniss refused on the grounds that he needed to retain editorial independence.

It was only when *Fatal Vision* was published that MacDonald learnt unequivocally of McGinniss's change of mind. MacDonald sued, citing a clause in their agreement exempting the journalist from libel claims, 'providing that the essential integrity of my life story is maintained'. The breach of contract case was heard in 1987 before a judge and jury. What intrigued Malcolm was that, by her account, 'five of the six jurors were persuaded that a man who was serving three consecutive life sentences for the murder of his wife and two small children was deserving of more sympathy than the writer who had deceived him' (1990, p. 6). I say by her account because her statement was contested by McGinniss, a point to which I will return. Malcolm quoted extensively from a series of around forty of McGinniss's letters to MacDonald in jail and from his cross-examination at the trial, as they showed in great detail the rarely exposed underbelly of journalistic practice. In his first letter McGinniss sympathises that anyone could see MacDonald had not received a fair trial, and laments:

> Goddamn, Jeff, one of the worst things about all this is how suddenly and totally all your friends—self included—have been deprived of the pleasure of your company. What the fuck were those people thinking of? How could 12 people not only agree to believe such a horrendous proposition, but agree, with a man's life at stake, that they believed it beyond a reasonable doubt? In six and a half hours? (Malcolm 1990, p. 36).

If McGinniss often presented himself to MacDonald as a friend, he later told Malcolm that the former army doctor was clearly trying to manipulate him and that he had been aware of this from the outset. 'But did I have an obligation to say, "Wait a minute. I think you are manipulating me, and I have to call your attention to the fact that I'm aware of this, just so you'll understand you are not succeeding"' (Malcolm, 1990, p. 17). He acknowledged to another journalist who had covered the murder trial that he felt 'terribly conflicted'. He had come to like MacDonald, but asked himself 'how can you like a guy who has killed his wife and kids?'. In response to the *Newsday* journalist's question about whether he had betrayed MacDonald, McGinniss said: 'My only obligation from the beginning was to the truth'. McGinniss was arguing that the ends justified the means, but MacDonald's lawyer, Gary Bostwick, swooped on the switch in McGinniss's behaviour. To some, it may appear axiomatic that a journalist is not a friend, but Malcolm interviewed four of the six jurors in the case, reporting them worried by the slippage between friendship and journalism. One tells her:

> 'The part I didn't like was when MacDonald let McGinniss use his condominium, and McGinniss took it upon himself to find the motive for the murders,' she said. 'I didn't like the fact that McGinniss tried to find a motive for a book that was a best-seller, and that's *all* he was concerned about' (1990, p. 44).

Well-known writers such as William F. Buckley Jr and Joseph Wambaugh testified in support of McGinniss's practices, but they did not fare well under Bostwick's cross-examination. In his closing argument, Bostwick said that the practitioners' argument that they would do whatever was necessary to write their book was one that had been used by demagogues and dictators throughout history to justify their actions.

Journalists' ruthlessness in pursuing news is hardly news: what made Malcolm's work of media criticism 'newsworthy' was that she put under a microscope a rarely discussed aspect of journalist–source relationships. Journalists in newspapers and magazines sometimes present a friendly face to sources before attacking them in print, but the process is quicker, cruder and less ethically complex than in long-form projects where practitioners must go beyond a dazzling smile and create a deeper level of trust with principal sources. The evidence suggests MacDonald was manipulative and deceitful, but so too was McGinniss in lying about his belief that MacDonald was guilty after sending him letters giving the opposite impression and after apparently befriending MacDonald. The publishing contract protected McGinniss's editorial independence (Kornstein 1989, pp. 133–6), but once McGinniss agreed to share his book earnings with MacDonald he had, in effect, signed a Faustian pact. He surely knew it was always possible the charge would be upheld in court; when that eventuated McGinniss had to share his royalties with a convicted triple murderer.

McGinniss's editorial independence was crippled by the financial agreement he had with his principal source. If a news organisation had paid MacDonald for an interview it would have been seen as chequebook journalism. McGinniss could perhaps have mitigated his problem by disclosing the agreement, but he did not mention it in *Fatal Vision* when recounting how he came to write the book (1989, pp. 3–7), nor in an afterword written two years after the first edition, by which time MacDonald had sued. The financial agreement drew the ire of respected practitioners, such as David Halberstam and even one who had testified on McGinniss's behalf (Gottlieb 1989).

Where McGinniss had few defenders for the financial agreement, the questions of when practitioners might be justified in deceiving their principal sources and the fine line between trust and friendship are murkier; Malcolm made a significant contribution to exposing and exploring these issues. Such is the persuasive power of her prose, however, that it almost obscures from view the more conventional interpretation of the MacDonald–McGinniss dispute, namely that MacDonald tried to use McGinniss to push his claims of innocence and when McGinniss reached the opposite conclusion, MacDonald sought to punish him. Few journalists of more than a couple of years' standing would not have experienced the wrath of a source about whom they had written something unfavourable. Imagine instead the case not through the prism of the deceitful journalist but through that of the murderer. Leaving aside whether MacDonald is a murderer or has been wrongly convicted, what kind of good faith did he show by agreeing to cooperate fully with McGinniss, only as long as McGinniss portrayed him in a way that met MacDonald's approval? At a pretrial hearing for the civil suit, federal magistrate James McMahon said MacDonald wanted the services of a 'kept journalist' or a 'PR man' (McGinniss 1989, p. 675). At the trial, MacDonald admitted that despite his contract, he would have ceased cooperating with McGinniss if he had learnt unequivocally the writer believed him guilty (Kornstein 1989). Malcolm's skill as a writer means she supplants the standard reading of the McGinniss–MacDonald case that would draw on the long history of valiant struggles for journalistic freedom in the face of opposition. The term 'Watergate' is today shorthand for just such a masterplot, as we saw in Chapter 3. The

standard reading of the case would have seen McGinniss the journalist as David and MacDonald the murderer as Goliath, but somehow
Malcolm makes the murderer David and the journalist Goliath.

By pushing out of view the standard reading of the case, Malcolm
opens the question of the journalist–source relationship, but she also
distorts the MacDonald–McGinniss relationship. First, as mentioned
earlier, one of Malcolm's most potent assertions is that at the civil
trial, five of the six jurors were more sympathetic to the murderer
than the journalist. McGinniss and his lawyer, Daniel Kornstein,
both argue this seriously misrepresents the trial, which they emphas-
ise Malcolm did not attend. To reach their decision, the jurors were
instructed by the judge to answer thirty-six questions about issues
heard in the trial. They needed to reach unanimous agreement on a
question before moving to the next one. The first question concerned
not McGinniss but MacDonald. It asked whether the convicted
murderer 'had performed all of the obligations and conditions on
him under the contract'. One juror found MacDonald had broken his
contract; others were unsure and confused about a 'thicket of legal-
ities' (Kornstein 1989, p. 132). The jury was deadlocked and the judge
had to declare a mistrial. None of the other questions, which, among
other things, went to McGinniss's behaviour towards MacDonald,
was voted on by the jury. The jury forewoman was quoted in the
news media saying that, despite widespread assumptions that the jury
sympathised with MacDonald and 'were going to give him the
Earth', that was not so. She would have welcomed the opportunity
to say that 'MacDonald got what he asked for and McGinniss did
what he said he'd do' (Kornstein 1989, pp. 132–3). One media outlet
quoted several jurors, saying they would not have awarded damages
against the journalist and another, in its report of the trial, printed a
photograph of McGinniss accompanied by the caption: 'Writer Wins
Court Victory' (Kornstein 1989, p. 133). If McGinniss and Kornstein
themselves have distorted the evidence, Malcolm, to my knowledge,
has never responded to their arguments.

Second, by underplaying the extent to which sources may be
able, not to mention willing, to manipulate journalists, Malcolm mis-
characterises MacDonald. She marvels that despite all the problems
MacDonald had with McGinniss, he was happy to talk to her and to

other journalists, and draws an analogy with psychoanalysis where the patient regresses in their relationship with the therapist. There is something to be said for this idea, but an alternative explanation has equal force. MacDonald has been sitting in jail convicted of murder. He believes he is innocent and is desperate to find someone to write his version of events and help win him a new trial. He has only one card in his hand—access to him—and he plays it to maximum effect. Third, Malcolm characterises the journalist–source relationship in one way—seduction followed by betrayal—and aims to avoid such behaviour in her own practice, putting the needs of her 'text' ahead of the 'feelings' of her sources, but she also writes that McGinniss's decision to stop being interviewed by her freed her from any 'guilt' she might have felt in portraying him harshly. This is tantamount to saying there are only two possible ways practitioners can engage with their principal sources: seduce then betray them, or stay clear so that you can treat people as 'characters' in a 'text' rather than autonomous human beings. Errol Morris, in his book about the MacDonald case, is exaggerating but not wrong, I think, when he writes that Malcolm's characterisation of the journalist–subject relationship is 'like creating a general theory of human relationships based on Iago's relationship with Othello' (Morris 2012, pp. 392–93).

Malcolm rightly excoriates McGinniss for deceiving MacDonald, but her own practice does not envisage the possibility of practitioners openly disagreeing with principal sources and continuing to work with them. After all the intelligence and courage Malcolm shows in opening up the journalist–source relationship, she closes it down by writing, in a paragraph added to the original article when *The Journalist and the Murderer* was published in book form, that 'nothing can be done' about the falseness built into the journalist–source relationship, and in the afterword describing it as 'the canker that lies at the heart of the rose of journalism'. This is a pity, because not only is Malcolm an acutely perceptive critic and superb prose stylist, but the affect of her brilliant but narrow framing of the journalist–source relationship is to provoke strong agreement or disagreement, leaving little space for other ways to think about it.

To begin opening up this space, then, consider the common (but not universal) newsroom practice of not showing sources what has been written before publication for fear of the source trying to retract what they have said on the record or of taking pre-emptive legal action. The development of online communication technologies that encourage greater interactivity, plus the time available to those working on long-form projects, means practitioners have greater scope to make and fulfil agreements, whether verbal or written, and to ensure sources have an opportunity to correct factual errors and put forward their view about the writer's interpretations. Sources may well sue for libel or take legal action to prevent a book's publication, but this strategy often backfires, drawing even more attention to the book. On this question, Boynton's interviewees in *The New New Journalism* are divided. Three of them—William Finnegan, Jon Krakauer and Susan Orlean—do not allow sources to see what has been written before publication, but five of them do— Richard Ben Cramer, Alex Kotlowitz, Richard Preston, Lawrence Weschler and Lawrence Wright. A writer's willingness to read back a source's quotations will depend on the volatility of the subject being written about, as well as a desire for accuracy. The key point is that the time available, plus growing media literacy in society, gives—or insists on—more flexibility in dealings between practitioners and sources; sometimes the checking process with sources leads to better understanding and even fresh material because it demonstrates the writer's commitment to accuracy. For Preston, the 'fact-checking interview' becomes another interview in which 'often the most important and interesting material flows forth'. Checking material with sources does not include giving them power of veto over the book's contents, according to these five practitioners.

There is broad agreement that once practitioners enter into financial relationships with sources their editorial independence is open to compromise, as is vividly illustrated by the McGinniss–MacDonald case. Sometimes practitioners act as 'ghostwriters' either on behalf of or in cooperation with the principal source, usually a celebrity of some kind, and in these cases royalties are shared or the ghostwriter is paid a one-off fee. The expectation of this particular sub-genre is that the ghostwriter is acting as an agent of the subject and will include in the book only what the subject wants included, which means the practitioner gives up their editorial independence. There are some cases of a peculiar hybrid between ghostwriting and editorial independence, as when former Australian Prime Minister Malcolm Fraser's memoirs were co-authored by Margaret Simons. She did independent research and, at Fraser's insistence, he was referred to in the third person as if the book was a biography rather than memoir. Simons discussed the oddness of the arrangement in 'A Note from the Narrator'. *Malcolm Fraser: The Political Memoirs* won a New South Wales Premier's literary award for non-fiction, and praise from the judges for using 'literary craft' to 'transcend the usual limitations of political auto/biography'. It was also criticised for ignoring or underplaying or misrepresenting some controversial episodes in Fraser's public life, a shortcoming common in political memoirs.

The spread of celebrity culture and of people using new media technologies to make their own media has prompted a keen sense of the commercial worth of people's own experiences and stories. It is possible, then, that journalists working on book-length projects will encounter a principal source represented by an agent aiming to extract the maximum amount of money for the minimum level of scrutiny; in other words, requiring a ghostwriter. Those unwilling to act as ghostwriters may still question the convention of never paying for information on the ground that principal sources, and perhaps other sources too, involved in a book-length project may give the journalist months of their time and energy, emotional and otherwise. Krakauer told Boynton in *The New New Journalism* that the blanket opposition to paying sources that is widely taught in journalism schools is a self-serving axiom:

> According to the accepted standards it's okay to buy a subject a nice dinner, but it's not okay to pay them cold hard cash? That's so patronizing. We have the right to enrich ourselves off of these people whose lives we may ruin, but we never, under any circumstances, owe them anything? Give me a fucking break (2005, p. 169).

What Krakauer did when researching *Under the Banner of Heaven*, a book about fundamentalist Mormon brothers who had slain a sister-in-law and niece in a ritual murder was, he felt, a step forward, but still a compromise. He bought one-off literary rights to a fundamentalist Mormon woman's memoir that he did not really need because she had already told him everything in it during their interviews. She was poor, however, and he wanted to compensate her for her time.

One way to combat the difficulties posed by paying sources is to disclose any financial relationship, giving readers the opportunity to assess whether payment affects the quality of the book. Krakauer did not disclose in *Under the Banner of Heaven* the payment he made for the memoir, but it appears journalists who write books rarely do. McGinniss's agreement became public only because of MacDonald's civil suit. On occasion, practitioners make clear they did not pay their principal sources for information, which is what I did in a biography of author Paul Jennings (2000, p. 304). Writers' reluctance to disclose financial agreements with principal sources may stem from a desire to preserve their own privacy as much as their anxiety over readers perceiving payment will taint the book's independence. One practitioner who probably regretted the decision to disclose is Gitta Sereny who, in 1998, wrote a book entitled *Cries Unheard* about Mary Bell, who in 1968 as an eleven-year-old girl had murdered two boys aged three and four in Newcastle, England. Sereny had reported on the murder trial, which not surprisingly stirred enormous public interest, and had written a book about it at the time. She had since followed Bell's life in special detention centres and prison as she grew up.

By 1995 Bell was in a stable relationship with a man and had a young daughter; her mother had died and she began to feel able to confront her past, including her mother's four attempts to kill her as a child and sexual abuse that occurred by being included in her mother's work as a prostitute. Sereny, who died in 2012, was a distinguished practitioner who wrote extensively about Nazi Germany, notably *Into That Darkness*, about the commandant of Treblinka extermination camp, Franz Stangl. Her continued preoccupation with Bell's case derived from her belief that parents, the judicial system and society as a whole do not heed the cries of disturbed children until it is too late. She considered sharing her advance and book royalties with Bell in the hope that the money would be used to help support Bell's child and because without Bell the book could not be written, which echoes Krakauer's view. Sereny also knew it would be deeply distressing for Bell to relive her childhood experiences.

Both Sereny and Bell knew the families of the murdered boys would find it very difficult to condone Bell receiving any payment for the book; they suspected the daily news media would be outraged, even though various news organisations had previously offered Bell more than UK£100,000 for her story, offers that often had been solicited by Bell's mother. The predicted media frenzy ensued and though Bell's identity and whereabouts were protected by law—she had changed her name several times because journalists had found her—she was found again by the news media. She and her daughter were forced to flee under blankets as the cameras whirred. The Press Complaints Commission heard a complaint about the payment to Bell, as the book had been serialised in *The Times*, bringing it into the commission's bailiwick. The commission dismissed the complaint as, under the law, payments to criminals extend only to crimes committed within the past six years and, though it had received no formal complaint about the media's harassment, the commission expressed great sympathy for the plight of Bell's daughter (Sereny 1998, pp. 406–14).

Paying a convicted child murderer presents a thicket of questions; what is clear, though, is the careful way Sereny tried to steer her way through them, not with unqualified success, as she acknowledges. Her publication record shows a journalist committed to exploring rather than sensationalising issues, and she chose profoundly disturbing issues to explore. Sereny raised the possibility of payment to Bell not, it appears, as a way of persuading her to cooperate, but in recognition of the cost, both material and emotional, to Bell of cooperating with her between 1995 and the book's publication in 1998. It is important, too, that she talked through, with Bell and others, the problem posed by the proposed payment, and she disclosed the arrangement to readers at the outset of the book. The point is not that Sereny's payment to Bell was the only course of action available; other practitioners might have decided otherwise. It is hard to fault the seriousness and sincerity with which Sereny considered her choices. It is also hard to find anything but fault in the actions of Sereny's daily news colleagues who not only repeatedly invaded the privacy of Bell's innocent daughter, but swiftly and sanctimoniously condemned the agreement after themselves routinely offering money for the 'story' of the person they described in headlines as an 'Evil Monster', as she recounts in an introduction to a subsequent paperback edition.

If the forming of a financial relationship between journalist and source is at best vulnerable to misinterpretation and at worst untenable, then the forming of a personal relationship between practitioner and source throws up equally thorny issues. We have already seen, with *In Cold Blood* and *The Journalist and the Murderer*, what happens when a writer feigns a personal relationship with a principal source or so blurs the line between the personal and the professional that the writer or the source, or both, are confused about the nature of their relationship. At one end of the spectrum are sexual relationships. None of the practitioners interviewed by Boynton or by me advocate forming sexual or intimate relationships with sources, but it would be naïve to think such relationships do not occur or that they do not add something to the texture of a work of narrative non-fiction. But clearly a writer's judgement would be coloured, probably clouded, if they have a sexual or intimate relationship with a source; if the practitioner and principal source wanted to complete the project, the relationship should be disclosed to readers regardless of the privacy implications.

The Australian journalist and novelist Blanche d'Alpuget had an adulterous affair with Bob Hawke before she wrote a biography of the trade union leader that not only sold well, but was important in persuading people within the Labor Party that Hawke was a serious contender for the party's leadership, from where he won the 1983 federal election and became prime minister. D'Alpuget's biography played down his womanising and made no mention of their affair. Long rumoured in political and media circles, these details were only confirmed twenty-six years after publication when d'Alpuget, by then Hawke's wife, gave an interview to publicise an essay she wrote entitled *On Longing*, in which she referred to Hawke as 'the Muse' and, later, 'M'. Regarded as the most successful of several books about Hawke, d'Alpuget's biography is, I think, diminished by her failure to disclose important, relevant information to readers and by her willingness to fashion the book for party political advantage (Legge 2008b).

Writing about friends and family raises complex issues, but such works are moving closer to memoir or autobiography, which, although a popular and valuable form of true story, is not one I will spend much time on in this book, mainly because the focus of a memoir is one person's experience of the world rather a practitioner's exploration of it. Both are valid forms of writing, but the latter not only reflects my background in journalism but my interest in discussing the issues inherent in telling other people's true stories. So, writers who form a personal relationship with a source—who become a friend, in effect—face a choice when writing of putting their new friend's interests ahead of the reader's interests. If they choose the former they are unlikely to write anything that reflects poorly on the source/friend, and so weaken the book's claims to veracity. If they opt for the latter, they may offend or upset the source/friend because, at some point in a true story, the source's flaws or foibles or blind spots will, in all likelihood, need to be written about. It is important to note that writing something revealing about a source in a poor light is no more a precondition than revealing the source in a good light. Examining people and issues in a book-length project is aimed at portraying them in their complexity. Neither the writer nor the source will necessarily know how the source will be presented until the book is written; friendship between the two is unlikely to help either party. Practitioners seeking friends through their projects are probably asking for trouble; it does seem a roundabout way to build your social circle.

Sometimes, however, the process of working together on an extended project as writer and source leads to a personal relationship. The question arises, will the journalist write about the source again, or does their personal relationship preclude this? John McPhee and Bill Bradley both attended Princeton University, but a dozen years apart, and in 1965 when Bradley was establishing himself as a college basketballer of rare skill and grace, McPhee profiled him for *The New Yorker*. The article was published in book form with the title *A Sense of Where You Are*. An updated edition outlining Bradley's professional basketball career was published in 1978 and was updated again in 1999 to include photographs and captions about Bradley's political career as a senator. By then the two men had known each other for more than three decades and their relationship was, by McPhee's description, brotherly. He said he had not written about Bradley since they became friends, with the exception of the brief material included in the updates to his original profile and a lightly observed piece about a day Bradley spent campaigning in New Jersey. There is clearly a lot more McPhee knows and could say about Bradley, but the effect of him becoming friends with Bradley is to circumscribe what he is willing to publish.

Instead of becoming personally involved, writers can resolve the issue by maintaining a professional relationship, but how exactly does the journalist establish a professional relationship with a source, and how do the journalist and the source negotiate its boundaries? The term 'professional' carries connotations of an established code of behaviour, an accrediting body with the power to include or exclude, guidelines for the exchange of money between the parties, promises of confidentiality and a prescribed level of personal interaction between the parties. Taking these one by one, the codes of ethics for newspaper and magazine journalists do not envisage the kind of relationships practitioners of book-length projects may develop with principal sources. There is no accrediting or licensing body for writers in English-speaking countries. Where most professional relationships are predicated on a client paying the professional, in narrative non-fiction no money changes hands or, if it does, it is from the professional (journalist) to the client (source). As to confidentiality, the various codes of ethics have clauses protecting the identity of sources, but the purpose of journalism is to make information public.

The impetus for *The Journalist and the Murderer* was Kornstein's letter to Malcolm and other journalists, but usually it is the practitioner who needs to persuade the principal source to be involved in the project, and at first glance it is not an especially alluring pitch to make. The practitioner will ask the source to spend dozens, perhaps hundreds, of hours with them, ask them sometimes personal and confronting questions, will scrutinise their answers from alternative perspectives, and then write a long article or book, where it is entirely possible the source will be portrayed unfavourably. In return, the writer offers publicity, an outlet for the source to give their version of events or views on the subject at hand and the satisfaction of contributing to what in many cases is a socially useful project. It is not hard to see that a dash of charm goes a long way for those working on book-length projects. Charming or charmless, though, writers are unlikely to gain full cooperation from principal sources unless they establish a trusting relationship. Some will demonstrate their bona fides by showing prospective sources examples of their previous work (Sims and Kramer 'Breakable Rules for Literary Journalists' 1995, p. 26), but as several have found, the fact that the journalist is working on an extended project carries weight. Malcolm Knox says: 'A journalist sort of buzzes in and buzzes out and never gets it quite right because they haven't put the time in. If you say to somebody that you are writing a book, you are paying that subject the same respect they have for the topic.' Echoing Knox, Lawrence Wright told Boynton: 'People are naturally interested in talking about themselves and their pursuits, and if you can convince them of the genuineness of your interest, it's a rare person who doesn't want to satisfy your curiosity' (2005, p. 443).

If, to rephrase Goethe, curiosity has a power and a magic of its own, it can also be applied to politicians, though a shrewd strategy is needed to pierce politicians' resistance to the media, as Richard Ben Cramer found in researching what grew into a 1047-page book entitled *What It Takes*, which one reviewer dubbed 'What It Weighs'. It is an account of the 1988 American presidential campaign contested by George Bush Sr for the Republicans and Michael Dukakis for the Democrats. Cramer gradually gained access, first by being around for long periods simply watching while other journalists asked the standard journalistic questions about policies and gaffes and backflips. Eventually the candidates became so comfortable with his presence that they would lean over after an interview and say, '*Damn*, I fucked up that agriculture question *again*!' At that moment, Cramer recalled, he had differentiated himself from the other journalists who needed to be given the 'message of the day' and he began to get the kind of material he was seeking. The impetus for his project had been the gap he observed between the wooden performance of politicians on television and the vibrant politicians he had known in his home town. He was interested in exploring what happens to politicians on the journey to the White House. Cramer's second strategy was to introduce himself to all the candidates at the outset then go away for a year to research their backgrounds. This had the dual effect of impressing on the candidates his diligence and, he told Boynton, he also found interesting material by interviewing the candidates' friends, families and schoolmates:

> What amazes me is that most journalists won't bother talking to the people who *love* these guys. They only want to talk to the critics … But they are missing the point. The important question is *how* is he wonderful! If you want to understand how someone got to the point where he is a credible candidate for president of a nation of 250 million people, you'd *better* goddamn-well know *how* he is wonderful (2005, p. 41).

Even assuming you've been successful in persuading one principal source to cooperate, that person's involvement may make it harder to persuade other key sources to participate. Jonathan Harr, for instance, gained excellent access to one side of the legal team in the lawsuit featured in *A Civil Action* and moderate access to the other side. A reviewer criticised him on this point, and was entitled to do so, but among the controversial and difficult issues and events that attract practitioners of book-length projects it is rare for *all* the significant sources to make themselves available. Book-length projects exist along two intersecting lines, one representing full immersion in a principal source's world, the other representing a panoply of perspectives on an issue. Most practitioners aim to occupy the furthest end of both lines; usually they find themselves stretched somewhat painfully between the two, leaning towards one end or the other. Adrian Nicole LeBlanc opted to completely immerse herself in the lives of several Latino families in the Bronx over an astounding eleven-year period for *Random Family*, while Ron Rosenbaum succeeded in covering an exhaustive range of historians, filmmakers and propagandists who have written about Nazi Germany for *Explaining Hitler*. David Marr's biography of Nobel Prize-winning Australian author Patrick White is a rare example of a practitioner gaining excellent access while retaining almost total independence. White was still alive while Marr did his research so he had access to him, but

White did not seek to prevent Marr speaking to any of his numerous enemies. White read the final manuscript but did not attempt to veto it, instead uttering his famous words 'I must be the monster of all time' after finishing it.

The consensus of Boynton's nineteen interviewees and the Australian practitioners I have interviewed is that the relationship with principal sources has both personal and professional elements. This is not surprising, given that both parties work closely and intensely together on a project that both regard as important, albeit from different perspectives. It is easy for either party to blur the kind of relationship that might develop from legitimate personal inter-action and the kind of interaction that might jeopardise the project. A framework outlined by Justin Oakley and Dean Cocking (2001) in their work about ethics and the legal and medical professions offers a way for practitioners to navigate this path that can be applied to this field. Practitioners of this form of writing identify with their role to both learn as much about their chosen subject as possible—which may mean becoming close to principal sources—and to disclose material that in other contexts would remain private. Relationships they form with principal sources are seen, and should be seen by others, in the context of their professional role rather than the context of a personal friendship.

If the McGinniss–MacDonald and Capote–Smith relationships alert us to the perils of the journalist–source relationship, there are numerous examples throughout Boynton's book of journalist–source relationships that marry ethical responsibility, personal engagement and revelatory material. The same applies to some Australian prac-titioners' relationships with principal sources: Estelle Blackburn worked closely with John Button when investigating the murder for which he had been wrongly convicted, Margaret Simons worked closely with various Ngarrindjeri women involved in the Hindmarsh Island bridge affair and David Marr became close to Patrick White when writing a biography of him. During his research, Marr success-fully applied for a A$25,000 grant from the Australian Bicentennial Authority but warned White about its imminent announcement because he knew White opposed the nation's then coming bicen-tenary, in 1988. White said to him: 'It's your decision of course but I would prefer it if you turned it down'. Marr did so; he could see how White's opposition could be misrepresented if the government-funded bicentennial authority was financially support-ing a biography of him. Marr describes his decision as both 'personal and strategic'. He needed White's cooperation to be able to draw on letters for which the author held copyright but he had also 'come to like him, in a wary sort of way'. When White subsequently learnt how much money Marr had given up, 'he was flabbergasted and there was almost nothing that he wouldn't do. Boy, was that the right decision on my part.'

Some of Boynton's interviewees (such as Kotlowitz, Orlean and Talese) place slightly more emphasis on the personal qualities of the relationship, while others (such as Dash, Harr and Krakauer) lean more towards the professional qualities. Juggling the various elements is what makes the relationship 'very ethically sticky', as Harr puts it. It is noteworthy that Malcolm's characterisation of the journalist–source relationship is not dismissed out of hand by Boynton's interviewees, as it has been by many newspaper and magazine journalists. Most have clearly considered it in arriving at their own positions and some, such as Harr and Krakauer explicitly endorse it. Says Krakauer: 'I tell the person I'm interviewing that he'll have no control over the process, that I won't show the article [or book] to him before publication, that he will tell me things he'll regret … and none of that deters anyone!' (Boynton 2005, p. 167). Malcolm makes a similar point at the end of *The Journalist and the Murderer* when she compares sources to young Aztec men and women selected for sacrifice. 'And still they say yes when a journalist calls, and still they are astonished when they see the flash of the knife' (1990, p. 145).

Where sources' propensity to 'sacrifice' themselves prods Malcolm to condemn the relationship as a 'canker', what impresses me about Boynton's interviewees is how their reflections enact Aristotle's notion of the golden mean, whereby 'the middle course occurs at the right time, towards the right people, for the right motives, and in the right manner' (Christians et al. 1995, p. 14). For instance, when at the World Trade Center disaster area in 2001 William Langewiesche thought he heard people saying things in his presence without knowing he was a journalist, he ensured they did know who he was and told them he would not report what they had said (Boynton 2005, p. 217). LeBlanc could have been present when one of the principal sources in *Random Family* returned to her family after ten years in jail but chose not to, as she felt she would have been intruding (2003, p. 245). When Conover was working undercover as a prison guard at Sing Sing prison another officer invited him home after work to spend time with his family, but Conover declined. A reviewer of his book in *The New York Times* asked: 'Where are the stories of the men he is guarding and the officers he is guarding them with?' Conover acknowledges the gap but as he was working undercover he felt he needed to distinguish between the work and private lives of his (then) fellow officers. 'I didn't think it was morally defensible for me to secretly learn about people's private lives for the sake of the book.' Defensible though his decision is, perhaps as a way of compensating for this apparent gap, in *Newjack* Conover gives readers an insight into how working undercover in a demanding job seeps into his private life, affecting his marriage and relationship with his young children.

In all three cases, it is easy to imagine the writers putting the needs of their project ahead of those they were writing about. All three knew the potential value of the material they were giving up but did so anyway. All demonstrated an ability to weigh the claims of legitimate competing interests. Nor, I would argue, were their books any poorer for these omissions. Langewiesche's *American Ground*, LeBlanc's *Random Family* and Conover's *Newjack* offer vividly detailed and revelatory accounts of, respectively, the clean up at ground zero after the 11 September terrorist attacks, life for impoverished Latino families in the Bronx and the work of prison guards. Conover's account illustrates not only the calibre of his decision-making but the real cost to him and his family of his project. The three practitioners' works and experiences illustrate the force of a remark made by Walt Harrington, a fellow practitioner and a journalism academic, that those who do not encounter issues in writing what he terms 'intimate journalism' are not digging deep enough; alternatively, 'you're either a schmuck or not really facing the ethical dilemmas' (eds Sims & Kramer 1995, p. 154).

Implicit in the acknowledgement by leading practitioners that their relationship with principal sources contains both professional and personal elements is a sense of the boundaries between and around the two ways of engaging with sources. Researching her book about the Hindmarsh Island controversy, Simons sometimes shared a meal with her principal sources, but always made clear her purpose for being there—gathering material for a book. 'If you do become a friend I think at that point the ethical problems are huge. There is a degree to which I would say you shouldn't become a friend, but that is not the same as saying that you don't become friendly.' Leon Dash developed strict rules for his in-depth reporting about urban poverty in predominantly black neighbourhoods in which he lived for months at a time getting to know those he was writing about for a multi-part series for *The Washington Post* that was later published in book form. He did not accept Christmas gifts from the adolescent mothers he was writing about in *When Children Want Children* because, he explained to them, he was working. He found the experience painful and difficult, but 'I don't want them to see me as their friend. I'm a reporter'. Working on another project about a woman named Rosa Lee, who was a heroin addict, mother of eight and grandmother of two, he said he never gave her any money as he believed she would use it to buy drugs, and told her he would not be witness to any crimes, but she stole anyway and he was angry at her and, later, at himself. 'It was very egotistical of me to insist that when she was with me she behave so differently from the way she normally behaved.' Like anthropologists, writers of narrative non-fiction immersing themselves in the lives and cultures of their principal sources may find themselves becoming personally involved, but the experience of Boynton's interviewees and others is that they retain a commitment to writing about what they find, even if that distresses or offends their principal sources. By comparison, in anthropology the goal of 'telling a story as intimately as possible from the standpoint of the groups being studied' can lead to 'a certain measure of idealization' (Cramer & McDevitt 2004, p. 132). For instance, Simons argues in *The Meeting of the Waters* that the work of Diane Bell, a prominent anthropologist, while detailed and useful, also 'sugar-coated' the Ngarrindjeri women. One was portrayed only as a 'softly-spoken Elder. There was nothing of her bite, her wiriness or her anger'. Bell's book also had little about 'the bitter factional battles that explained some of the reasons the Ngarrindjeri had behaved as they had' (Simons 2004, p. 424).

In the light of these practitioners' careful negotiation of their relationships with principal sources and their commitment to readers, how do they fare with the issue that flummoxed McGinniss, namely that if he was honest with MacDonald he would lose his precious access? None of Boynton's interviewees said they had been as duplicitous, but a minority said they had allowed sources whose views they found repellent to continue talking without offering their own view. Finnegan describes this as 'one of the not-very-secret tawdry little secrets of journalism' (Boynton 2005, p. 95), while Kramer and Conover say they are not by nature confrontational and are more inclined, as Conover says, to understand a racist's point of view rather than 'teach him about mine' (Boynton 2005, p. 16). The majority, though, said they were willing to confront interviewees if they disagreed with them over an issue or when they believed they were lying. Michael Lewis, author of thirteen non-fiction books, says, 'If I've got criticisms, I find it useful to lay them out and see how they respond. It's all good material' (Boynton 2005, p. 262), while Preston, author of the bestselling book about an Ebola virus outbreak, *The Hot Zone*, says he has learnt from interviewing FBI agents for another book-length project the importance of remaining calm in the face of lies. The FBI agents, he says, simply 'point out contradictions between the evidence and the suspect's statements' (Boynton 2005, p. 310).

Where Lewis's stance appears essentially pragmatic and Preston has learnt an effective way to confront difficult sources, Kotlowitz keeps in mind the needs of his readers. Researching the death of a black teenage boy found floating in a river that ran between a black community and a white community in south-western Michigan, Kotlowitz was told by one black woman it was inconceivable the boy had tried to swim because 'we don't swim. We don't run to the water' (Boynton 2005, p. 140). Kotlowitz says the comment brought to mind a remark made on national television by Al Campanis, general manager of the Los Angeles Dodgers, that black people lacked the natural buoyancy to swim. He says he had to challenge the woman's remarks 'because otherwise I'd be left thinking, as would my readers, "Why didn't I ask her the next logical question?" I'd risk losing my connection to my reader' (Boynton 2005, p. 140). Equally important, these statements prompted Kotlowitz to think about why such views prevailed. 'And I learned much of it had to do with the ambiguous place of rivers in African American history' (Boynton 2005, p. 140). Cramer has firm views, saying he learnt from newspaper reporting in Baltimore that if he needed to criticise a source in print he should let the source know ahead of deadline. 'One politician who was my *friend* was sent to jail because of what I and others wrote in the paper. But I told him what I was doing every step of the way … I told him he might want to tell his wife before it hit. And he appreciated that. He sent me gifts from jail' (Boynton 2005, p. 44). Perhaps even more bracing is to see the lengths that Sereny went to to inform Bell about the likely additional problems Bell would face if Sereny agreed to Bell's proposal that she give her version of how she committed murder at the age of eleven:

> Did she realize, I asked her, that such a book was bound to be controversial? That people would think she did it for money? That both of us would be accused of insensitivity towards the two little victims' families by bringing their dreadful tragedy back into the limelight and, almost inevitably, of sensationalism, because of some of the material the book would have to contain? Above all, did she understand that readers would not stand for any suggestion of possible mitigation for her crimes? (1998, p. 16).

Sereny has deep compassion for Bell, as is evident throughout *Cries Unheard*, but she does not hesitate from confronting her when she believes Bell is lying or being manipulative. It is entirely possible, then, for writers working on book-length projects to disagree with their sources *and* maintain a working relationship. It could be argued that openness between practitioner and principal sources about the project and a preparedness to discuss disagreements are barometers of good practice.

What emerges from examining various works and the reflections of those who wrote them is how important the research phase is to the success or otherwise of true stories. In *The Journalist and the Murderer* Malcolm opens up the MacDonald vs McGinniss lawsuit in uniquely interesting ways even as she distorts its facts. Her work has spurred many leading writers to think about the nature of the journalist–source relationship, which is an inherently healthy activity. Their experiences make them only too aware how complex and subtle a process it is to find the point along the continuum between the professional and the personal that works for them, for their principal source and for their project. Where Malcolm characterises the journalist–source relationship as inescapably enacting a pattern of seduction and betrayal, these leading writers know that may have happened with some colleagues, but that it does not have to. In their experience writers can enter into and maintain a relationship with principal sources that takes on elements of ethnography, such as informed consent, and that continues common journalistic understandings of editorial independence. In many cases they will allow their sources to check material for accuracy, and in some cases they will remunerate principal sources for their extended commitment and will disclose that to readers. For Malcolm, 'nothing can be done' about the falseness inherent in the journalist–source relationship; for many others a good deal can, and is being, done.

Chapter 6

The value of thinking about what is fact and what is fiction *before* writing

I have never been impressed by the argument that, as complete objectivity is impossible in these matters (as, of course, it is), one might as well let one's sentiments run loose. As Robert Solow has remarked, that is like saying that as a perfectly aseptic environment is impossible, one might as well conduct surgery in a sewer.

Clifford Geertz, *The Interpretation of Cultures*

What is fact, what is fiction and the relationship between the two are questions that have preoccupied philosophers for years, and I don't pretend to have any definitive answers on that score, but I do think the questions matter—a lot. I am keenly aware that scholars have long dismissed the notion that there is some neatly drawn line separating fiction from non-fiction, but that does not mean these two ways of representing the world are indistinguishable. That the representing of actual people and events in words spins off complex questions about the difficulty or even the possibility of separating them from our perception or construction of them does not mean we should be indifferent to the task of distinguishing them or, worse, delight in the blurring of boundaries between fact and fiction as some ineffable cosmic irony.

Words matter. As Mark Twain once said: 'The difference between the right word and the almost right word is the difference between lightning and a lightning bug'. His aphorism is used to exhort practitioners to write clearly, but it was another disciple of clear writing, George Orwell, who also showed repeatedly in his journalism, such as *Homage to Catalonia*, his essays, such as 'Politics and the English Language', and in his fiction, whether *Animal Farm* or *1984*, the very real connections between words and political actions and their consequences for ordinary people. More recently, as alluded to in Chapter 2, the devastating consequences of misused and deliberately misleading words can be seen in how former United States president, George W. Bush, publicly justified his decision to invade Iraq in 2003 on several spurious grounds. The Bush administration's campaign to persuade people around the world of the invasion's validity proved to be fraudulent (Rich 2006), and by the end of 2006 the number of American troops who had died in the war in Iraq had surpassed the number of people killed on 11 September 2001—just below 3000 (www.icasualties.org). Nor should it be forgotten, either, that this figure, which was well over 4000 by the time the United States formally withdrew forces from Iraq, is far exceeded by the deaths of Iraqi civilians. A decade after the invasion this figure had reached 122,000 (www.iraqbodycount.org).

This may be an extreme example of the importance of words, but is no less real for that; it can serve to anchor a discussion of the relationship between fiction and non-fiction writing that can waft off into abstraction. A starting point, then, is to ask how readers know whether they are reading fiction or non-fiction. The answer is that they don't unless they are told, according to H. Porter Abbott, in the *Cambridge Introduction to Narrative* (2nd edn, 2008, pp. 147–50). That prompts a further question: does it matter whether the reader knows or believes they are reading fiction or non-fiction, which opens into a larger debate about whether journalists can, however imperfectly, report on events in the actual world, or whether in the face of crumbling belief in positivist notions of a simple objective reality, journalists are seen as one group among several in society that construct reality through words and images. These debates are critical to narrative non-fiction, which is grounded in the practice of representing in words actual people, events and issues in print. These debates, I have found, are bedevilled by the conflating of various concepts, which has the effect of muddying rather than clarifying what are already complex ideas. In Chapter 2 I argued that the choice by some to study non-fiction works according to their literary merit has the effect of submerging the question of whether the issues arising in representing events hinges on the taking of a narrative approach rather than the practitioner's literary ability. Here I want to highlight the effect on readers of conflating notions of fiction with notions of literariness, of narrative with fiction and of fiction with non-fiction.

Hayden White's work on the use of literary elements in historical writing has been influential; it is relevant here because in history, as in narrative non-fiction, an attempt is being made to represent in words actual people and events. His approach has been applied to narrative non-fiction by, for instance, Kathy Smith, in her analysis of John McPhee's work (ed. Sims 1990, pp. 206–27). 'Historical situations are not inherently tragic, comic, or romantic', but only made so, writes White, 'by the historian's subtlety in matching up a specific plot structure with the set of historical events that he wishes to endow with a meaning of a particular kind' (1978, p. 85). White's argument, developed over several works, has been important in undermining belief in a naïve historical realism and in drawing attention to the extent to which historians, and by extension those who write true stories, construct plots and meanings for the events and people they write about. The value of the work of White, among others, has been to shake 'narrative theory out of the complacency with which it has long approached non-fiction. If rhetorical devices produce meaning in fiction, so do they in non-fiction', writes Marie-Laure Ryan in *The Routledge Encyclopedia of Narrative Theory* (2005, p. x).

White's argument about emplotment is displayed routinely on commercial television current affairs programs, such as Australian shows *Today Tonight* and *A Current Affair*. That is, as Jonathan Holmes demonstrated on ABC television's *Media Watch* in a 2010 item entitled 'Tweed Tales on TT', plots are imposed on a set of events and people rather than arise out of inquiry into them. Holmes showed how an item about a man, portrayed as a victim of 'youth gangs' 'terrorising entire neighbourhoods' in Tweed Heads on the

New South Wales–Queensland border, had actually been attacked by three men in their twenties, as he himself told the producers of *Media Watch* after the item ran on *Today Tonight*. The man, Ron Roberts, admitted 'the feud started with a neighbourhood dispute'. For this item Roberts had been portrayed as an elderly, garden-loving victim, but several years beforehand, on another *Today Tonight* program, he had been 'exposed' as a 'brutal bully' for hitting a fifteen-year-old who picked one of his prized roses, and chastised for allegedly inventing his past as a decorated Vietnam veteran. This is by no means an isolated example, as regular viewing of *Media Watch* testifies. If the *Today Tonight* item dramatically illustrates the potency of White's insight, it also opens the door to its limitations.

Lubomír Doležel draws attention to how White's argument is founded on a non sequitur. White writes that endowing a set of historical events with a specific plot structure is 'essentially a literary, that is to say fiction-making operation', which means, as Doležel points out: 'The equating of history and fiction is smuggled into the postmodernist paradigm by a tautology. Emplotment is a literary operation; therefore, history is tantamount to fiction-making' (1999, p. 251).

Doležel argues that White's position founders when he is asked, and agrees, to take what Doležel calls 'the Holocaust test'. That is, can the Holocaust, like other historical events, be plotted as a comedy, or must it be seen as a tragedy? White shifts the argument from a consideration of how the facts of the genocide of six million people can be represented in a limited number of ways to a broader consideration of whether there are any limits 'on the *kind* of story that can responsibly be told about these phenomena?' (1992, p. 37). There is a logical hole in the assumptions underlying White's position; if historians draw from concepts usually associated with fiction—tragedy, comedy, romance—presumably these concepts originated in novelists' experience, and re-imagining, of the world. That is, life preceded fiction. The interplay between life as experienced and as rendered in fiction is more complicated than White's argument allows; equally, the dividing line between historical facts and historians' interpretation of them is not definitively drawn but continually feeds back and forth, enriching both the finding of facts and the making of interpretations.

In taking the Holocaust test, though, White continues to distinguish between facts and 'poetic and rhetorical elements by which what would otherwise be a list of facts is transformed into a story', as if facts did not need to be unearthed in the first place by historians and that those facts may surprise practitioners and run entirely counter to any preconceptions they have about an event. If the belief that historians' portrayal of events can accurately reflect objective reality is naïve and simplistic, so too is the belief that there is no reality but only our representation and 'emplotment' of it.

The use by Doležel of possible worlds semantics is valuable in teasing out and clarifying the points of difference between fiction and non-fiction (1999, pp. 247–73). Possible worlds semantics acknowledges the inability of language to express reality directly: 'The only kind of worlds that human language is capable of creating or producing is possible worlds'. From the outset, writers of fiction are 'free to roam over the entire universe of possible worlds, to call into fictional existence a world of any type', including fantasy worlds and the supernatural. Verisimilitude is required in some kinds of fiction but is not a universal principle of fiction, whereas historians engage in a continuous refining of historical worlds, supplementing or rewriting history according to the state of available sources.

An apt example, given Doležel's invoking of the Holocaust test in his discussion of White's thesis, is a work of history entitled *The Destruction of Dresden* that was written by David Irving and published in 1963. Even after Irving became a public and virulent Holocaust denier, his book on Dresden continued to be well regarded by historians until 1999, when Irving sued American author Deborah Lipstadt over her portrayal of him in her book *Denying the Holocaust*. For the trial another historian, Richard Evans, conducted a forensic examination of all the primary and secondary sources Irving relied on and demonstrated that Irving's work on Dresden was fraudulent. Evans found Irving had fabricated evidence, had used a forged document that gave a wildly inflated number of bombing victims even after he had been told it was a fake, and had refused to use a genuine document that provided a more accurate number of victims. What this example illustrates, courtesy of a lucid work of narrative non-fiction by D.D. Guttenplan entitled *The Holocaust on Trial*, is not only the potentially ever-changing nature of historical study, but the real dangers of historians allowing some gaps to remain unfilled. By contrast, where gaps in knowledge exist in fictional works, they have nothing like the same impact, even though they may be impossible to fill. Doležel cites the example of *Macbeth*; no amount of textual analysis will yield whether Lady Macbeth had children because Shakespeare simply did not provide the information in his drama.

Doležel is happy to say the boundary between fiction and history is open, but 'possible worlds semantics is curious about what happens when the boundaries are crossed', and points to three well-known border-crossings: historical fiction; counterfactual history; and what Doležel terms 'factual narrative', and what is called in this book a true story or narrative non-fiction. Writers of historical fiction, for instance, can include representations of both actual and fictional characters, but fictional characters cannot exist in the actual world. Factual narrative is 'the most remarkable manifestation of the open boundary between fiction and history' because the possible worlds of factual narrative are 'models of witnessed present', but its mode of presentation is 'fictional' (1999, pp. 267–68). Questions can be asked about the factuality of factual narrative, but they can be explained by the practitioner's 'skilful and patient reporting' and, where that is shown to have failed, the work has violated the norms of its genre and, Doležel writes, can be reclassified as fiction. The question of exactly how works of narrative non-fiction are shown to have failed may be more complicated than Doležel allows, but that will be dealt with in a later chapter.

A clearer sense of the boundaries between fiction and fact enables us to apply White's argument about emplotment more productively, I think. Where Ryan takes from White the notion that rhetorical techniques are present in non-fiction as well as fiction, I turn to the research phase in works of fiction and non-fiction. However much factual material is included, a work of fiction remains primarily a work of invention. That is, following Doležel, authors invent plots for their novels. An historian or a narrative non-fiction author cannot—or should not—invent a plot for the subject of their work. White is right to point out that some historians do impose plots on their raw material; that is at least partly what I have argued about both *The Final Days* and *In Cold Blood*, and what is shown in the *Today Tonight* items. Many of the most engaging works of narrative non-fiction, however, are imbued with a well-deep sense of curiosity about the world and its people; intellectually, and emotionally, the practitioner has travelled a long distance from their original idea via their research to the final argument. As Margaret Simons says: 'If you go through the entire process of writing a book without having changed your mind on anything then my instinct would be to question whether you really engaged in the process. You should be surprised by your material.'

Eric Heyne and Daniel Lehman have made significant contributions to developing a theoretical underpinning for this area of writing. Heyne begins by flatly rejecting as grandiose assertions that there is no difference between fact and fiction, and argues for core differences between fiction and literary non-fiction that need to be recognised by 'any theory that hopes to do justice to powerful nonfiction narratives' (1987, p. 480). Drawing on John Searle's work that the distinction we commonly make between factual and fictional statements derives not from the statements themselves but our perception of the type of statement being intended, Heyne argues it is the author who decides whether a book is fact or fiction and it is left to the reader to determine whether the book contains good or bad fact. He uses the terms 'factual status' and 'factual adequacy' respectively to distinguish between these two kinds of truth. Heyne acknowledges there is no 'transcendent connection between space/time events and narrative of those events', but 'recognizing we are students of human constructions shaped by human purposes need not make us afraid to talk about truth. We make decisions every day based on our evaluations of competing versions of reality' (p. 489). Lehman, in his book *Matters of Fact*, agrees with much of Heyne's argument. 'The confession that, finally, it is impossible to delineate an exact boundary between fiction and nonfiction does not mean that the boundary does not matter' (1997, p. 5).

Lehman builds on Heyne's binary model of factual status and factual adequacy by setting up the four-way framework that was discussed earlier. He uses the term 'implicated' to describe the complex strands of relationships inherent in non-fiction between, on the one hand, practitioners, the events they write about and the texts they produce, and on the other readers, their knowledge of the events written about and their engagement with the text. The relationship between writer and reader operates differently in non-fiction to fiction because of the overt and claimed relationship between the book and actual people and events. Lehman openly acknowledges there is no simple equation between actuality and non-fiction, or even actuality and fictional texts; even if such an equation was possible the 'genre police', as he calls them, would need to account for the existence of narratives in an 'intertextual milieu' that make the relationship between actuality and its reproduction almost indistinguishable. Even so, the decision by an author or the publisher to label a book non-fiction remains an important key to how it is written and read. Heyne, in a second journal article, concedes his binary model is oversimplified, then develops Lehman's work by offering a mental map for discerning the relationship between fiction and non-fiction:

> One way to recognize the kind of narrative truth that we associate with nonfiction is by the presence of a certain kind of caring. If the reader is prepared to assert an alternative version of events, to engage actively in a certain kind of dialogue, then we are dealing with something we might all be willing to call non-fiction … When we can talk about different stories competing, and when we genuinely wish to choose among them rather than allowing them to peacefully coexist, then we have left the realm of fiction (2001, p. 330).

This is a particularly helpful switching-point for discerning readers' differing responses to fiction and narrative non-fiction. It illuminates an aspect of the public response to Helen Garner's *The First Stone*, for instance. Some read the book as fiction, and Garner used pseudonyms, but she intended the book to be read as non-fiction and overwhelmingly readers and critics read it that way, and passionately argued about the events at Ormond College and Garner's interpretation of them.

If the first point to be clear about is that fiction and literariness are not one and the same, the second is to avoid conflating fiction with narrative. No less a theoretical figure than Gérard Genette noted that narrative studies have focused 'almost exclusively on fictional narrative alone', acting as if there is 'an implicit privilege that hypostatizes fictional narrative into narrative par excellence, or into a model for all narratives' (1991, pp. 54–5). Such has been the emphasis in narrative studies on fiction that he believes his work *Narrative Discourse Revisited* ought to have been retitled 'a restricted narratology'. Genette uses the framework he developed in his earlier work, *Narrative Discourse*, to compare fiction with what he, like Doležel, terms 'factual narrative'. His framework provides valuable insights into, for instance, the question of omniscient narration in factual narrative, but Genette acknowledges he has not done the 'empirical investigation that remains eminently necessary in this arena'. Genette's unfamiliarity with the range and history of journalistic writing prompts him to discuss the 'indexes of fictionality' in the opening of an article published in *The New Yorker* in 1988, as if such an anecdotal lead, as it is known in the media industry, is noteworthy rather than commonplace, not just at that magazine since at least the 1930s, but a common practice in newspapers as well as magazines for decades in English-speaking countries. Not that Genette is alone; as Mitchell Stephens comments, in *A History of News*, too often journalism historians 'seem like theater historians who have never studied Shakespeare or Sophocles' (1988, p. 1).

Conflating the words fiction and narrative bears on discussion about this field of writing, in that one of its defining elements is said to be the *application of fictional techniques* to writing about actual people and events. Tom Wolfe was probably the first to use this description in his 1973 essay, 'The New Journalism', but later scholars, such as Norman Sims and Barbara Lounsberry, have repeated it. I've done it myself in various writings, but now believe the phrase to be misplaced. Specifically, the problem with the phrase is, first, the word 'technique' connotes the simple plucking of techniques from the writer's toolbox and applying them to a set of facts. Following this line of thought can lead people to view research and writing as separate and distinct processes rather than organically linked to each other. I know that in this book, discussion of the processes of research, writing and reception are separated into various chapters, but that has been done for the purpose of making them more understandable; in reality, they are interconnected. Practitioners will, in all likelihood, keep talking to their principal sources as they write, and at the same time they probably will be thinking about the kind of relationship they want to develop with readers.

Second, and more important, implicit in the words *fictional techniques* is a reaction against the dominant way people and events are presented in the print media, especially newspapers; that is, in news reports. This form of writing, fact-driven and formal in tone, is good for the brisk transmission of information, but any impact it has on readers is carried by the force of the news rather than an attempt to engage the reader beyond that level. The news report, too, has been the predominant print media form since near the end of the nineteenth century (Mindich 1998; Schudson 1995). So familiar, even formulaic, are its conventions that it has been satirised since at least 1965, when former journalist Michael Frayn wrote a novel called *The Tin Men* in which scientists use a computer program to produce a newspaper. They find newspaper headlines can be written almost at random and show a sample of headlines to readers such as 'Row Hope Move Flop', 'Leak Dash Shock' and 'Hate Ban Bid Probe'. Most claim to understand the headlines but cannot say what the stories were actually about, which meant 'a computer could turn out a paper whose language was both soothingly familiar and yet calmingly incomprehensible'. Our familiarity with the form and tone of news reports invites the belief that it is a naturally occurring phenomenon, but it is actually the result of a complex history that includes, but is not limited to, the unreliability of the early telegraph that impelled journalists to send the most critical piece of information first in their dispatches, and the rapid expansion of newspapers that gave rise to a journalistic class. Previously, most publishers had used newspapers to express their partisan political views; they did not want to grant their employed journalists similar freedom, which led in turn to the development of a mode of writing that sought to erase the identity and ideology of the journalist and present the world dispassionately (Schudson 1978; Stephens 1988; Mindich 1998).

It may be more productive, though, to see the taking of a narrative approach not only as a reaction against the fixed form of news reporting, but to look before the rise of the inverted pyramid. What this shows is, while all forms of writing are an abstraction from the reality they seek to describe, the hard news report is, more than many, a circumscribed form of writing. News reports do not offer analysis, they do not set events in context and they exclude atmosphere and emotion, or where they do report atmosphere and emotion, they snap-freeze them in phrases such as 'visibly upset'. In Norman Mailer's memorable line, they are forever 'munching nuance like peanuts'. The limitations of the hard news report, as James Carey suggests, are a key driver behind the continued existence of other journalistic forms:

> Journalism must be examined as a corpus, not as a set of isolated stories. The corpus includes not only the multiple treatments of an event within the newspaper—breaking stories, follow-ups, news analysis, interpretation and background, critical commentary, editorials—but also the other forms of journalism that surround, correct and complete the daily newspaper: television coverage, documentary and docudrama, the newsweeklies and journals of opinion and, finally, book-length journalism (1986, p. 151).

Before the rise of the hard news report in the second half of the nineteenth century, daily newspapers presented their reports in a variety of forms written in a variety of narrative styles. In 1836 James Gordon Bennett, editor of *The New York Herald*, pioneered the eye-witness true crime report when he wrote about his viewing of the 'beautiful female corpse' of a murdered 23-year-old prostitute in the city 'that surpassed the finest statue of antiquity', and drawing on his sources, recreated the death from the moment the murderer 'drew from beneath his cloak the hatchet' (Stephens 1988, p. 231). It was common then for newspapers to present their reports in the form of a chronological narrative. On 8 December 1854, *The Age* newspaper in Melbourne began its report on war in the Crimea as follows: 'To render the narrative of events clear to our distant readers, we must trace it from its commencement' (eds Hutton & Tanner 1979, p. 5). Michael Schudson studied the historical development of the coverage of the American president's state of the union address from

1790 to the twentieth century. By the mid-nineteenth century it was common for newspapers to reprint the president's address in full, accompanied by an editorial commentary that was written from 'an engaged and partisan stance', and a news report about the 'spectacle' of the opening of Congress. *The New York Times* began its report in 1870: 'A beautiful Indian summer sun, a balmy atmosphere, and crowded galleries, resplendent and brilliant hues of gay toilettes, greeted the return of the Congress to its chambers' (Schudson 1995, pp. 57–8).

What emerges from this historical context are three points relevant to narrative non-fiction: first, the use of the hard news report has never been the sole form in which news has been presented; second, the use of a range of modes of writing usually associated with fiction are not the sole province of fiction; and third, the use of the word fiction in the term fictional techniques sends a misleading message to practitioners and readers alike because the word fiction is, according to the Oxford English Dictionary, 'that which is feigned or invented; invention as opposed to fact'. Granting that the line between fact and invention is nowhere near as tidily drawn as lexicographers would have us believe, using the word fiction flies in the face of what writers, including Boynton's interviewees and mine, believe they are doing. As Tracy Kidder, winner of a Pulitzer Prize for general non-fiction, says, the techniques of fiction writing never belonged to fiction: 'They belong to storytelling' (eds Sims & Kramer 1995, p. 19). It is preferable, then, to avoid any potential confusion by seeing what practitioners do as drawing on a range of narrative approaches to research and writing about actual, as distinct from invented, people, events and issues.

An important corollary of this reorientation in which fiction and literariness are kept separate is that it allows us to see how many of the issues that arise do so because of the decision to take a narrative approach. The question of how well the book is written is a second, and in some ways a secondary, issue. This is one of the key conclusions that flows from analysing the work of Woodward and Capote, as discussed in Chapters 3 and 4. Just because a work of narrative non-fiction is superbly written would not necessarily mitigate or eliminate the ethical issues. It could be argued that a superbly written work would intensify them, as it would lodge deeper in the reader's consciousness. I do not want to argue there are fixed links between ethics and levels of literary skill, as that connotes a mechanistic relationship between them, whereas the act of researching and writing is an organic as well as a mechanical process. It is possible for a practitioner to be a gifted wordsmith and unethical, and for the reverse to hold also. It is entirely possible that more complex interrelationships exist between any given practitioner's literary ability and their practice of ethical decision-making; the range of possibilities that could exist is beyond the scope of this book. The key point here is that the decision to take a narrative approach to writing about actual people and events triggers certain ethical issues in the writing that need attention before, or at the very least alongside, attending to literary issues.

Chapter 7

The narrator's voice: more than a question of writerly choice

To keep ourselves open to what is before us, we must not become too obsessed with asking ourselves, 'What's the story here?'—and thus fall victim to the reporter's paranoia that we've got to produce something out of this mess and we better figure it out fast. That undermines our ability to grasp the story, because it means we'll inevitably fall back on well-worn themes and observations—interpretive clichés—and not give ourselves the time or frame of mind to see anything beyond that.

Walt Harrington, 'A Writer's Essay'

Cyril Connolly, in his book of critical essays and autobiography, *Enemies of Promise*, famously writes: 'Literature is the art of writing something that can be read twice; journalism what will be read once, and they demand different techniques'. Narrative non-fiction sits somewhere in between. It is longer than most journalism, it aims to explain the complexities of events and it is imbued with the subtleties, resonances and emotional freight of storytelling. Whether narrative non-fiction is literature is not my point here; certainly, many works of narrative non-fiction require close reading and many reward re-reading. With this in mind we can think about

129

what happens when you begin writing. You have around you the material you have gathered; you are thinking about how to represent it and about what kind of relationship you want to create with readers. During the research phase of narrative non-fiction the practitioner's knottiest issue is the relationship between them and their principal sources, because writers gather all their material not for a private diary, but for a public act of communication. The relationship writers seek to establish with readers, and readers' expectations of true stories, will be discussed in later chapters.

For those aspiring to write narrative non-fiction, though, it is helpful to disentangle the many interconnections so as to see the nature of individual strands and how they knit together. The subject of this and the next three chapters is the issues that arise for practitioners in representing through words on a page what they found in their research about actual people and events. In the writing, practitioners need to find a balance between their desire to write in a narrative style that deeply engages readers' emotions and one that engages readers' minds as well as their emotions. The former runs the risk of sensationalism; the latter more faithfully reflects people and events in their complexity. Whichever approach the practitioner favours, their work needs to be underpinned by a commitment to veracity. The demands of balancing these goals exist in a range of practices, such as the use of quotations, but they show up most sharply in how writers present their narrative voice, how they describe people and when they reconstruct events as scenes. Practitioners need to think about whether some narrative methods are unavailable or unsuitable to narrative non-fiction, such as trying to convey their sources' thoughts and feelings in interior monologues.

The first choice to be made by practitioners who write in a narrative style is whether they make claims to represent events and people as they are or draw attention to the impossibility or, at least, the difficulty of doing this. David Eason's framework for analysing representation in the New Journalism is relevant here. He proposes two main approaches: the first he terms realist, the second modernist (Sims 1990, pp. 191–205). The first approach claims to represent reality as it is, the second draws attention to the inherent difficulty of this task, and makes clear to the reader that the meaning of events is constructed by both journalist and reader. Eason argues Talese, Wolfe and Capote take the realist approach while Didion, Mailer and Thompson take the modernist approach. The former group acknowledges that 'reality, though elusive, nonetheless waits to be discovered', which they achieve by immersing themselves in their subjects' worlds and writing in a narrative style about what they find. The second group believes image and reality in the world are so entwined as to entangle common understandings. The modernists write in a narrative style that calls 'attention to storytelling as a cultural practice for making a common world'.

Eason links how writers explore representation with their approach to research and argues that, where realists describe their firsthand observation as a professional act that poses 'only manageable ethical problems', modernists explicitly examine such assumptions. For realists, a clear distinction must be maintained between the observer and those being observed. Wolfe may have been a strong advocate for New Journalism practiced by both realists and modernists, but in his own work he hewed strongly to realism and paid little direct attention to ethical issues. It is worth quoting in full what he did write on the topic:

If a reporter stays with a person or group long enough, they—reporter and subject—will develop a personal relationship of some sort, even if it is hostility. More often it will be friendship of some sort. For many reporters this presents a more formidable problem than penetrating the particular scene in the first place. They become stricken with a sense of guilt, responsibility, obligation. 'I hold this man's reputation, his future, in my hands'—that becomes the frame of mind. They may begin to feel like voyeurs—'I have preyed upon this man's life, devoured it with my eyes, made no commitment myself, etc.' People who become overly sensitive on this score should never take up the new style of journalism. They inevitably turn out second-rate work, biased in such banal ways that they embarrass even the subjects they think they are 'protecting.' A writer needs at least enough ego to believe that what he is doing as a writer is as important as what anyone he is writing about is doing and that therefore he shouldn't compromise his own work. If he doesn't believe that his own writing is one of the most important activities going on in contemporary civilization, then he ought to move on to something else he thinks is ... become a welfare eligibility worker or a clean-investment counselor for the Unitarian Church or a noise abatement surveyor (1973, pp. 67–8).

It may be, as Wolfe asserts, that journalists can become 'overly sensitive' to those they write about, but it is fair to say that, in the history of media criticism, seldom has such a charge been levelled at journalists. Wolfe's loaded language—'stricken with guilt', 'voyeurs', 'preyed upon this man's life'—trivialises a very real issue facing writers of true stories. He glibly forecloses the often competing interests of those for whom the practitioner writes, and those they write about, in favour of the former, with barely a thought for the latter beyond his complacent assertion he knows what is best for them.

In contrast, Eason cites John Gregory Dunne's *Vegas: A Memoir of a Dark Season*, published in 1974, that began as a conventional realist attempt to write about the underside of Las Vegas through the lives of a prostitute who attends beauty school by day, a private detective and a small-time comic, but becomes a questioning of his own voyeurism, which Dunne decides is sanctioned by the apparatus surrounding realist journalism. Eason does not argue his binary framework covers all New Journalists. While valuable, it is overly schematic. For a start, Eason's framework draws too neat a line between the approach practitioners take in representing people and events and how they engage with them during their research. For instance, Malcolm's *The Journalist and the Murderer* is a modernist text by Eason's framework but, as argued in Chapter 4, she distorts certain key events in the *Fatal Vision* case, and she appears unable to conceive of the journalist–source beyond either a pattern of seduction and betrayal or disengagement from the source. Conversely, *Random Family* is presented as a realist text, yet the available evidence suggests LeBlanc went to great lengths to respect the humanity of the principal sources she worked with over eleven years (Kelliher 2004). LeBlanc may look like one of Wolfe's 'overly sensitive' types, but far from turning out second-rate work, LeBlanc's *Random Family* was named one of the best books of the year by *The New York Times*.

Eason does not appear to allow for the possibility of a practitioner being fully alive to the difficulties of representing events and people yet choosing to present their findings in a realist narrative. Conversely, a practitioner's self-conscious demonstrating of the difficulties of representation can have the effect of obscuring the subject or, consciously or otherwise, of foreclosing their inquiry. How a writer of narrative non-fiction chooses to represent events and people and issues, then, is not a failsafe guide to how they researched their topic or even necessarily of their worldview. It does follow, though, that a reader (or a critic) will draw conclusions from the book with or without the benefit of knowing how it was researched, and this should prompt writers to reflect on their choices in representing their topics. Conceiving of narrative non-fiction existing along a continuum rather than a binary framework, it can be seen that realist texts sitting near one end of the continuum ask for greater trust from readers and have fewer ways of signalling that they offer one version of events rather than an inviolable truth. At the other end, modernist texts make clear the limits of representation, but this is a first step, not the final word. What happens if the practitioner's narrative voice so dominates the book that it squeezes out alternative perspectives?

A writer of fiction is free to choose any narrative voice they want, and to move between a range of voices when inventing their fictional world; a writer of narrative non-fiction needs to be mindful of the nature of the events, issues and people they are portraying. Is an omniscient narrative voice appropriate in narrative non-fiction when, by definition, a writer cannot possibly know everything about the actual events they are portraying? The danger of the omniscient narrative voice in true stories has already been alluded to in the discussion of *The Final Days* and *In Cold Blood*. Gérard Genette goes so far as to describe its use as 'disrespectful' (1991, p. 67).

Many authors of narrative non-fiction, though, come from a background in journalism where they have been trained in a writing style that emphasises the importance of the subject matter, not the journalist's subjectivity. It is common for textbooks to advise journalists to keep themselves out of their articles unless they believe their overt presence will add something useful; I have repeated such advice myself in *Writing Feature Stories*. It has been dispensed in newsrooms since at least the 1950s, when E.B. White's essay 'An Approach to Style' was added to a new edition of William Strunk's *The Elements of Style*: 'To achieve style, begin by affecting none—that is, place yourself in the background. A careful and honest writer does not need to worry about style. As he becomes proficient in the use of language, his style will emerge, because he himself will emerge'. The goal of what Strunk called the 'plain English style' was solely to serve the meaning of the intended communication and to leave no trace of an individual voice. 'One measure of this doctrine's weirdness', observes Ben Yagoda in *The Sound on the Page*, 'is its absolute inapplicability to E.B. White's own prose style, which, although outwardly plain, simple, orderly, and sincere, is also idiosyncratic, opinionated, and unmistakable' (2004, p. xx). Yagoda and other critics, such as Hugh Kenner, are alive to the agendas and assumptions that can be hidden beneath the transparent style, though Yagoda is also attuned to the virtues in prose of clarity and simplicity. Despite the influence of the New Journalism and the rise to prominence of opinion(ated) columnists, there remain many in news organisations with an unblinking belief in simple notions of objective journalism that tends to translate in long-form projects to a belief that objectivity can be achieved by adopting an omniscient narrative voice. A moment's thought lets you see this is a ropey idea, but it is what happens when journalists don't stop to think about the implications of what they do and how they do it.

A good way to see the problems of using the omniscient narrative voice is to look at John Bryson's *Evil Angels*, because it is an award-winning and much-praised work (later adapted for film) and because it was written at a time when ideas about narrative non-fiction, especially in Australia, were relatively undeveloped. Bryson's work questioned the jury verdict that found Lindy Chamberlain guilty of murdering her baby daughter, Azaria, in the central Australian desert in 1980. The case stirred an ugly brew of long-held fears about lost children in the outback, prejudices against little-understood religions and unspoken agreements between police and reporters. Lindy Chamberlain was released from gaol after a vital piece of missing evidence was found in 1986 that supported her long-held belief that a dingo had stolen Azaria. The following year a Royal Commission found the evidence presented in the original trial insufficient to justify the guilty verdicts. Adrian Howe, author of a detailed retrospective of the case, describes *Evil Angels* as 'the most influential miscarriage-of-justice book ever written in Australia'. In 2012, a fourth coronial inquest into the case unequivocally cleared the Chamberlains of any role in their daughter's death and stated that a dingo was responsible (Bryson 'Four coroners').

Bryson had freelanced as a journalist and had been spurred to cover the case because he felt the police had mishandled the investigation and mistreated the Chamberlains by leaking inflammatory material to the news media. Early on, the Chamberlains cooperated with another journalist, Steve Brien, in telling their story, but felt his 'quickie' book betrayed them, retailing misleading rumours about their faith and arguing they were guilty. After this, Lindy Chamberlain sent a message from gaol to Bryson offering to tell him her version of events. Bryson interviewed her, as well as other members of the family, and was able to convey their perspective in detail. He defrayed the research costs for his book by covering the second coronial inquest and the trial as a freelancer for radio and television.

He wanted to make the book, which was already long, running to 550 pages, 'an easy journey' for the reader. 'If you want to touch a lot of people with a book, you've got to draw them in, with a sense of "Hey, come and listen to this story."' Bryson's approach certainly foregrounds the Chamberlains' plight in ways that earlier books do not, but what is lost is a sense of transparency between writer and reader. The book's tone is calm and even-handed, perhaps reflecting Bryson's background as a criminal lawyer; his questioning of the trial verdict was certainly vindicated by later official inquiries. Bryson writes about numerous episodes he witnessed and wrote about, but he never openly acknowledges his presence in the book. On occasion the text refers to a stringer for the *Today* show on television or the radio station Fox FM without identifying the stringer as Bryson. These events were minor, and it was probably immaterial whether the person described is Bryson or someone else.

In at least one other instance, however, readers would have bene-fited from knowing Bryson's role in events. After the jury found the then seven months pregnant Lindy Chamberlain guilty, Bryson writes about the parties held in Darwin. The journalists gathered at one hotel where:

> The waiter refused to serve three journalists who were rolling joints on a dinner-plate in full view of a nearby party hosted by a uniformed superintendent of police. [Malcolm] Brown [of *The Sydney Morning Herald*] knew those journalists were upset with the verdict, and plainly he was observing some calculated gesture of insolence, more than anything else. When he walked through to the garden-lounge, things were peaceful enough, until two radio reporters who were otherwise firm friends got up, grey-faced and shouting, from a poolside table and knocked each other into the water (1985, pp. 529–30).

Bryson was one of the two grey-faced, anonymous reporters. He told me:

> What happened was that there was a party at the Hotel Darwin after all the journalists had filed their stories and everyone was letting down. They were tired and getting drunk and smoking dope and I was very upset about the verdict because I thought it unfair and wrong and this other journalist, who is an old friend but I won't tell you who he is, said: 'Look, Johnny, it's not that bad really and you've got to remember that for us this is the best result, because it is a sensational story.' I thought that was cruel, so I hit him. We started fighting and punched each other into the hotel pool.

The contrast between the cool, magisterial tone of the book and Bryson's violent reaction to his friend's remark is stark. I found it hard to imagine this slight, softly-spoken man getting so passionate about his work that he would start throwing punches but, as he says, his anger over the treatment of the Chamberlains was his original impetus. Margaret Simons admits she was shocked when she learnt that Bryson had 'played' (her term) with the relationship of trust between journalist and reader.

Whether Bryson's anger distorts his book is difficult to assess. It appears not; Bryson has an acute sense of fairness. For instance, after the jury returned its guilty verdict, defence counsel were invited to the judge's chambers. As an orderly opened the door Justice Muirhead, pouring himself a whiskey, said to them: 'Well, I didn't think I exactly summed up in favour of a conviction, did you?' The orderly withdraws, 'closing the door on the rest of the conversation'. Bryson had been reliably told by sources what had been said in the judge's chambers but chose not to report it because he distinguished between reporting an important fact about the judge's attitude and attempting to take the reader into the privacy of the judge's chambers. He also knew that since the trial, Justice Muirhead had expressed similar views. 'I took the reader to what could have been overheard but what was said in chambers was their business. It also did not throw any *further* light on his views and thinking.'

The problem is that none of this decision making is made available to the reader, either in the book, in endnotes, in a note to the reader or even in promotional interviews, which some use to discuss the issues raised in researching and writing their books. Bryson says he enjoys footnotes himself, but felt they would have clogged the book. In this I would argue he did himself a disservice, because the available evidence shows he took great care researching and writing *Evil Angels* and his readers are asked to invest a high level of trust in his integrity over an event where many journalists had performed poorly. To learn that Bryson disguised his identity in the poolside fight provokes, if not the terror that John Hersey argues readers feel when writers distort the truth by adding invented material, then at least a sense of disquiet that comes from the reader's desire to trust a journalist's account of events (1989, p. 249).

Does criticism of Woodward, Capote and Bryson's use of an omniscient narrative voice mean it is impossible to use? As it is a common feature of realist texts, how much doubt does it cast on such books? It certainly means the writer offers the reader the reassurance that their work reveals exactly how things happened, which is a false reassurance, but does that mean all true stories need a narrative voice continually waving disclaimers at the reader that nobody really knows what happened? This may be an exaggeration, but one of the pleasures and the benefits of a narrative approach is that it helps us make sense of the chaos of life. Nowhere was this more apparent than in John Hersey's account in *The New Yorker* of the impact of the dropping of the first atomic bomb on Hiroshima to end World War II. In this account, subsequently published by Penguin, and in his criticism of aspects of the New Journalism, Hersey showed himself to be a realist in Eason's framework. *Hiroshima* was ranked first on the list of the Best American Journalism of the Twentieth Century and remains in print many decades after publication, but it was also attacked by critics as the prime example of an all-pervading understatement in *The New Yorker* whose 'denatured naturalism' and 'antiseptic' prose becomes a 'moral deficiency'. The novelist Mary McCarthy accused Hersey of avoiding the event's unique nature by treating it like a natural disaster rendered through the standard journalistic lens of 'human interest stories' (Lifton & Mitchell 1995, p. 89).

Understatement does characterise journalism in *The New Yorker*. When Hersey's report was published in 1946 the magazine's editor, Harold Ross, took the rare step of including a short note to readers suggesting that 'everyone might well take time to consider the terrible implications' of the dropping of the first atomic bomb (Hersey 1946a, p. 15). You might well say that is something of an understatement. It is important to recall the historical context, though. World War II had ended just a year before and Japanese people were still primarily seen as a defeated enemy. Most of the people killed by the bomb blast were civilians, not soldiers, but after Wilfred Burchett's initial reporting of the bomb's impact there had been almost nothing about the long-term effects on the people of Hiroshima, at least partly because of a confidential request by President Harry Truman to media outlets (Lifton & Mitchell 1995, p. 55). Hersey later recalled he initially considered an article documenting the bomb's power and its destructiveness but decided he wanted to 'write about what happened not to buildings but to human beings' (Lifton & Mitchell 1995, pp. 86–7). Hersey travelled to Hiroshima, where he interviewed several dozen survivors. It would have been entirely understandable if Hersey had felt overwhelmed by their horrifying accounts. He did feel terrified throughout his three weeks in Hiroshima, but this prompted him to reflect: if that was what he experienced eight months afterwards, how must those in the city on 6 August 1945 have felt? Instead of expressing directly how *he* felt, then, Hersey channelled his energy into enabling the reader, as far as possible, to sympathise with the bomb survivors' experience. The bomb attack, another critic argues, demanded Hersey 'provide forms for understanding what has been called history's least imaginable event' (Jones 1992, p. 214).

A closer reading of *Hiroshima*, then, reveals not an omniscient narrator but one concerned to describe the event as far as possible through the eyes of the six survivors, implicit in which is their limited knowledge beyond their own experience of, say, the political context of the decision to drop the bomb. During the story's editing, Ross raised this in one of his many queries: 'This is a story throughout of what people see firsthand and (except for a few parenthetical remarks) only that. Did this woman see her dead husband and know it that way? If so, it should be told that way. If not, it should be out' (Yagoda 2000, p. 189). Only occasionally does Hersey comment on the horror he describes, either directly, as when he says of his survivors that they knew they 'lived a dozen lives and saw more death' than they ever thought possible, or indirectly, when at the end of the first section, 'A Noiseless Flash', Hersey writes: 'There, in the tin factory, in the first moment of the atomic age, a human being was crushed by books'. The absence of open signals to the reader about the article's reportorial underpinnings, combined with Hersey's conscious decision to, as far as possible, remove himself from the narrative, undoubtedly increases the likelihood of it being read as 'antiseptic', but a fuller understanding of the context in which Hersey wrote shows he was anything but uncaring and that sometimes in prose less affect can make a more powerful impact. I have often set *Hiroshima* for classes and been surprised and gratified by how many students are deeply moved by it, more than half a century after publication and half a world away.

The point remains, though, that most readers know little of the background to the creation of *Hiroshima*; for those wanting to use an omniscient narrative voice, are there other means by which they can signal to readers they understand the limits of what they are presenting? In *Dark Victory* David Marr and Marian Wilkinson show there is by making clear to readers the information they are relying on and where it came from. *Dark Victory* is a narrative reconstruction of the response of the federal government, led by Prime Minister John Howard, to the arrival of asylum seekers on Australia's northern shores just weeks before he called an election. The 2001 federal election was the third of four consecutive elections that Howard, leading the Liberal National Party coalition, would win before his government lost office, and the prime minister his seat, in 2007. *Dark Victory* is not a work of polemic, but it is clearly the work of two politically engaged journalists who, after investigating the events in question, have reached firm conclusions that are infused throughout their chronologically organised narrative. The returned government and its supporters did not agree with the journalists' evidence or findings, but no lawsuits were lodged. Government ministers made no comment about the book, but nor were they pressed about it by daily journalists, as *Dark Victory* was launched during the week that the United States invaded Iraq in March 2003.

Marr believes anyone writing a book is just as obliged to reach conclusions as they are to investigate an issue from as many perspectives as possible. He points to the American biographer of James Joyce, Richard Ellmann, who, he says, is more concerned to lay out fifteen views of his subject than offer his own. 'It drives me beserk. Mr Ellmann, you have been studying this subject for years, you've read everything on it, you've talked to the descendants, you've read the letters, what do *you* think?'

Marr and Wilkinson were co-authors, but I interviewed Marr, who spoke about *Dark Victory* on behalf of both of them and who, as a former host of ABC television's *Media Watch*, is an articulate critic of practice. He says he has an 'explainer's imagination' rather than a 'creator's imagination'. He enjoys the possibility in narrative non-fiction of taking readers into new and complex areas. Marr and Wilkinson interviewed numerous asylum seekers and gained important testimony from them, but they did not need to become close to them for their project. Much of the material in the book came from documents, whether government documents obtained under the Freedom of Information Act, academic papers on refugee policy or, most extensively, the volumes of witness statements and testimony for the Senate Select Committee on what was coyly entitled 'A Certain Maritime Incident'. Much of this material goes unreported in the news media, even when it is being covered daily, as the committee's hearings were. Marr sees the potential in such seemingly unpromising raw material. 'If you bring all these sticks and old boxes together, these branches and rubble and some old newspapers, you can put it all together in a heap, and if you know how to build a fire with narrative it *will* ignite, like a bonfire.' Marr's 'explainer's imagination' enables him to sift through the thousands of pages of material to find the key threads of the events—the proximity of the arriving asylum seekers to an election, the pitting of longstanding maritime codes against a political leader willing to push conventions and rules to breaking point, the misuse of intelligence services, the government's suborning of the military for political ends, the dehumanising of the asylum seekers' plight by preventing journalists from photographing them and the setting up of an expensive, political rather than public, policy-driven scheme to process asylum seekers, the Pacific Solution.

The book deals with urgent public issues and its events were well known at the time, but it reads like a novel, which is reflected in the dust jacket copy's description of the book as 'a thrilling and provocative account of events'. Later editions reprinted reviews from critics who agreed: 'When a non-fiction book reads like the scariest, most horrifying thriller, you know you're on a winner' (*Sunday Telegraph*), 'A gripping, ripping yarn—alive with detail and rich in analysis' (*Eureka Street*) and, in *The Age*, former foreign correspondent and Pulitzer Prize-winning novelist Geraldine Brooks described it as a 'breathtaking read'. To Marr, these were compliments. He wanted *Dark Victory* to reach the broadest possible audience, but its subject matter—federal politics and immigration—are 'such relentlessly uncongenial material' that he believed the book needed to be written like a thriller if it were to have any chance of engaging a broad audience, and in this he and Wilkinson succeeded, selling more than 35,000 copies over two editions. Marr was not wanting to reach a broad audience for the sake of it, or for commercial success, but because he believed the issues were important and that they should be discussed with a deeper understanding of the meaning of events that had taken place amid the clamour of competing voices in the election and against the backdrop of the 11 September 2001 terrorist attacks. *Dark Victory*, then, does not read like an escapist thriller but one that fully engages the reader's mind and emotions, because the journalists have made a narrative out of a vast amount of material. By the end of its 293 pages the book prompts, in me and many other readers, a boiling outrage at how dishonestly the government had acted and how ruthlessly it had manipulated the flow of information to its citizens during an election campaign. As Marr says, 'We thought that if we presented the facts in a compelling narrative, the result in a fair observer would be fury and shame'.

Marr and Wilkinson's book is their interpretation of events and, as such, is open to debate; unlike Bryson's *Evil Angels*, though, *Dark Victory* provides readers with ample means to scrutinise its sourcing and methods. It has twenty-eight pages of endnotes that source information to particular documents, papers and interviews. With the exception of seven sources granted anonymity, all sources are named. The journalists also included six pages of acknowledgements that provide more detail on how they obtained information, and thank those who spoke to them off the record. Governments change hands for many reasons, but at least one strand of the growing disaffection with Howard's eleven-year-old conservative government was how it dealt with asylum seekers. *Dark Victory* played a key role in articulating and cementing in readers a belief that Howard had drawn on longstanding and deep-seated fears in Australians about border security to take electoral advantage of the arriving asylum seekers. There seems little doubt that the book's page-turning narrative played a major role in its success. Equally important, if less remarked on, is the means given to readers to assess the work's veracity and, if they choose, question the authors' interpretations.

Turning now to practitioners who decide to foreground their presence in a narrative, their decision may have stemmed from their belief that effacing themselves from what they write is itself dishonest, or at the least unrealistic. In *Slouching Toward Bethlehem* Joan Didion refuses to be simply a 'camera eye', and Norman Mailer argues objective news reporting hides as much as it reveals, beginning *The Armies of the Night* with a quotation from a news magazine before commenting: 'Now we may leave *Time* in order to find out what happened'. If issues arise when practitioners ignore or suppress their subjective response to people and events they write about, so at the other end of the spectrum problems arise when they fix on their subjective response at the expense of people and events they write about. Where one kind of narrative style denies the people being written about their full humanity by an inability or unwillingness to engage with them, the other kind denies subjects their full humanity by treating them as less important than the writer's own subjectivity. Hunter S. Thompson illustrates both the value and the problems of a practitioner writing in an avowedly individual narrative voice. Thompson was continually at odds with orthodox objective journalism, which he regarded as utterly incapable of getting at what was happening in the world ('the phrase itself is a pompous contradiction in terms', he once wrote), but throughout his life Thompson identified himself as a serious journalist. This may seem odd in light of his epic (and lovingly chronicled) hedonism, but he once threatened to sue *Esquire* magazine after it (mis)quoted him saying that only '45 per cent of what I write is true' on the ground that it would cripple his *credibility as a journalist* (Thompson 2000, pp. 642–3 italics in original). Thompson distinguished between his political journalism and *Fear and Loathing in Las Vegas*, which he acknowledged moved freely between fiction and verifiable fact.

Thompson's narrative non-fiction work, *Hell's Angels*, however, provided readers with a great deal more accurate information about the gang and a great deal more insight into its members than had the mainstream news media. His book *Fear and Loathing on the Campaign Trail '72* was described by Frank Mankiewicz, the political director of Democrat candidate George McGovern's campaign, as 'the most accurate and least factual book' written about the 1972 American presidential election (Carroll 1993, pp. 153–4). Mankiewicz was referring to Thompson's now widely-known 'gonzo' style, whose main elements are the foregrounding of the journalist's subjective response to what they are writing about, the possibility they will be as much participant as observer and the process of getting the story will be discussed, to the point where it may become the story itself (eds Wenner & Seymour 2007; McKeen 2008). Thompson's political journalism, which first appeared in *Rolling Stone* before being published in book form, differed wildly from that of the regular White House correspondents who, as Timothy Crouse showed in *The Boys on the Bus*, were unreflective, reactive and prone to a herd mentality. Thompson wrote what the other correspondents thought but could not—or would not—write. For instance, failed Democrat candidate Edmund Muskie 'talked like a farmer with terminal cancer trying to borrow money on next year's crop'. As a novice to political journalism, Thompson worked hard to understand the political process and took trouble to explain it for general readers (Dunn 2007).

The value, then, of Thompson's approach to narrative non-fiction is clear and enduring; the problems it created eventually overwhelmed his work and, eventually, him. Sometimes, the practitioner's subjective response is not the most important thing about an event, as the bombing of Hiroshima exemplifies, and over time Thompson's focus on the difficulties he faced doing his work became contrived, even counterproductive, as when he was sent by *Rolling Stone* to Zaire to cover the George Foreman–Muhammad Ali heavyweight title match but chose to smoke marijuana in the hotel swimming pool, and did not file a word on one of the most remarkable bouts in boxing history (McKeen 2008). Over time Thompson became known less for his writing than for his lifestyle. His gargantuan intake of drugs, whiskey and cigarettes curtailed his ability to get out of his Woody Creek compound and participate in events he wanted to write about. Originally a serious, diligent practitioner, Thompson ended up trapped by the myth he had created. Douglas Brinkley, Thompson's literary executor, says that, tragically, Thompson chose to commit suicide in 2005 rather than seek help because he believed if the headline 'Thompson Put in Detox Hospital' was ever written his fans would see him as just another frail old man (eds Wenner & Seymour 2007, p. 417).

It would be a mistake, though, to think that all practitioners who foreground their subjectivity do so as dramatically and with, over time, such self-destructive effects as Thompson. Helen Garner is widely regarded in Australia as a leading writer of both fiction and non-fiction. The narrative voice in her non-fiction—sometimes rhapsodic, other times querulous, always wincingly honest—is immediately recognisable and welcomed by her many readers. Where Bryson hid behind his omniscient narrator, Garner continually draws attention to what she thinks and feels about what she is learning, to the point where some critics have read her non-fiction as fiction. As Australian novelist Marion Halligan says of Garner's *The First Stone*: 'It's a novel whose main character is Helen Garner, acting out the role of the journalist' (Taylor 2005, pp. 77–8).

The First Stone was Garner's account of a sexual harassment case brought in 1992 by two students living in Ormond College at Melbourne University against the college's master. Garner's interest in the case was sparked when she read a newspaper report about it and impulsively wrote a letter to the master, Dr Alan Gregory, expressing her sympathy, and writing that whatever the truth of the allegations, 'This has been the most appallingly destructive, priggish and pitiless way of dealing with it. I want you to know that there are plenty of women out here who step back in dismay from the kind of treatment you have received.' Garner reprinted her letter in the book; many readers, especially women, were shocked that Garner, a long-time libertarian feminist, would side with the older man rather than the young women, especially when he was in a position of power and had a fiduciary duty of care towards them. Others cheered Garner's blunt questions—'He touched her breast and she went to the *cops?*—and her willingness to sandblast political correctness. 'Look—if every bastard who's ever laid a hand on *us* were dragged into court, the judicial system of the state would be clogged for years.'

Before discussing the case any further, it is important to note that, while some like Halligan read *The First Stone* as fiction, most read it as non-fiction because, apart from some names Garner invented to avoid a defamation suit, all other factual details cor-related—or purported to correlate—with specific incidents that occurred to actual people at Ormond College's 'smoko' night in 1991 that led to actual consequences. Throughout the controversy provoked by the book, supporters and detractors, readers and those involved in the case all discussed the book as an account of real events and people. They demonstrated Eric Heyne's 'certain kind of caring' about competing accounts that show when a work has left the domain of fiction.

The First Stone sold more than 73,500 copies, but did not win any major literary awards, perhaps because of the controversy surrounding Garner's research methods and how she represented people in the book. Garner began investigating the case soon after sending her letter to the master, but the two complainants heard about the letter's contents and refused to be interviewed, believing Garner did not have an open mind on the issue. Garner continued, and the drive of much of her narrative comes from her inability to speak to the complainants and other women at Melbourne University who supported them, notably Dr Jenna Mead, a tutor at Ormond. Garner argues that if the two young women really believe in their case they should be willing to defend it. As she struggles to understand why they went to the police over what she perceives as a minor matter compared to rape, she attacks them, in increasingly violent terms, writing at one point that she wanted to '*shake them till their teeth rattled*'.

Garner wrote her letter as a citizen, which is her right, but it is hard to see how she could fail to appreciate that sending such a strongly worded letter into an emotionally charged atmosphere would jeopardise her chances of getting interviews. It was certainly unreasonable for her to expect the young women to agree, and deeply unfair to attack them so personally for their choice. It is not simply the fact that Garner was unable to interview the young women that weakens her book, but the way she treats them thereafter. She lashes them and she lashes the women in the college who supported them. 'The warmth of her manner on the phone had congealed into the permafrost of a feminist who'd been shown my letter to Colin Shepherd [the pseudonym she gave Gregory in the book]' and 'But feminism too is a conduit for Eros ... It is not the exclusive property of a priggish, literal-minded vengeance squad that gets Eros in its sights, gives him both barrels and marches away in its Blundstones, leaving the gods' messenger sprawled in the mud with his wings all bloody and torn'.

Garner's narrative voice, and her extraordinarily vivid and intimate portraits of people, whether in *The First Stone* or in a later account of a murder trial, *Joe Cinque's Consolation*, are two traits that deeply engage many readers. As Kerryn Goldsworthy (1996) perceptively notes, Garner is one of few writers who could attract a mass audience with a book debating feminist theory and gender relations. The dangers shadowing this rare quality in Garner's work are twofold: first, Garner has not shown herself able or particularly willing to do the kind of detailed research that characterises much successful narrative non-fiction (Ricketson 1997, pp. 95–9) and, second, her highly personal approach leaves itself open to the charge that she believes her subjective response is more important than the events she is writing about or, at its strongest, that she is preying on other people's misfortunes for her own edification. As one woman supporting the complainants is quoted saying to her: 'Helen, this story is *not* being played out for the benefit of *your* finer feelings'. Garner is honest enough to include the line and it is characteristic of her narrative voice, but I wonder whether she realises exactly what she reveals about herself. No sooner has Garner quoted these words than she mocks them for making her feel like a fourth-former getting worked over by a headmistress. If that conveys something of the woman's approach to the case, so it does of Garner, whose refusal to see how her initial letter to the master cruelling her prospects of an interview comes across as a fourth-former's adolescent narcissism.

None of this is to say practitioners should ignore their subjective response to the people and events in their writing, as others before Garner, such as Joan Didion, and since, such as Margaret Simons, have shown. In *The Meeting of the Waters*, her re-investigation of the Hindmarsh Island affair, Simons presents a less certain persona in her narrative non-fiction, often foregrounding her uneasiness about the limits of what can be known about an event or issue, and picking at the unexamined assumptions underlying people's justifications for their actions. The case concerned two developers' plans to build a bridge across to Hindmarsh Island from the South Australian coast; the plans were initially blocked by the Aboriginal Affairs minister, Robert Tickner, after women of the Ngarrindjeri people protested that the island held spiritual significance for them as the site of secrets known only to women to do with childbirth, menstruation and burial of the dead. Another group of Ngarrindjeri women came forward saying the 'secret women's business' was fabricated, and their views were accepted by a Royal Commission. The commission's findings were used as ammunition by conservative newspaper columnists and others to further their argument that the federal Labor government, of which Tickner was a member, was soft-headed about indigenous people, putting more weight on spiritual beliefs of a minority group squabbling among themselves than on the developers' legal property rights. The developers brought a lawsuit against the federal government but, ironically, it was this case, heard in the Federal Court in 2001, which found the Royal Commission's findings substantially flawed. It was not within the court's remit to make a finding about the validity of the controversial secret women's business, but Justice John von Doussa was clear that 'it had not been proved that it had been fabricated'.

Simons had not covered the case, but because she was willing and able to spend time on it, she gained access to Aboriginal women who had not spoken to other journalists in detail. Simons brought no specialist knowledge of the issues to her investigation but this disadvantage was offset, she says, by the recognition among various people involved in what had become a bitter partisan struggle that she was not seen as allied to any party. She was anxious to continue to be seen as unaligned to any group, even though in the end Simons's book strongly argues that the supporters of the 'secret women's business' were treated almost as badly by the judiciary, the news media and the professional experts—in this case, anthropologists—as Lindy Chamberlain before them. When she first met the Aboriginal women Simons had already examined the Royal Commission's report and evidence presented to it, and found it wanting, but knew because of the trenchant support given it by various commentators that anything she wrote questioning it would be attacked. 'I knew it was essential for the credibility of the story that the journalism had integrity. I wanted to understand the Ngarrindjeri women's point of view, and I certainly wanted information from them, but I didn't want anybody to be able to say that I was doing the book for them.' She stressed this to the women on the first evening she met them, saying she did not know whether the 'secret women's business' was fabricated, though she says she did express her doubts about the Royal Commission. When writing her book Simons checked various interviewees' quotations with them, but says none of the women or any other people represented in the book had power of veto over its contents.

Simons maintained the independence that journalists value, but during the four years she worked on the book she came to question the assumptions underpinning it, writing in *The Meeting of the Waters*: 'Journalists and their sources are human beings, and the boundaries between empathy and independence are always complicated' (2003, p. 266). The use of a Royal Commission to inquire into spiritual beliefs is an irony that underlies much of *The Meeting of the Waters*; a further, unspoken irony is the intense scrutiny of Aboriginal spirituality but of no other spirituality, such as Christianity. The commission, steeped in Enlightenment ideals of rational thought and objective inquiry, struggled to understand the complex relationships between land, people and culture in Aboriginal society and how these relationships evolve over time, taking account of changing circumstances since the arrival of Europeans at the end of the eighteenth century. Opponents of the secret women's business viewed suspiciously its proponents' revealing of secret knowledge in stages; to them, this seemed like a way of changing the story to make it more likely to persuade a government minister to recognise its special status. Journalists covering the issue found this reasoning persuasive. 'Why didn't they just stick to one thing, and they would probably have gotten away with it', one told Simons. Apart from the sense of cultural superiority ingrained in these remarks, Simons notes how galling it is to journalists for events to remain hidden. 'Secrets exist in order to be uncovered, and published on the front page. It is particularly important that powerful people's secrets be revealed. This is called accountability.' Yet, this is not the only purpose of secret knowledge, as Ngarrindjeri beliefs and practices demonstrate, she writes. Simons agonised over how much of the secret women's business to include in her book. By commonly agreed journalistic standards, anything that had been put on the public record could be used, but the Ngarrindjeri people had been upset by what some anthropologists had already revealed, and among the Ngarrindjeri there were different views too. Simons tried to pick her way through this minefield, but admits that it was impossible for all those involved to agree with her editorial choices. What she decided to do was make this plain to readers, in the first paragraph of an author's note, and elsewhere in the book. She also points to how she has written about 'white men's secrets here as well, because our society and our attitude to knowledge are not as transparent as we like to think. I have offended uniformly.'

The Meeting of the Waters is written in a narrative style, but instead of an omniscient narrator, Simons adopts an open, first-person narrative voice. Simons' persona is reflexive, sometimes self-consciously so, but also unafraid to confront difficult issues, as the passages just quoted show. The anxieties she expressed are more tightly tied to the issues she is writing about than is evident in Garner's narrative voice, where events in her own life, such as a marriage breakdown, are discussed alongside the events she is writing about, to the point that at times they overwhelm the narrative. Simons says she sees her narrative voice as a representation of herself that she wants to be as accurate as those of other people she writes about. Her questioning of herself and her practices in the book are not simply or not only a rhetorical stance, but also an expression of her subjectivity and her struggles with the many nebulous strands of the issues she writes about. In *The Meeting of the Waters* Simons, unlike Garner, also makes full use of material such as an author's note and acknowledgements (three pages), endnotes and references (twenty-five pages), a timeline (seven pages), a cast of characters (eight pages) and a map, to make the nature and the depth of her research accessible to readers. What becomes clear in a reading of the book is her deep-seated commitment to investigating the issue with an open mind and a similar commitment to balancing her obligations to a wide range of sources with her obligations to readers. She achieved her goal, which means *The Meeting of the Waters* has been recognised as the most thorough, fair-minded and revelatory account of the Hindmarsh Island affair; it won the Queensland Premier's prize for best non-fiction book in 2003.

The writers interviewed by Boynton have developed narrative voices in their work that avoid the pitfalls evident in the work of Woodward and Capote at one end of the spectrum and Thompson at the other. Individual narrative voices differ, of course, but Ted Conover's *Newjack* illuminates just how far current practitioners have advanced. As an exercise in journalistic participation–observation, *Newjack* is every bit as dangerous as Thompson's riding with Hell's Angels. Most of the book is written in a first-person narrative voice, but there is none of Thompson's relentless self-dramatising. Thompson was twenty-seven when he met the bikers; Conover was twelve years older when he spent eleven months working as a guard in Sing Sing prison, and the author's photograph on *Newjack* shows him as a plain-looking man with friendly eyes. That Conover presents himself as an everyman helps readers identify with him. His vivid description of his struggle to manage more than sixty inmates accompanied only by a similarly inexperienced colleague induces in the reader heart-pounding anxiety. Not only do you fear what might happen to Conover, you begin imagining whether you could cope in the same circumstance. Deeply engaged in Conover's experiences, the reader is willing, eager even, to learn more about the American prison system, which Conover provides in thoroughly researched detail woven into his first-person narrative voice. Conover rarely discusses the impact his assignment has on his home life, so when he does it is all the more powerful. He is minding his two small children one evening when one begins misbehaving and he smacks him, something he had never done before. Immediately remorseful, Conover reads a book in bed to his son, who sobs for an hour before settling. Over time, Conover settles into a pattern of falling asleep on his son's bed after reading the night time story. His wife is sceptical, but Conover finds it 'the sweetest thing in my day', even as he knows 'It was an excuse, an evasion, a way not to examine the fact that I'd never been meaner or more vulnerable' (2000, p. 245).

What becomes clear, then, examining various writers' approaches to the question of narrative voice is, first, that the nature and aims of narrative non-fiction affects the choice of voice. A novelist is free to choose any narrative voice they like when inventing their fictional world. Certain aesthetic 'laws' of fiction exist, but they do so in inverted commas. There are no black letter laws governing narrative non-fiction either, but writers do need to think about the implications of their choice of narrative voice because their explicit aim is to represent actual people, events and issues. Apart from thinking about what kind of voice will best suit the content of the story, they need to understand the misleading signals that an omniscient narrative voice sends in non-fiction and about when and in what ways such a narrative voice could be used. They also need to be open to their own subjective response to the material they are exploring and think about how much their presence affects the events they write about. Finally, they need to think about how much and in what ways their subjective response is necessary to tell their true story.

Chapter 8

Description: finding the balance between vivid intimacy and unnecessary hurtfulness

If you aren't learning intimate details about your ordinary subjects that you believe are too personal for print, you're probably doing a poor job of reporting. If you don't often struggle with the ethics of what you will include in your profiles of ordinary people, you're either a schmuck or not really facing the ethical dilemmas.

Walt Harrington, journalist and teacher

One of the great strengths of narrative non-fiction, not to mention one of its pleasures for the writer, is describing people and events in words. Compared to the formal and purportedly objective words of the news report, these are words that convey the flavour of an event or the sense of a person so readers feels like they were there too or would recognise the person if they met them. Easier said than done; you don't have to read too widely before you realise that for every poet there are a dozen wordsmiths, and that for every word-smith there are two dozen journeymen hammering clichés into a flat and soggy state. Editing *The Faber Book of Reportage*, John Carey acknowledges that journalism cannot get beyond language because it is language itself, but found himself trudging through countless accounts of battles containing phrases like 'Our horse inflicted severe punishment on the enemy's right flank' before selecting those that contained 'unusual or indecorous or incidental images that imprinted themselves scaldingly on the mind's eye' (1987, p. xxxii).

He listed nearly a dozen examples, including an ambassador peering down the front of Queen Elizabeth I's dress and noticing the wrinkles, boxer Joe Louis's nostrils flared like a double-barrelled shotgun and the starving Irish, whose mouths were green from a diet of grass. Such descriptions combat the 'inevitable and planned retreat of language from the real'. Different writers will observe and describe different things, depending on their training, experiences, culture and psyche, but it seems undeniable that some practitioners observe more acutely than others; some are more intellectually and emotionally honest than others. How much of this is innate and how much learned is an open question, but I know from my own experience the value of practise, reading and reflection. Careful and honest observation of principal sources and events may not convey everything about them, but it will convey something and, in the hands of a good writer, will convey something powerful about them.

Let's start by looking at especially noteworthy passages of description and then ask what issues arise from this power. Helen Garner has an extraordinary ability to unfold the meaning of unexamined everyday events. One memorable scene in *The First Stone* is the hearing in the County Court of a (successful) appeal against the conviction of Ormond College's master for indecent assault. Garner attended and seems to notice everything: the sarcasm beneath the barrister's use of the chivalrous word 'madam' in cross-examining one of the two complainants, the needle beneath his elaborate show of ignorance of how young women wear their hair today, the two 'Ormond men' who push hard against Garner's legs as they seek to sit behind Gregory and the 'strange reflex of helpfulness' that prompts the master's wife to look around her for a chair when, from the witness box, one of the young women who had accused her husband of sexual harassment asks for a seat. Most writers would unconsciously censor this oddly poignant detail but Garner seizes on such moments, which has characterised her approach, whether in feature articles or in her narrative non-fiction.

In one newspaper piece about a visit to the city morgue, Garner watches from a raised and glassed-in viewing area as two gowned and masked technicians perform an autopsy on a hepatitis-infected young man. Again, in a horrifyingly precise and lengthy description she seems to notice everything: how the pathologist moves as swiftly and lightly as a dancer; how the technician scours out the man's hollowed skull 'using the same rounded, firm, deliberate movements of wrist and hand that my grandmother would use to scrub out a small saucepan'; and how, finally, the technician hoses down the body, wiping the man's mouth, which 'moves under the force of the cloth just as a child's will, passively, while you wipe off the Vegemite or the mud' (1996, pp. 146–8). These images do indeed imprint themselves scaldingly on the mind's eye, as Carey says. Death may be a universal human experience, but many of us have little contact with it; certainly, we have little exposure to how those for whom death is a workday experience deal with it. Autopsies are common fare on television shows like *CSI* or *Law and Order*, but a good deal of the power of Garner's piece comes from her being an eyewitness to an autopsy. This is not imagined; this happened in front of my eyes, she says, positioning herself openly in the narrative as an everywoman whose emotional responses to the autopsy we can share. Through the metaphors quoted above Garner conveys both the strangeness and the universality of the autopsy. A grandmother cleaning a saucepan and a parent wiping clean a child's mouth are instantly familiar, but when paired with a corpse are jarringly incongruous. They are also poignant, putting us in mind of memories of family food and children's small resistances to parental authority, even as we wonder about the past life of the man on the table who died infected with hepatitis C.

A powerful piece of writing, then, no doubt; it is important to underline that, for practitioners, the origins of good descriptive writing lie in observing people and events with an open mind and unflinching eye. It means, as Garner says, quoting Henry James: 'Be someone on whom nothing is lost'. Not everything you observe will be relevant or interesting or resonant, but even once you have culled the material, are there issues that arise in descriptive passages? These are not simply 'technical' issues, as Capote and, for that matter,

Harold Ross of *The New Yorker*, labelled them, though they certainly involve the techniques of writing. To say they are only technical is to ignore the ethical dimension, which requires writers to keep in mind the virtues inherent in narrative non-fiction—truthfulness, independence and social justice—with the capacity of these elements of narrative to engage readers emotionally as well as intellectually. That is to say, the purposes of narrative non-fiction and fiction are not identical, though they may overlap in parts. Description is a potent part of writing in a narrative style, as it can draw a reader deep into an event or a person's life. Its potential for intrusiveness raises issues, though. How do we describe people, their appearance, actions, gestures, mood, behaviour and interaction with others? How do we balance our obligation to the reader with our obligation to those we write about? In general, readers want vivid, intimate description, while sources, understandably, want to be presented in the best possible light, or at least in a tactful way. If a person's actions are rendered in a narrative style, how can writers know what particular actions mean and how readers will interpret those actions when they are represented in a true story? In this area novelists clearly enjoy greater freedom, and not simply because of questions about accuracy in representation. Novelists can and do create characters who are physically disgusting or morally repugnant or, at a more mundane level, have foibles and blind spots. Characters in novels have every possible human attribute. One of the pleasures a novel offers is the depth of observation of a character; a work of narrative non-fiction may well contain sharp observations of the people in it, but here practitioners need to find a balance between honouring the virtues of honesty and compassion.

Detailed and vividly written description of people and events will induce in readers a strong emotional response that could be considered manipulation, but to try and cauterise emotions from a description is also manipulation, though it is manipulation by omission rather than commission. That is actually what happens in news reports, as has been discussed earlier. Most writers value time they spend observing events and people at firsthand, and detailed descriptions of what they have observed are well recognised as one of the strengths of narrative non-fiction. Readers, too, value vivid description: who would choose to read the official report of an autopsy over Garner's gripping account? The choices writers make about what to exclude, what to include and how to describe it are not neutral because they are representing actual people and events. People get upset and angry when they are portrayed inaccurately, especially in a work conveying emotional texture as well as everyday facts. We have already seen how distressed Dick Hickock's son was at how Capote represented his father as a 'sex fiend' as well as a murderer in *In Cold Blood*, and for years the Chamberlains endured misleading media coverage fed by police leaks. Even when they gave their version of events in detail to a Sydney journalist, Steve Brien, he wrote in his 1984 book, *Azaria: The Trial of the Century*, that: 'Ever since I had known the full ramifications of the police case I had always believed Lindy was guilty' (p. 369). He suggested two 'scenarios' for what happened at Uluru in 1980. In one, Lindy Chamberlain killed her baby in a 'crime of passion', while in the other the murder was premeditated, with Lindy atoning for her sins by sacrificing her child in the desert. Lindy Chamberlain, in her autobiography, *Through My Eyes*, was scathing of Brien who, she wrote, 'said we were some of the nicest people he had ever met—and claimed he was our best friend—later authored one of the most scurrilous books ever written about our case with incorrect evidence and rumours put in as fact' (Chamberlain-Creighton 1990, pp. 196–200). How events are interpreted can be, and often are, contested, but Bryson's *Evil Angels* showed both the failings of police and the willingness of the news media to print rumour as fact and to put sinister connotations on innocuous information.

Writers can ask themselves several questions to help guide their writing choices. First, is the description relevant? In one of the 'quickie' books released soon after Lindy Chamberlain was convicted of murdering baby Azaria, Jim Simmonds refers to how he and other journalists indulged in the 'not-unpleasant past-time of Lindy-watching' during her trial: 'When she wore a filmy apricot dress with thin straps over the shoulders, male onlookers ogled her shamelessly, many tipping that she was braless underneath', he writes in *Azaria: Wednesday's Child* (1982, p. 127). Simmonds's description is prurient rather than relevant, which is evident in other passages describing her physical appearance in detail (on pages 27–8, 46, 138, 161 and 177).

Lindy's then husband Michael was described too, but less often, in less detail and with little attention paid to his sexual appeal.

These references may be obviously gratuitous description, but no less a writer than Janet Malcolm is similarly guilty in *The Crime of Sheila McGough*, her account of a lawyer disbarred for apparently collaborating with a conman client, when she recounts an unproductive interview with a former acquaintance of the conman. Malcolm is met at the door of the interviewee's house by an old woman who 'looked at me with suspicion, almost with hatred. When I explained my errand, she continued to stare at me wordlessly. Then she allowed me to enter the house' (1999, p. 97). The interviewee is an old and ailing man who remembers little. As Malcolm leaves, 'through a door that stood ajar in the hallway and showed a darkened bedroom, I saw the suspicious old woman again, standing bent over beside the bed, taking off all her clothes' (1999, p. 98). Does this passage add anything to the book? If Malcolm's point is to show the many leads she pursued that turned up nothing, the 240-or-so word passage could have been reduced to one sentence. If her point is to contrast the old woman's secrecy with her nakedness, it is a small point made about two people of little consequence to the overall story. It is also cruel in its calculated disregard for the woman's privacy. Malcolm does not name her, but she does list the man's former employer, probably making them identifiable to local residents, which count for more than for readers like me living on the other side of the world.

An equally intimate detail in a newspaper feature story by Barry Siegel was more confronting to read than Malcolm's passage but succeeded, I think, because the details were so relevant. The story, which won a Pulitzer Prize for feature writing in 2002, was about a father haunted by the death of his son he inadvertently left alone for too long while they were in the wilderness scouting for deer. Here is the passage where Siegel describes the end of the search for the boy.

It was the longest night Wilkes [the searcher] ever spent. He feared falling asleep, afraid he'd never wake up. Near 5am, he rose and began to walk. Within minutes, Dino's nose went down. The schnauzer darted up a slope to the base of a pine tree.

From below, Wilkes could see his dog licking a mound of snow. Then, as he approached, he saw two little feet. By the time Wilkes reached the tree, Dino had cleaned off Gage's face. Six inches of snow covered the small body. Gage lay in a fetal position, his hands clenched, his eyes wide open. His pajama legs were up to his knees; his feet had worn through his thin booties. His throat was blue. In his eyes were frozen tears (cited in Craig 2006, pp. 73–4).

A second question writers can ask about description is whether a particular action of the subject of the passage fairly indicates their overall behaviour. You can see this phenomenon most easily in interview articles written to a tight deadline, where journalists are susceptible to over-reading offhand remarks and everyday incidents. In a sharp piece headlined 'Notes on the Death of the Celebrity Profile' (2001), Tad Friend writes that, when an interview in *The New York Times* with the former lead singer of Fleetwood Mac began, 'The miniature cheesecake sat in front of Stevie Nicks like a cruel temptation'. It transpires that 'the wee pastry must bear the weight', Friend writes, 'of being an indication that the onetime substance-and food-abusing "Ms Nicks knows something about indulgence, and about paying the price for it"'.

Those working on long-form projects should be able to overcome this hurdle because they spend more time with their principal sources. Researching a biography of bestselling Australian children's author Paul Jennings, I spent many hours interviewing him and those who knew him, and in tagging along with him on school visits and literary events. With his young readers Jennings was unfailingly polite and solicitous, but he was also prone to bouts of depression and seemed to have grown up with one less layer of skin than most. This was central to his writing; seemingly at will Jennings could re-experience childhood memories, which meant that his stories, with their child's eye worldview, connected instantly and resonated deeply with his readers. As something of a man-child, though, Jennings was not always easy to live or work with. Portraying him was less about revealing the private man beneath the public face, which teeters on the brink of biographical cliché in any case, but learning over time how much weight to put on individual episodes so that the book was as fair as possible to all parties. Fairness does not necessarily equate to niceness, as Jennings acknowledged in an afterword I asked him to write after beginning to appreciate how confronting it is to have someone trampling about in the entrails of your life while you are still living it. He found it painful to read that he was not as nice or kind or wise as he thought, but he acknowledged that, unlike many biographies, this one sought neither to destroy nor hero-worship.

That a bracing honesty can coexist with compassion is even more evident in Julie Salamon's extraordinary work, *Facing the Wind*, which is about a married couple, Bob and Mary Rowe, one of whose children is disabled. They become part of a close-knit group of parents of disabled children. After years of caring for the boy, Bob Rowe becomes depressed, then delusional, and one day kills his wife and three children with a baseball bat. He is found not guilty of the crime by reason of insanity. After spending more than two years in a psychiatric hospital he is released, remarries happily and eventually dies of cancer aged sixty-eight. Near the end of the book is a scene describing a meeting between Rowe's second wife, Colleen, and the families from the self-help groups, whose disabled children are now adults. It occupies thirty-four pages of *Facing the Wind* and is as harrowing as it is compelling to read. Colleen loved Rowe, and the women from the self-help groups loved Rowe's first wife and were still angry and grieving over the deaths. What had happened to the Rowe family was, writes Salamon, 'a monstrous story', but Rowe was not 'a monstrous man'. Salamon's rendering of the scene quivers with the participants' intensely felt, sometimes ugly, emotions. It discloses far more than is published in most newspaper and magazine articles, and probably still would have been draining for the participants to read, but the descriptive passages are respectful of the vulnerability of both Colleen and the families.

A third question practitioners can ask is whether their descriptions are aimed at evoking an emotion or if they are being used as a substitute for an argument. In *The Journalist and the Murderer*, for instance, Malcolm describes in detail McGinniss's own description in an earlier book of him stealing a can of crabmeat from novelist William Styron, which he had been saving for a special occasion. She writes that it signifies 'the dire theme of Promethean theft, of transgression in the service of creativity, of stealing as the foundation of making' (1990, p. 14). Perhaps it does, but without wishing to defend McGinniss's decorum as a houseguest, I would argue Malcolm uses the description to provoke readers' disgust at McGinniss's apparent selfishness. Further, a single incident is asked to carry a disproportionate amount of weight for an argument that Malcolm has not really developed beyond a sharp observation. In narrative non-fiction, practitioners usually inquire into the underlying meanings of the events they write about and, in so doing, develop an overall argument, but they are also telling a story. At one end of this continuum sits something akin to an academic thesis; at the other is what is known in journalism as 'one hell of a damn story', as Nick Lemann puts it. Ambitious practitioners such as Lemann aim to marry the two, but not all are equipped to do this. Similarly, some events and issues are so dense and complex as to resist being told in an accessible narrative. For instance, Margaret Simons had to deal with the potential threat of lawsuits in composing *The Meeting of the Waters*, and so included exhaustive detail ensuring her text was defensible. She also had what is called a Russian novel problem: there were simply too many people involved in the case for it to be comprehensible to many readers. 'If this were fiction, one would surely amalgamate a few', she writes wryly. Other events and issues attracting writers' attention are simpler and may well not carry meanings much beyond their surface. The implication for writers is to be as clear as possible in their own minds about the relationship between meaning, argument and story in their work.

A fourth, and final, question practitioners can ask is to consider how their presence—or nominal absence—in the descriptive passage affects how it will be read. As we have seen with Woodward and Capote's work, the use of an omniscient narrative voice heightens the reader's sense that the passage represents events and people as they are; it erases awareness of any possible gaps and of the writer's role in interpreting the material for the reader. In *Stasiland*, Anna Funder's account of life for ordinary East Germans since the fall of the Berlin Wall, Funder renders a series of interviews as they were experienced rather than remove her presence from the narrative and convert the interviews into either the interviewees' firsthand account or into a third-person narration of the interviewees' experiences.

The content of the interviews is disturbing enough, as we learn the full extent of the German Secret Police's intrusion into people's lives, but it is underscored by Funder's framing of her interviewees' stories. When one woman tells her how she was called in to a meeting with a Stasi officer, who read out loud the woman's love letters to an Italian boyfriend, Funder tells us: 'The hairs on my forearms stand up. I have stopped looking at Julia now because in this dimness she ceased addressing her words to me some time ago. I am humbled for reasons I cannot at this moment unravel. I am outraged for her, and vaguely guilty about my relative luck in life' (2002, p. 109).

Among Funder's interviewees is another woman who had been forced to choose between informing on a man helping others to get over the wall and reuniting with her severely disabled infant son, who was receiving treatment in a West German hospital. She refused to be an informer, was tortured by the secret police, and imprisoned for four years. Funder comments:

> It is so hard to know what kind of mortgage our acts put on our future. Frau Paul had the courage to make the right decision by her conscience in a situation where most people would decide to see their baby, and tell themselves later they had no choice. Once made though, her decision took a whole new fund of courage to live with. It seems to me that Frau Paul, as one does, may have overestimated her own strength, her resistance to damage, and that she is now, for her principles, a lonely, teary, guilt-wracked wreck (2002, p. 221).

Frau Paul helped numerous people escape to West Germany but did not see herself as brave, which to Funder was the most tragic element of her account, 'that the picture she has of herself is one that the Stasi made for her' (2002, p. 229). Funder's comments could be read as personal, even invasive, but coming at the end of sixteen pages closely describing the interview, they read to me as deeply compassionate. That Funder was able to devote to Frau Paul the time mostly unavailable to newspaper and magazine journalists is critical; so, too, is a commitment to researching people and events with empathy and telling stories as truthfully as possible (Joseph 2007).

Chapter 9

What if you weren't there?
The difficulties of reconstructing
scenes and dialogue

Deputy Dwight 'Dewey' Riley: 'Page 32, "Deputy Dewey filled the room with his Barney Fife-ish presence."'
Gale Weathers, author of *The Woodsboro Murders*: 'You read my book?'
Dewey: 'Well, yes, I do read Miss Weathers.'
Gale: 'Dewey, don't take it so seriously. It's a character in a book.'
Dewey: 'Page 41, "Deputy Dewey oozed with inexperience."'
Gale: 'Don't you think you're overreacting just a little bit?'
Dewey: 'You're a money-hungry, fame-seeking and, forgive me for saying, mediocre writer who's got a cold storage shed where her heart should be.'

From *Scream 2*, directed by **Wes Craven**

Scenes are integral to narrative non-fiction; they're what distinguish narrative non-fiction from news reports on one side and textbooks on the other. Scenes present the unfolding of events and the interplay of people. As a form of storytelling they have been with us since the plays of ancient Greece, but are more recognisable to tellers of true stories in the development of the socially realistic novel and in cinema. Almost all the descriptive passages discussed in the previous chapter came from scenes. Many of the most celebrated moments in the history of narrative non-fiction—what the six survivors were doing at the exact moment the atomic bomb dropped on Hiroshima, George Orwell getting shot during the Spanish Civil War, Norman Mailer protesting on the steps of the Pentagon—are contained in scenes.

For some scenes the writer was present and describes what they observed; for others they weren't and they opt to reconstruct them, which poses problems that are the focus of this chapter. Even for those scenes the writer witnessed, they have a choice about whether they present themselves openly in the narrative or seek to remove themselves from it. Bill Kovach and Tom Rosenstiel, in their excellent book *The Elements of Journalism*, provide five guidelines for 'trying to navigate the shoals lying between fact and fiction' that are underpinned by a discipline of verification (2nd edn, 2007, pp. 78–112). They are, first, never add anything that was not there; second, never deceive the audience; third, be as transparent as possible about your methods and motives; fourth, rely on your own original reporting; and, fifth, exercise humility. Before continuing, a note of caution: I am talking about scenes as if they exist before, and independent of, the practitioner who simply wanders in and picks one off the shelf. A scene, like a story itself, is the result of the interplay between events and those observing them. Two practitioners might observe the same set of events and write different accounts; one of them might even think there is nothing of note to write up.

It is a common experience among writers, though, that if they tag along with those they are writing about they will see things of value to their true story; the longer they tag along the more likely it is they will witness the fine grain of people's lives. They may want to present what they witnessed without drawing attention to their presence and so create an illusion that readers, like an invisibility-cloaked Harry Potter, can watch the scene at close quarters unseen by participants. A similar illusion is created in fiction (and in cinema) that follows Percy Lubbock's argument in *The Craft of Fiction* for showing over telling. For Lubbock, dramatising events was preferable to describing or picturing them because 'other things being equal, the more dramatic way is better than the less. It is indirect, as a method; but it places the thing itself in view, instead of recalling and reflecting and picturing it' (cited in ed. Herman 2007, p. 15). Written more than half a century ago, Lubbock's views have been influential, especially in newsrooms, in much the same way as William Strunk, Jr and E.B. White's advocacy for the 'plain style', because it plugs into the idea abroad that you can offer readers stories clean of any static interference. Lubbock's ideas have been superseded by later scholars, beginning with Wayne Booth, who exposed problems with the premise of the show-versus-tell debate. As narrative theorist David Herman recounts, Booth 'characterised showing as an effect promoted by certain, deliberately structured, kinds of telling, organised in such a way that a narrator's mediation (though inescapably present) remains more or less covert' (Herman, 2007, p. 14). In other words, you can't really show without telling; you are simply disguising the telling from the reader. As such, showing rather than telling has drawbacks as well as benefits. Whatever these drawbacks and benefits in fiction, they take on new weight in narrative non-fiction, where we need to consider not only how writers gather the material, but how they represent it and how it is read.

Lillian Ross's work illustrates these issues. She was one of the first writers to be labelled a 'fly on the wall'; the critic Edmund Wilson used a similar term when he called Ross 'the girl with the built-in tape recorder'. Both were intended as compliments; Wilson meant that Ross not only had rare powers of observation and description, but that she could use those powers without appearing to judge those she wrote about (Yagoda 2000, p. 251). Few disagree about Ross's observational powers, but in the absence of clear authorial signals, her work has been open to a range of interpretations by readers, some of which jarred with her intentions. In her famous profile of the writer Ernest Hemingway, headlined 'How Do You Like It Now, Gentlemen?', Ross tracked Hemingway over a few days while he and his fourth wife, Mary, visited New York, showing him in the mundane business of getting from the airport to a hotel, ordering room service, shopping for a new coat, visiting an art gallery and meeting his publisher about the manuscript for his new novel, *Across the River and Into the Trees*.

Nothing of great consequence happens yet the profile is revealing, partly because Ross creates the illusion we are seeing Hemingway up close and partly because Hemingway is always talking about himself, making pronouncements about life and the world, relating everything to sport and big-game hunting, and regularly dropping into a cheesy mock native American dialect. Here is the moment when Hemingway meets Ross at the airport, one arm clutching an old briefcase containing the manuscript, the other wrapped round a small, profusely sweaty man named Myers who had sat next to Hemingway on the flight:

> Myers made a slight attempt to dislodge himself from the embrace, but Hemingway held on to him affectionately. 'He read book all way up on plane,' Hemingway said … 'He liked book, I think,' he added, giving Myers a little shake and beaming down at him.
>
> 'Whew!' said Myers. 'Book too much for him,' Hemingway said. 'Book start slow, then increase in pace til it becomes impossible to stand. I bring emotion up to where you can't stand it, then we level off, so we won't have to provide oxygen tents for the readers. Book is like engine. We have to slack off gradually'. 'Whew!' said Myers. Hemingway released him. 'Not trying for no-hit game in book,' he said. 'Going to win maybe twelve to nothing or maybe twelve to eleven.' Myers looked puzzled. 'She's better book than *Farewell*,' Hemingway said. 'I think this is best one, but you are always prejudiced, I guess. Especially if you want to be champion.' He shook Myers' hand. 'Thanks for reading book'. 'Pleasure,' Myers said, and walked off unsteadily.
>
> Then he turns to Ross and says moodily that after finishing any book he feels dead, though no one knows it. 'All they see is the irresponsibility that comes in after the terrible responsibility of writing.' (2002)

When the profile was published in *The New Yorker* in 1950 it provoked an uproar. Many thought it a 'devastating' portrait of a self-obsessed bore, a borderline alcoholic, an unrelentingly macho writer whose best work was behind him. Ross was shocked, as she revealed in a note accompanying the profile when it was reprinted in a collection of her work, *Reporting*. She maintained she liked Hemingway and had written a sympathetic piece that 'tried to give a picture of the man as he was, in his uniqueness and with his vitality and his enormous spirit of fun intact' (1966, p. 171). She felt such readers did not want Hemingway to be Hemingway. 'They wanted him to be somebody else—probably themselves. So they came to the conclusion that either Hemingway had not been portrayed as he was, or, if he was that way, I shouldn't have written about him at all' (1966, p. 171).

Hemingway himself had seen an advance galley proof of the profile and he told Ross he thought it funny and good; he also wrote to his publisher that the profile would make him 'plenty good new enemies' and presented them both as 'horses' asses', albeit well-intentioned ones. After the furore he wrote to Ross to reassure her that he still regarded her as a friend; later, though, he used the profile as a scapegoat for the poor reviews he received for *Across the River and Into the Trees* (Baker 1969, pp. 737, 742). There is evidence in the profile to support both Ross's view and that of Hemingway's detractors. For my part I could see both interpretations, and enjoy the profile the more for it, but what is interesting is that Ross struggled with the vagaries of readers' interpretations. A clue lies in her response to being complimented for her 'fly-on-the-wall' approach. She thought the term misguided. Practitioners, she argues in her memoir *Reporting Back*, cannot 'pretend to be invisible, let alone a fly; he or she is seen and heard and responded to by the people he or she is writing about; a reporter is always chemically involved in a story' (2002, pp. 5–6). This is surely the case, but it is odd she cannot see that by removing as much of her 'chemical' self as possible from the narrative she leaves a gap into which readers project their own views.

Helen Garner is a prominent example of a writer who leaves no such gap. Instead, in almost every scene she presents herself openly as the narrative sensibility through which readers see what she sees, which for critics like Willa McDonald, is Garner's signature appeal, while others find it distracting or overwhelming (eds Bak & Reynolds 2011). In *Joe Cinque's Consolation*, which concerned the killing of Cinque by his then girlfriend Anu Singh, Garner attended Singh's trial in an effort to understand her actions. One morning during the trial, while those in court wait for the judge to arrive, Garner watches as Singh puts up her hair:

> Although her back was turned to us, it was an almost inde-cently intimate and histrionic display, a series of age-old, deeply feminine gestures. First, the raising of both arms and the gather-ing of the hair in two hands. Then the twisting and rolling and flicking and doubling back of its dark mass, redder towards the tips, into a thick club; the binding of it with a broad black stretchy band; then the patting, the sensitive roaming of the flattened palms against the smooth round curve of her head; the feeling for loose strands at the temples and the anchoring of them over and behind the ears. All was in order. Satisfied, the small flexible hands flew up, out, and down to her lap, where they would lie, hour after hour, neatly clasped and occasionally twisting, while her inner life (or lack of it), her disturbances, her madnesses and cruelties were stripped bare and paraded before a small, intent cluster of strangers (2004, p. 46).

Reviewers were divided about this passage when the book was published in 2004. In *The Australian* Emma-Kate Symons, a staff journalist, wrote that she was mesmerised by the 'intimate domestic detail' in the passage, which reminded her of paintings by the seventeenth-century artist Jan Vermeer. Maryanne Dever, director of the Centre for Women's Studies and Gender Research at Monash University, found the passage manipulative. 'Singh's pleasing appearance becomes a finely calibrated measure of her apparent moral degeneracy, and as she sits in court the arrangement of her fine, serpent-like limbs and her "dark mass of hair" are obsessively monitored by Garner' she writes in *Hecate's Australian Women's Book Review*. Garner defends the scene; she told me:

> It wasn't as if I sat there looking at her thinking, 'Now, what did she do today to make her look narcissistic?' It doesn't work like that. One of the things that makes courts interesting is that there *is* a mode of behaviour, there is a glaze of formality over

everything, and what people do to disrupt that glaze is very interesting and it tells you a lot about them. For Anu Singh to do something *that* intimate, that intensely feminine in the middle of a court room where she was on trial for murder was, for me, completely staggering.

For Garner, then, the description is not gratuitous but relevant and representative of what she observed of Singh. That Garner had such a visceral response to the sight of a woman rearranging her hair in court may say something about her, as she acknowledged in our interview, but for Dever to describe Garner's firsthand observation as 'obsessively' monitoring Singh says something about her too. To me, Garner's choice in the way she presented this scene was defensible, but it also shows how her journalism is primarily driven by her personal response to people, events and issues.

If practitioners face questions about their presence in scenes they observe, they face a good deal more when they reconstruct scenes they did not see for themselves. How can they do this with any real confidence, and how can they convey this to readers? We have seen the difficulties Woodward and Capote got themselves into, and scholars such as Russell Frank are sceptical about the integrity of reconstructed scenes, arguing that the quest for reader involvement can push aside the need to attribute information to its source. Where practitioners collapse 'the distinction between a story based on eyewitness reporting and a story based on other people's stories, the writers of reconstructions privilege storytelling over reporting, preserve artistic integrity at the expense of journalistic integrity' (1999, p. 155). For his book, *The Ethics of the Story*, David Craig, a former newspaper copy editor who became a journalism academic, interviewed sixty practitioners at three major newspapers, who told him about their efforts to balance the two, which included subtler forms of attribution than the reflex 'she said' at the end of each paragraph and editors' notes or story boxes that outlined journalists' sources and research methods. But Frank argues such notes are insufficient unless they specify which parts of the reconstruction came from which sources.

Both Frank and Craig are primarily discussing newspaper and magazine articles, but their concerns carry probably even more weight in book-length true stories, where writers have more time and space to ensure accuracy and where greater accountability to readers is a reasonable expectation. The questions for writers to consider in reconstructing scenes include: how important is the scene to the book, is the scene straightforward or highly contested and is it everyday or intimate? At a practical level, you need to consider whether you have access to all those present in a scene, whether they are cooperative or hostile and whether there is any documentation to support memories which, by their nature, are fallible? (Lorenz 2005). These questions go to the gathering of material; there are other questions concerning where along the continuum you sit in either drawing the reader deep into the narrative style or signalling to them the limits of the representation. Among the nineteen writers interviewed by Boynton, twelve said they have reconstructed scenes or, where they were not asked the question directly, it is clear from statements in their own work or from critics that they have. These writers are Cramer, Finnegan, Harr, Kotlowitz, Kramer, LeBlanc, Lewis, Orlean, Preston, Rosenbaum, Trillin and Wright. Of the other seven, they either did not discuss the issue or their works are grounded mostly in their own firsthand observation and in documentary evidence. Among the Australian writers all but one, Garner, say they have reconstructed scenes in their narrative non-fiction.

The majority of these writers may have reconstructed scenes, but all preferred to observe events firsthand, and most were acutely conscious of the difficulties. For instance, Lewis says 'What *really* makes the scene swing on the page are the little things that nobody but the writer would ever notice', but if unable to be present, he is 'happy to reconstruct it after talking to everyone else who was'. Orlean is anxious to make clear to the reader that in any reconstructed scenes, 'the construction shows' and is 'repulsed' when a practitioner writes a scene as if they had been present when they were not. Between these two is LeBlanc, who spent eleven years researching and writing her account of impoverished families living in the Bronx. She accumulated vast files and observed her principal sources hundreds of times, but on occasion she reconstructed events she had not witnessed. To do this she would get information from as many sources as she could, interview them repeatedly and, where possible, ask them to take her

Telling True Stories

to visit the place where the scene happened and show her who stood where, and even draw pictures and charts. Two of the people in the book, Cesar and Coco, spent a weekend at a hotel in the Poconos. 'To verify whether they gave me the right details I drove up to the hotel and took photographs of their room and interviewed the hotel management. I asked, "Were the bedspreads that color? Was the décor the same then?" Then I showed the pictures to Cesar and Coco in order to stir their memories.'

Thinking about the checklist of questions above, we can see the weekend in the Poconos was a relevant, but far from central, scene in *Random Families* while, for instance, Capote's reconstruction of Hickock and Smith's flight from the crime was central and so raised the stakes for his reconstruction. LeBlanc's scene was straightforward rather than contested. She had good access to Cesar and Coco, who were cooperative, and she could buttress their accounts relatively easily by visiting the hotel. The events described were certainly personal, but given how well LeBlanc knew her principal sources, not overly so. Capote did have excellent access to Hickock and Smith, and could compare their versions of events, but he did not have access to all the people they encountered along the way and relied on memories of events that occurred months, even years, beforehand. Like LeBlanc, he knew his principal sources well, but Capote was also reconstructing contested and highly charged events, such as Hickock deliberately running over a dog on the road and his alleged sexual depravity.

From this it is clear LeBlanc's approach is careful and thoughtful; she is not an exception, though. Others have been equally painstaking in their efforts, as Walt Harrington shows in an article about his and others' practices, 'The Writer's Choice'. Where LeBlanc's comments illustrate the thoroughness of her efforts, Rosenbaum says his views have changed as he has learnt that, no matter how much material he gathers, he cannot write a 'seamless narrative'. He now expects to hear conflicting points of view. 'It is often from the seams of the narrative that the really interesting questions emerge. *Why* do these people's stories conflict? *What* are their agendas?' This is particularly evident in *Explaining Hitler*, his long, engrossing inquiry into the origins of Adolf Hitler's evil where, amid his close readings of the extensive Hitler historiography, Rosenbaum interviews two people holding polar opposite views: David Irving, a Holocaust denier, and Claude Lanzmann, the purpose of whose epic nine-hour film, *Shoah*, is to definitively document the final solution. Rosenbaum's account of his interviews fairly crackles with tension as first he challenges the disingenuousness of Irving's rhetoric and then runs foul of Lanzmann, who proves inordinately proprietorial about not just the film, but the Holocaust itself. There is much more that could be said about these encounters but the relevant point here is that, even though Rosenbaum's interview scenes are firsthand rather than reconstructed, they exemplify the value of asking '*Why* do these people's stories conflict? *What* are their agendas?' rather than creating a seamless narrative.

To see how you might reconstruct a scene *and* show some seams in the narrative, let's look at Sebastian Junger's *A Perfect Storm*. The book is about a freak confluence of weather that produced what meteorologists call a 'perfect' storm—that is, one that could not be worse—which claimed the lives of six men on board a sword-fishing boat, the *Andrea Gail*, in 1991. The book became a bestseller and was subsequently filmed, starring George Clooney and Mark Wahlberg. The question, of course, is how did Junger know what happened when none on board the *Andrea Gail* survived? His task looks like the scene-reconstructing equivalent of a triple twisting somersault in pike position. The events are central to his story but they are con-tested, literally of life or death importance, and he has to gain the close cooperation of grieving families. In a foreword and an acknowledge-ments section, Junger makes clear the limits of what could be known about the event. He interviewed the dead fishermen's families and friends, as well as those on other boats who had survived the storm. He interviewed people who had been in similar situations to gain an appreciation of what might have happened on board the *Andrea Gail*. Any dialogue quoted in the book is drawn from interviewees' recol-lections; none was made up, he writes. Junger does write about how the fishermen died, but he does not appear to step over the boundary into writing fiction. He gathered as much information as he could from experts and describes over eight pages what happens when a person drowns, from how the instinct not to breathe underwater is so strong that it overcomes the agony of running out of air, to how the body responds to the first involuntary breathing in of water, and how the panic of dying is mixed with a peculiar sense of disbelief. 'Having never done it before, the body—and the mind—do not know how to die gracefully. The process is filled with desperation and awkwardness. "So this is drowning," a drowning person might think' (1997, p. 180). Critically, as Rebecca Rule and Susan Wheeler argue in *True Stories: Guides for Writing from Your Life*, writing what a 'drowning person might think' differs from putting that thought into the mind of a particular person. Junger buttresses his informed speculation with an account from a medical journal of a man who survived a near drowning; it has the added effect of reminding the reader that *The Perfect Storm* is non-fiction. This section of the book is nonetheless deeply discomfiting to read because the level of detail Junger provides forces the reader to stop and imagine a universally terrifying prospect—drowning.

What is interesting reading this passage is how, in its own way, it is as deeply engaging as a work of socially realistic fiction. Where the suspension of disbelief means novelists need to create a credible fictional world, the reader's corresponding disposition to believe the veracity of non-fiction means writers do not always necessarily need to make their true stories read like thrillers. That the events actually happened will lay some claim on the reader's attention.

That said, I would like to finish this chapter by drawing your attention to the power of a reconstructed scene that does read thrillingly. It comes from Adrian Hyland's *Kinglake–350*, his account of the 2009 Black Saturday disaster that caused the worst loss of life from bushfires in Australian history. Instead of centring the book on those who died, as Junger had done in *The Perfect Storm*, or on a sample of survivors, as Hersey did in *Hiroshima*, Hyland makes Roger Wood, the police officer on duty in the small country town of Kinglake, the person through whom we readers see, hear and smell the fires that raged across the state of Victoria. Of the 173 people who died in the fires, 120 came from Kinglake. Hyland's is an inspired choice, and not simply because Wood and his fellow officer, Cameron Caine, won Victoria Police's highest valour award for leading a convoy of fifty people out of Kinglake to safety, but because through him the reader sees just how little, as well as just how much, a country cop can do to protect the community they serve in such a horrific event.

Mobile phones worked spasmodically that day; midway through a call home with Wood's wife, Jo, screaming at him that the fire had arrived at their home, the signal died. Wood furiously punched redial but the phone rang out, the ringtone 'tolling like a funeral bell'. From what he is able to see, the road to his wife and two young children is cut off by flame; not that he can even try to get home because there are so many others he is duty-bound to help. It is only after he and Caine have led their extraordinary convoy off the blazing mountain to safety that Wood tries his phone again:

> For the first time all night, it's answered. 'Oh Rodge ...' Jo's voice is drawn, weary. Enormously relieved. 'I've been so worried about you. Been trying to call you all night.'
>
> 'Same here. Worried you were dead.' He blinks back tears. 'Kids okay?'
>
> 'They're fine.'
>
> He slumps forward in the seat: the long-held tension slackens like a cut rope, and he's suddenly aware of the terror he's been struggling with for so many hours.
>
> 'It was that wind that saved us.' Jo is still talking. 'It was only seconds away when it turned around.' He is struck by the irony of that. The southerly buster that diverted the fire from St Andrews and saved his own family had driven it up the escarpment to wipe out Kinglake.
>
> 'When are you coming home, Rodge? Everything's still on fire down here.'
>
> 'Soon, honey,' he says. A wrenching need to be there. 'Not just yet.'
>
> 'How's Kinglake?'
>
> 'Pretty much wiped out.' A brief silence.
>
> 'You do what you have to, Roger.'
>
> 'Love you.'
>
> 'Yes' (2011, pp. 206–7).

The scene conveys Wood's experience: his twin loyalties to family and community and the enormity of what he endured. It provides a glimpse of the fire's toll on him and his family, physically and emotionally. Thinking of the questions we should ask, the reconstruction is central rather than peripheral to the narrative, is intimate rather than mundane and there appears to be no corroborating documents or eyewitnesses to the phone calls, unless Caine observed the second one. The stakes, then, are high, but there are only two people in the scene and Hyland has interviewed them both at length. Notice, too, that the reconstruction goes no further than what the Woods experience. On the book's release, Woods and Hyland were interviewed on ABC Radio National's *Life Matters* program and Woods praised the writer's account without qualification. Nor is *Kinglake–350* simply or solely a reconstruction of the day's events. Hyland is determined to explain and explore the context of events he describes, whether it is the physics of fire or the organisation of the Country Fire Authority. Deeply affecting though Hyland's narrative is, he moves beyond that to offer sharp but measured comments about the puzzling lack of preparedness for fire among many people despite abundant warnings, and to ask difficult questions about the prospect of more fires as severe as Black Saturday because, as a society, we are ignoring scientists' predictions that global warming will lead to a rise in extreme weather events.

Chapter 10

Interior monologues: are they 'one more doorbell to push', or the province of fiction?

Invariably, the most profitable conversations are ones that come after a degree of trust has developed between the journalist and his source. This relationship is fraught with problems, since trust and friendship go hand in hand. Knowledge is seductive; the reporter wants to know, and the more he knows, the more interesting he becomes to the source. There are few forces in human nature more powerful than the desire to be understood; journalism couldn't exist without it. But the intimacy that comes with sharing secrets and unburdening profound feelings invites a reciprocal degree of friendly protection that a reporter cannot always offer. By the conspicuous use of a tape recorder and extensive note-taking, I try to remind both of us that there is a third party in the room, the eventual reader.

Lawrence Wright, *The Looming Tower: Al-Qaeda and the Road to 9/11*

Where reconstructed scenes prompt concern among some writers, interior monologues raise alarm. It is the most controversial element of the narrative approach in non-fiction, as it aims to take readers inside someone's head. This chapter looks at whether it is possible for writers to do this and, if it is, whether they should.

By this stage I hope you can see this debate needs to be seen in the context of this book's two central themes. The first is that, whatever narrative approach you take, it should sit within the goal of telling a true story, or one that is as true as you can make it. If that goal is not uppermost in your mind you really should make that clear to the reader, as Martin Flanagan did when writing about Australian Rules football pioneer Tom Wills in *The Call*. In an author's note, Flanagan writes: 'This book is an imagining of real events. It does not purport to be a history; rather, it is an interpretation of an historical drama in the manner of a work for theatre or the screen'. Flanagan drew on historical documents but wanted the liberty to fill gaps in the record with his own imaginative speculation. Wills is an actual historical figure and Flanagan writes regularly about football for *The Age*, so he wanted to make clear to readers the book's status. The second theme flows from the first: there are boundaries and there are differences between fiction and non-fiction, even though the boundaries are, at times, blurred, and there are probably as many similarities as differences.

The interior monologue, according to Chris Baldick's *The Concise Oxford Dictionary of Literary Terms*, is 'the written representation of a character's inner thoughts, impressions and memories as if directly "overheard" without the apparent intervention of a summarising and selecting narrator'. Its aim, then, is to give the reader access to the thoughts and feelings of a character. A related concept is stream of consciousness, which is sometimes confused with interior monologue but which Baldick distinguishes as a particular kind of interior monologue: 'While an interior monologue always presents a character's thoughts "directly" … it does not necessarily mingle them with impressions and perceptions, nor does it necessarily violate the norms of grammar, syntax, and logic; but the stream-of-consciousness technique also does one or both of these things' (Baldick). Stream of consciousness is most famously associated with modernist novelists James Joyce in *Ulysses* and Virginia Woolf in *Mrs Dalloway*, both published in the 1920s.

Thinking of non-fiction, at one end of the continuum is a news report quoting a person expressing their thoughts or (less commonly) feelings and at the other is an interior monologue. In between is a narrated account of a person's actions, appearance and dress, as well as their words. We have already seen, in Ross's profile of Hemingway, among others, how much can be conveyed by describing a person's actions, appearance and dress, as well as how using actions as a direct index of state of mind opens a piece to a range of interpretations by readers.

One of the many claims in Tom Wolfe's influential, if widely contested, essay proclaiming a 'New Journalism' is that the interior monologue is a distinctive, perhaps unique, feature of the novel and that it is the element of narrative writing that is furthest from straight news reporting. This did not give Wolfe pause—no surprise to those who have read his brilliant, boisterously self-promoting essays. With a typically insouciant sweeping aside of concerns, Wolfe conceives of this level of intimacy in journalism as simply 'one more doorbell a reporter had to push'. He pointed to a profile magazine article he wrote in the early 1960s of Phil Spector that describes how the pop music producer felt as an airplane readied for take-off: 'All these raindrops are *high* or something. They don't roll down the window, they come straight back, toward the tail, wobbling, like all those Mr Cool snow heads walking on mattresses'. Asked about Wolfe's hyperkinetic portrait, Spector confirmed the passage was 'quite accurate'. This did not surprise Wolfe, as it was founded on his long interview with Spector (1973, pp. 33–4).

Conversely, thirty-five years later, when H. Porter Abbott, a leading scholar of narrative, came to update his *Cambridge Introduction to Narrative*, he took the opposite view. For this second edition he included a chapter dealing specifically with the relationship between narrative in fiction and narrative in non-fiction, and he writes that unless historians and biographers—and by implication those writing narrative non-fiction—are making things up, they cannot report or record in the same way as a narrator in fiction can about their subjects' inner lives. Abbott cites a vivid internal account from Henry James's *The Beast in the Jungle*:

> But the bitterness suddenly sickened him, and it was as if, horribly, he saw, in the truth, in the cruelty of his image, what had been appointed and done. He saw the Jungle of his life and

saw the lurking Beast; then, while he looked, perceived it, as by a stir of the air, rise, huge and hideous, for the leap that was to settle him. His eyes darkened—it was close; and, instinctively turning, in his hallucination, to avoid it, he flung himself, face down, on the tomb (2nd edn 2008, p. 149).

Abbott comments that what works so well in James's novella 'Would raise all kinds of alarm bells if you found it in a text claiming to be history' (2nd edn 2008, p. 149).

A clear divergence of views, then. Wolfe says you can write interior monologues, no problem, while Abbott flatly declares them out of bounds. The historical context is relevant here: Wolfe was writing about an era of journalistic experimentation where 'the top rung is up for grabs. All the old traditions are exhausted, and no new one is yet established' (Wolfe, 1973, p. 51). As is their nature, some experiments left enduring legacies while others failed. Some New Journalists treated fact and fiction simply as two ingredients in the salad of their story. For instance, George Butler adopted a New Journalism approach for the documentary he directed about body-building, *Pumping Iron*: 'We took nonfiction material and gave it a dramatic structure'. What this meant was that when Butler heard a story about a boxer who had not attended his father's funeral because he was preparing for Olympic competition, Arnold Schwarzenegger took the story and pretended it was *his* father and *his* competition, according to his biographer, Nigel Andrews. This caused Big Arnie media grief when he became a famous film star, but that is another story. Today, though, for the overwhelming majority of writers and scholars, accuracy is a cornerstone of narrative non-fiction.

The implications of writing an interior monologue for a work of non-fiction are far more complex and challenging than Wolfe concedes, but for Abbott to argue that the interior monologue is 'strictly speaking, not available to the historian' and, by implication, to other writers of non-fiction, is to fly in the face of a body of narrative non-fiction that attempts to do just that. This includes works ranging from Gay Talese's portrait of boxer Floyd Patterson after losing a heavyweight title bout to Sonny Liston to Truman Capote's portrait of convicted murderer Perry Smith in *In Cold Blood* and, more recently, from Richard Cramer's extensive use of interior monologue in his account of an American presidential campaign, *What It Takes*, to Richard Preston's more modest use of it in his book about the Ebola virus, *The Hot Zone*. This is far from an exhaustive list. For instance, in Mark Kramer and Wendy Call's selection of talks given to the annual narrative journalism conference, Jack Hart, managing editor and writing coach at *The Oregonian*, describes the interior monologue as a 'staple for successful narrative nonfiction writers' (2007, p. 236).

Drawing on Boynton's interviews and on my own, though, I would argue that only a minority of writers practise the interior monologue in non-fiction today. An even smaller number write stream of consciousness interior monologues. A novelist can write interior monologues without qualm, as they create their own characters and can give them any thoughts and feelings they like; indeed, reading about the interior life of characters is one of the great pleasures of reading novels as well as a source of insight into humanity. In real life we know what we are thinking and, to a greater or lesser extent, feeling, but we cannot know for sure what anyone else is thinking or feeling because the only consciousness to which we have access is our own. People can tell us what they are thinking or feeling, of course, but beyond that we can only imagine. Novels create the illusion of being inside someone else's consciousness better than other forms, such as cinema, dance and art. For narrative non-fiction, which seeks to represent actual people, the question immediately arises: how does—indeed, how can—the writer know with any certainty what a person is thinking or feeling? As journalists are often accused of misquoting a person's spoken or written words, how can they be confident their efforts to represent a person's thoughts and feelings will be credible?

There is an important set of questions writers can ask themselves to guide whether or how they will use interior monologues: How important is the monologue to the article or book? Is it about everyday life or an important event? How much cooperation has the subject of the monologue provided to the journalist? How well known is the subject of the monologue to the reader? How honest and reflective is the subject of the monologue? Readers will also ask how they can trust the veracity of what they are reading, so what can writers do to build a relationship of trust with their readers? With these questions in mind, let us return to Wolfe's profile of Phil Spector, as a number of critics remain unconvinced by Wolfe's assurances. Jack Fuller, a journalist and novelist, asks whether the passage fairly represented what Spector thought and felt at the time or whether this was his apparently gleeful description of it later: 'The man on the other side of the door often lies about his inner state. He may even lie to himself' (1996, pp. 148–9). Fuller's point is apt but also not surprising, and prompts the question: why does Wolfe place unblinking trust in an interview as a means of understanding exactly what a person thought and felt at a given moment?

Wolfe does not address this question in any detail in *The New Journalism* but, to be fair to him, at the time he was writing few others were either. By 1980 John Hersey, a pioneering figure in narrative non-fiction, examined Wolfe's use of interior monologue and argued that the most distinctive element of the interior monologues Wolfe creates in his narrative non-fiction work, *The Right Stuff*, is how most of them sound like him. Whether these passages were the monologues of astronauts, their wives or even a chimpanzee test pilot, Hersey writes in his essay 'The Legend on the License', 'Right Stuffers who are alleged to speak nothing but Army Creole are garlanded with elegant tidbits like *esprit, joie de combat, mas allá*! … God help us, God becomes Tom Wolfe and with His sweet ear chooses the Wolfeish "ninny"' (1989, p. 255).

Hersey's answer is a good one, even if he understates Wolfe's ability to adopt different narrative voices, such as, for instance, the southern drawl of pioneering airman Chuck Yeager in *The Right Stuff*. Hersey also perhaps misreads the tone of Wolfe's interior monologues. That most of them hum with the current of Wolfe's energy and comic brio draws attention to Wolfe's artifice; that is, what Wolfe does is a form of impersonation that he performs for the reader and, with this in mind, the reader is not perhaps expected to take these passages as a literal attempt to render a person's (or a chimp's!) thoughts. This prompts a further question, though: does Wolfe always rely on in-depth interviewing and 'his sweet ear' to produce a fair and accurate representation of his subjects' thoughts and feelings? Not always, according to Daniel Lehman. In *Matters of Fact* he argues that in Wolfe's work about Ken Kesey and the Merry Pranksters, *The Electric Kool-Aid Acid Test*, Wolfe sometimes writes as if from inside the collective head of organisers of an anti-Vietnam War rally without any indication he interviewed them or attended the rally. What makes it worse, writes Lehman, is that Wolfe misrepresents and denigrates their views.

There is only marginal support among current practitioners for Wolfe's unclouded view of the ethical difficulty of writing interior monologues. Prominent writing coach Jack Hart, in his book *Storycraft*, may be as impressed as Wolfe by the power of interviews to reveal thoughts and feelings, but Roy Peter Clark of the Poynter Institute warns that use of the interior monologue is a 'dangerous strategy' that is permissible in 'the most limited circumstances' (eds Kramer & Call 2007, p. 168). Theodore Cheney, in his textbook on creative non-fiction, writes: 'In the hands of the inept, or the ept but unscrupulous, it is an easy device behind which to hide unethical writing behavior' (1991, p. 222).

Among Boynton's interviewees, only five said they write interior monologues or, where they were not asked the question directly, it is clear from statements in their own work or from other critics' work that they have. These practitioners are Cramer, Harr, Kramer Preston and Talese. Wright appears to have changed his view between 1994 when he included interior monologues in *Remembering Satan* and his interview with Boynton a decade later. Of the others, ten did not discuss it and the remaining three—Lewis, Orlean and Trillin—strongly oppose use of interior monologues.

Preston and Talese have written interior monologues without attracting the criticism levelled at Wolfe, but both appear to have gained full cooperation from their sources, including for extensive checking, and both write about relatively unknown people. Talese gained such complete cooperation from the son of a Mafia boss for his book *Honor Thy Father* that the criticism he drew was not for presuming to know another's thoughts but that he became so close as to lose his sense of perspective about organised crime. In *The Hot Zone*, Preston writes an interior monologue for vet and pathologist Nancy Jaax at the moment she fears (wrongly) that she might be infected with the Ebola virus, and she is annoyed she has forgotten to go to the bank that day. Preston told Boynton: 'It rang absolutely true when she first described her thoughts to me. But then I went over it again and again until I was finally sure that this was—to the best of her recollection—what she thought at that moment' (2005, p. 321).

The interior monologue is contained within a description over thirty pages of an experiment led by Eugene Johnson to find a vaccine for the Ebola virus. At the United States Army Medical Research Institute of Infectious Diseases, Johnson is accompanied by Jaax into the highest level biosafety laboratory rooms to examine monkeys infected with the Ebola virus. Preston builds suspense by describing in almost claustrophobic detail the precautions taken—the three layers of clothing, super restricted access to the labs, the extensive quarantine procedures for anyone believed to be infected—and the ease with which a person can become infected; Ebola is what he calls a 'slate-cleaner', as infectious as influenza, but with a mortality rate of the black plague in the Middle Ages. Here's the moment where Jaax fears she has become infected:

Son of a bitch! She thought. Aw, fuck! They'll put me in the Slammer [the biocontainment hospital]. And Tony will be filling out accident reports while I'm breaking with Ebola. And a week later, I'll be in the Submarine. Shit! Jerry's in Texas.

And I didn't go to the bank today. There's no money in the house. The kids are home with Mrs Trapane, *and she needs to be paid*. I didn't go to the market today. There's no food in the house. How are the kids going to eat if I'm in the Slammer? Who's going to stay with them tonight? Shit, shit, shit! (1994, p. 70)

It's vivid and, as Preston says, rings true. It is important to note, though, that this is the most extensive passage where the reader is given access to Jaax's thoughts and feelings, and it is only 105 words. Most of the thirty-page description positions the reader as an observer of Jaax and Johnson's actions, but not of their thoughts. As Preston intimates, representing a person's thoughts and feelings is inherently difficult and so should be limited to those elements that can be checked, should be used sparingly and should be buttressed by more easily verifiable information. Alternatively, the writer can signal to the reader through phrases such as 'she later recalled' that what they are reading is one person's memory, with all the vagaries that implies.

Cramer, however, writes interior monologues for presidential candidates, which attracts intense scrutiny both from the principal sources and from critics. It does appear, however, that Cramer is thorough. In a note to the reader in *What It Takes* he writes that he interviewed more than a thousand people and that 'In every case, thoughts attributed to the characters in this book have been checked with them, or with the people to whom they confided those thoughts' (1992, p. ix). Cramer provides no endnotes, however, and this, coupled with his habit of writing about well-known, important people with slangy intimacy—he refers to Republican Bob Dole as 'the Bobster'—drew criticism for reincarnating Wolfe's faded New Journalism technique. Jack Fuller agrees that the content of the interior monologue is relevant. 'It is one thing to infer certain feelings in a warm and flattering account of a father's pride at watching his son pitch his first professional baseball game and another to attempt to guess at what went through a policeman's mind as he fired a shot that killed an innocent boy' (1996, p. 153).

Of the Australian writers I interviewed, only two (Blackburn and Bryson) said they have written interior monologues, while four (Garner, Hooper, Knox and Marr) said they had not. One (Simons) was chary, but did not rule out the practice completely. Bryson's use of interior monologue is relatively circumscribed, whereas Blackburn's work contains the most extensive use of interior monologue—and the most problematic, primarily because of her lack of experience in writing narrative non-fiction. Her book *Broken Lives* is an important work, so it is useful to set out its achievement as well as its shortcomings.

Published in 1998, *Broken Lives* was the prime impetus for the reopening of the cases against John Button, convicted in 1963 of the manslaughter of Rosemary Anderson, and Darryl Beamish, convicted in 1961 of the murder of Jillian Brewer. At the time another man, Eric Edgar Cooke, had confessed to killing both women. Cooke, however, was a convicted serial killer and his confessions were disbelieved or ignored by police who had already obtained confessions from Button and Beamish. Button was sentenced to ten years and Beamish to life imprisonment after his initial death sentence was commuted. A chance meeting between Button and Blackburn in 1991 at a dancing class sparked her interest in the cases. Her research showed that the police cases against Button and Beamish had been misguided, perhaps deliberately so. It also showed that Cooke's confession had been sincere and that he was responsible for running down and injuring seven more young women. The police, however, had not connected these cases with the running down and killing of Anderson. *Broken Lives* prompted calls in the West Australian parliament for the cases to be reopened, which eventually were heeded, despite opposition from the police. In 2002 Button's conviction was quashed in the West Australian Court of Criminal Appeal, making legal history as the longest standing conviction in Australia to be overturned. Three years later the same result was achieved for Beamish. Rarely do works of narrative non-fiction have such a specific, substantial effect. Blackburn's efforts won a Walkley Award for the most outstanding contribution to journalism in 2001, and in the same year won the Australian Crime Writers Association Ned Kelly Award for best true crime book.

After that Blackburn wrote a book entitled *The End of Innocence* that reflects candidly and, for a journalist, at rare length on the issues, both professional and personal, that came up as she researched and wrote *Broken Lives*. It soon becomes clear she approached her investigation thoroughly and thoughtfully, interviewing more than 160 people and uncovering a wide range of police, judicial and government documents. As she sought out the women who had been run down but not killed by Cooke, Blackman felt both 'a journalist's excitement at what information I might glean' and nervousness about the 'shock and pain I would evoke' by asking them to revisit agonising memories. During some of these interviews she found herself crying along with her interviewees. Both Button and Beamish had been wrongfully convicted, she believed, but *Broken Lives* focuses overwhelmingly on Button's case, as he and his family were willing to take part while Beamish's family was not. Even the Buttons were willing to be involved only if Cooke's widow, Sally, supported the project, which she did after Blackburn discussed it with her.

These actions demonstrate Blackburn's care for those she was writing about; she was confronted by even more difficult decisions as the process continued. Button and Anderson, his girlfriend, were enjoying his nineteenth birthday until a misunderstood remark led to an argument. Walking home along the road, Anderson was run down by Cooke. The prosecution case had been that Button had made advances but Anderson resisted and, in a rage, Button hit her with his car. More than two years after Button had met Blackburn, Button told her that he and Anderson had been having sex for three months before her death. Button had not told anyone this because of the then taboo on pre-marital sex and because he 'wanted to protect Rosemary's honour and I didn't want to hurt her parents any more than they were hurting already. But you have to know everything. I trust you to do the right thing with it' (2007, p. 146). Blackburn was moved by Button's trust and convinced of his honesty, as the revelation went so much against his interests. But she also believed she had to use the information because it was vital to proving his innocence. She offered to continue research but not publish anything until after Anderson's parents had died. He then agreed to let her use it, trusting her to treat it sensitively.

Where Blackburn carefully balanced her goal of disclosing as much information as possible with a duty of care towards Button, she acknowledges she was not as sensitive to the needs of the Anderson family, who for four decades had believed Button had killed their daughter and were being told this was wrong. Early on she had told them that her investigation would have been easier if they were dead, meaning that they would not have to confront the pain of giving up their long-held belief, but her 'clumsy comment' intensified the Andersons' feeling that 'their daughter had been metaphorically dug out of her grave and tossed around in the air by the media, and they had no part in it'. Perhaps the obsessiveness that drove Blackburn's campaign to overturn Button's and Beamish's convictions also blinded her to the Andersons' plight. Researching and writing *Broken Lives* occupied her for more than six years.

Broken Lives reconstructs the accounts of the individual hit-and-run victims, and tracks between Button's life and Cooke's crimes, and his execution in 1964. The book's editor, Zoltan Kovacs, said the first draft read like a 'series of police rounds stories', prompting Blackburn to rewrite, trying to 'colour it up' and 'breathe life into the characters' (2007, p. 163). At Kovacs's urging she attempted to write an interior monologue for Cooke, not to excuse him but in an effort to explain. She interviewed a psychologist and two psychiatrists who knew Cooke and sought to imagine his thought processes as he committed each of his many crimes:

> A powerful new urge stole over him, rising from the deep bitterness within. He felt a surge of irresistible excitement as the idea took shape. It was more than his usual need to mock the mockers by taking the things they held dear. This was more—this was an urge for more power and a realization that he had more power (1998, p. 46)

> It was over. He'd had his fill of revenge. That feeling left him— that feeling of power that made him light, coming over him like a mantle or cloud, telling him he must use the gun. He didn't know where it came from, his heart or his head, but it was strong— stronger than an impulse or an urge; a power as though he was God, with power over life and death (1998, p. 164).

> She was sleeping on top of the bed, wearing just a flimsy nightie; virtually nothing to hide her nakedness. The feeling that had been stirring all night grew stronger. It was a balmy night, thoughts of young love had been on his mind since the previous day ... He could have her and avenge himself again (1998, p. 219).

Blackburn felt she had restored Cooke's humanity rather than repeat his tabloid portrayal as the cold-blooded Nedlands Monster. The attempt is clearly sincere, but to me the interior monologues read like a Gothic novel, in phrases such as 'a powerful new urge stole over him', 'that feeling of power', 'telling him he must use the gun', 'thoughts of young love had been on his mind' and 'he could have her and avenge himself again'. Cooke's family complained to her after the book's publication for daring to know what their father was thinking. She sympathised and explained her intention. She asked the family to specify what was wrong in her portrayal of

Cooke and interpreted their silence as suggesting 'an emotional basis to their complaint'.

Another way to interpret their silence is that they were unable to say what was wrong because they did not know what their father was thinking before he committed crimes for the simple reason that they were not him. That underscores the difficulty for any interior monologue in narrative non-fiction. If people feel proprietorial about their words when they are quoted, they feel doubly so about their thoughts and feelings being represented. To attempt an interior monologue of someone who is not only dead but also responsible for horrific crimes—Cooke committed necrophilia with the woman described in the passage above—seems close to impossible to achieve. Magnifying the problem, Blackburn had represented Cooke's thoughts and feelings from an omniscient narrative perspective. As novelist and literary critic David Lodge writes in *The Art of Fiction*, the representation of a character's inner life in a work of fiction undoubtedly tends to generate sympathy 'however vain, selfish or ignoble their thoughts may occasionally be; or, to put it another way, continuous immersion in the mind of a wholly unsympathetic character would be intolerable for both writer and reader' (1992, p. 42). In other words, Blackburn, for whom *Broken Lives* was her first attempt at narrative non-fiction, set herself a task bound to backfire. The potential benefit of gaining at least some understanding of Cooke seems outweighed both by the likelihood of offending the surviving families and appearing to be voyeuristic, despite her best intentions. She is still, in my view, a long way ahead of Joe McGinniss, who not only writes interior monologues for Senator Edward Kennedy without interviewing him for his biography *The Last Brother* but then 'seems anxious to cash in on the rhetorical power of factual narrative' (1997, p. 51), according to Daniel Lehman. In my assessment, *Broken Lives* will be remembered for the life-changing impact it had on the lives of Button and Beamish, whereas *Evil Angels*, which also included modest use of interior monologue, is remembered not only for its persuasive upending of received wisdom about the Chamberlain case but for the skill of Bryson's writing, which draws the reader deep into the events at Uluru in 1980 and their meaning.

It may not be impossible, then, to ethically write interior monologues, but it is certainly difficult and, accordingly, it is more common for writers to avoid them. Michael Lewis told Boynton he disapproved of journalists such as Bob Woodward claiming to capture their subjects' inner thoughts. 'I don't believe it for a second. His characters end up having the capacity to feel only what Bob Woodward feels. And it is always the *same* feeling'). David Marr, Chloe Hooper and Susan Orlean all say they are content to know that not every element of fiction writing is available to practitioners of narrative non-fiction, and Malcolm Knox says he feels no pressing need to write interior monologues 'because I am not a frustrated novelist who is writing non-fiction'. Knox has written several well-received novels as well as prize-winning narrative non-fiction, such as *Secrets of the Jury Room*. Similarly, Anna Funder, winner of both the Samuel Johnson Prize for *Stasiland* and the Miles Franklin Award for her novel, *All That I Am*, says: 'The purpose of the novel is to do what only novels can, which is to get inside someone else's consciousness, or pretty close to it. In non-fiction, you just can't do that'.

My analysis of interviews with nineteen American writers of narrative non-fiction and of the work of seven Australians offers suggestive rather than conclusive findings, but of these twenty-six, most (nineteen) avoid interior monologues in their work on the grounds that they are too difficult to do successfully, that the margin for error is too great, the consequences of failure too serious and, finally, because many believe the interior monologue sits more comfortably in the domain of fiction writing. There is a balancing power, of course, that accrues to a true story that novelists can never quite claim. As David Lodge puts it: 'For the reader the guarantee that the story is 'true' gives it a compulsion that no fiction can quite equal' (1992, p. 203).

Chapter 11

What do readers expect of narrative non-fiction?

Dear Inmate MacDonald,
My wife and I are here in beautiful and sunny Hawaii having a great time, and we have both read the novel *Fatal Vision* by Joe McGinniss. We are both, I must tell you, convinced beyond a shadow of a doubt that you are guilty as hell of the murder of your wife and daughters ... You are obviously a latent homosexual (or perhaps no longer *latent* now that you are where you are. Perhaps, by now, you may well be the 'Queen of the Hop' there in the joint, hm?) who hates women because you are an impotent faggot, true?......
    With best wishes. J_____H_____.
    Included in *The Journalist and the Murderer* by **Janet Malcolm**

Until this point, I have been saying that writers generally compose their true stories with intended readers in mind, but beyond stating the common goal of reaching the broadest possible audience, I have not examined the implications of that assertion. This, then, is the chapter where we look at how writers need to consider exactly what they are offering readers. So, you have completed the research and the writing phase and you are at the moment of publication. Your principal sources are present only as represented in the work, and you are present primarily as a narrative voice and secondarily as an author promoting your work. Just as the writer's conduct during the research phase influences how they represent people, events and issues, so their approach to the writing phase influences the kind of relationship they seek to establish with readers. The main questions a writer needs to think about at this stage of the process are: what am I offering readers or, to put it another way, what am I promising to deliver to readers? What expectations do readers have of a work of narrative non-fiction?

True stories can be published across various media forms, but here we need to explicitly consider readers' expectations of true stories published in book form rather than in newspapers, magazines or online. Will readers think the work is a novel, or do they readily distinguish between novels and works of narrative non-fiction? This is not an implausible question; for most people, journalism is what they read in newspapers, hear on radio, watch on television or do all three online. Similarly, non-fiction is associated with information and knowledge. Short stories used to be widely published in newspapers and magazines, but that happens infrequently today. For most of the past two centuries the novel has been a highly popular book form. For many, books are synonymous with novels. Do journalists, and their publishers, then, need to help readers see clearly what kind of book they are reading and, if so, how can they do this, whether in the text itself, or outside it in endnotes, notes to the reader, dust jacket copy and promotional interviews? If the nature of the book presented is ambiguous, what are the ramifications for readers?

Readers are accustomed to a high degree of playfulness about authors' claims for a work of fiction; the genre is predicated, after all, on what Samuel Coleridge, discussing poetry, termed a willing suspension of disbelief. There is less scope for such playfulness in narrative non-fiction, which makes claims to be representing actual people, events and issues. Practitioners have obligations to those they write for as well as those they write about, but regardless of how careful they are, ultimately writers cannot control how people will read their work. Readers may read a work as the writer hopes they will, or they may well find other meanings and interpretations. That we are unable to control exactly what readers make of our work does not absolve us of obligations to them. Indeed, I would argue that writers' obligations to readers are heightened because the readership for narrative non-fiction is general not specialist. That is, the average reader knows little about the people and events being written about in contrast to academic books, whose audience is almost entirely specialist and on more equal footing with the author. The narrative non-fiction writer has gathered the information and, if thorough, will know a good deal more about the topic than most of their readers. They have considerable power, then, to shape readers' perceptions of the people and events being written about. Some general readers, of course, will know a good deal about what is being represented in narrative non-fiction works, but the majority will not. In any case, because writers of true stories aim to reach the broadest possible audience, they need to assume readers have less rather than more knowledge of the topic. To put it another way, it does no harm to assume this, but there may be harm if you don't.

Why? Because once the reader begins reading, there is a range of ways the writer can signal the kind of book being offered. To the extent that they avoid endnotes, notes on sources and the like, and write primarily in a narrative mode, they increase the likelihood their book will be read as if it is fiction, especially given that the majority of readers—and at least some scholars, as we have seen—conflate a narrative style with fiction. This prompts a key issue. When a writer seeks to present the world as it is, their narrative style resembles that of socially realistic fiction. In such works, the writer wants to engage the reader's mind and emotions as fully as possible. They want to induce in the reader a dreamlike state of mind, as the novelist and creative writing teacher John Gardner termed it in *The Art of Fiction* (1983, pp. 30–8).

'If we carefully inspect our experience as we read, we discover that the importance of physical detail is that it creates for us a kind of dream, a rich and vivid play in the mind. We read a few words at the beginning of the book or the particular story and suddenly find ourselves seeing not words on a page, but a train moving through Russia, an old Italian crying or a farmhouse battered by rain. We read on—dream on—not passively but actively, worrying about the choices the characters have to make, listening in panic for some sound behind the fictional door, exulting in characters' successes, bemoaning their failures. In great fiction, the dream engages us heart and soul; we not only respond to imaginary things—sights, sounds, smells—as though they were real, we respond to fictional problems as though they were real.'

Gardner argues readers of fiction may feel powerful emotions and may vividly experience the novel's imagined world, but they know that the people and events as presented in the book are not real. There are novels that include actual people, places and events, such as Don DeLillo's *Libra*, which features a character named 'Lee Harvey Oswald' and concerns the assassination of John Kennedy, but they do not purport to be a verifiably accurate account of those people, places and events in their entirety. There are also novels, known as roman à clef, in which actual people and events are represented, but their identities are disguised, usually as a way of avoiding a libel suit.

The reader's experience of fiction stems from their imaginative engagement with a series of black marks on a page. But when readers talk about their experience of fiction and use phrases such as 'I couldn't put it down', 'I lost all track of time', 'I was off in another world' or 'I was lost in the book'—and these phrases have been used so often by readers as to be clichés—they are not voicing resentment but happiness (Nell 1988, pp. 1–2). The experience of being deeply engaged in a novelist's imagined world is welcome and pleasurable. To say a novel is enthralling is to praise it, yet the word gives a vital clue to the issue that arises when true stories are written with the aim of inducing in readers Gardner's fiction dream state. The word 'enthral' carries two meanings in the Oxford English Dictionary: 'to hold spellbound by pleasing qualities' and 'to hold in thrall; to enslave'. A reader in thrall, you would think, is in an inherently vulnerable state, but their 'enslavement' to the fictional world is felt as pleasure precisely because it is confined to the fictional world. It is a state of mind freely entered into, and though some novels may be keenly felt and remembered long after they have been returned to the bookshelf or saved on a tablet, the reader knows that however sad they may feel about, say, the death of Anna Karenina, she is a character existing only in their imagination from reading Tolstoy's eponymous novel. When readers give themselves over to, or are drawn into, this state of mind for a work of narrative non-fiction, ethical issues are triggered by the differing power relations between writers and readers. If you write in a narrative style, then, you have an obligation to readers because of your efforts to 'enthral' them. Should writers resort to invention or seriously misrepresent people and events in their work, they will have abused the trust readers place in them. David Craig quotes two journalists working in newspapers on the implications of Gardner's fiction dream state. One of them says: 'You want people to suspend their disbelief and be carried along with the story in kind of a dream state. And anything that disrupts that is working against your role as a storyteller, which makes the ethical obligation even greater, because once you have them in that dream state you could really screw with their minds' (2006, p. 65).

Applying Gardner's fiction dream state is a powerful idea, and can be expanded to take into account different readers' reading levels and the capacity of the narrative voice to engage us. In his examination of 'ludic reading' (that is, reading for pleasure) Victor Nell argues that what Gardner calls the fiction dream state and he calls a 'reading trance' can be experienced by reading novels ranging from what he terms 'trash' to those normally listed in literary canons. He also argues that 'for many sophisticated readers, a wide range of materials, from the trashiest to the most literate and demanding works, may induce reading trance' (1988, p. xiii). Nell explicitly includes readers' involvement in reading newspaper reports of major news events and argues that it 'cannot be distinguished from the way we lose ourselves in a novel' (1998, p. 51). There may be little doubt, as Mitchell Stephens's *A History of News* shows, that people's hunger for news is a common human yearning across societies and across time, but the experience of reading a hard news report does, as I have argued earlier, differ from reading journalism written in a narrative style. I think Nell is confusing form and content. A big news event lays a claim on the reader's attention and imagination; the hard news report is just the vehicle for conveying the news. Gardner is right to draw attention to the use of physical details as triggers for starting the fiction dream state, but the use of a narrative voice in a true story can also deeply engage readers. This is obvious in Thompson's and Garner's highly idiosyncratic, self-dramatising narrative voices; it is less obvious but still present in the narrative voice of Conover and of Chloe Hooper in *The Tall Man*, her deeply disturbing work about the death in a remote island police station watch house of an indigenous man and the subsequent clearing of the police officer charged with his manslaughter. It is not necessary to examine the full range of narrative forms or means by which authors engage readers. The point here is to highlight the potential issue created when writers of true stories induce in readers Gardner's fiction dream state.

Several practitioners have articulated the terms of their relationship with readers. McPhee, Malcolm and Garner all liken the relationship to a contract. In 'The Art of the Dumb Question', Garner distinguishes between her fiction and non-fiction:

Someone reading a novel wants you to create a new world, parallel perhaps to the 'real' one, in which the reader can immerse himself for the duration. But a reader of non-fiction counts on you to remain faithful to the same 'real' world that both reader and writer physically inhabit (1996, p. 6).

McPhee lists practices that he finds unacceptable in narrative non-fiction—making up dialogue, creating composite characters out of real people and interior monologues—and says, 'Where writers abridge that, they hitchhike on the credibility of writers who don't' (cited in ed. Sims 1984, p. 15). Any blurring of the line between fiction and non-fiction is anathema to McPhee, for whom the image connotes ignorance of where one field ends and the other begins. 'That violates a contract with the reader.' Malcolm draws an extended metaphor where novelists are masters of their own house and non-fiction writers are renters:

The journalist must abide by the conditions of his lease, which stipulates that he leave the house—and its name is Actuality—as he found it. He may bring in his own furniture and arrange it as he likes (the so-called New Journalism is about the arrangement of the furniture) and he may play his radio quietly. But he must not disturb the house's fundamental structure or tamper with any of its architectural features. The writer of nonfiction is under contract to the reader to limit himself to events that actually occurred and to characters who have counterparts in real life, and he may not embellish the truth about these events or these characters (1990, p. 153).

John Hersey, in his essay 'The Legend on the License', first published in 1980, writes that novelists and journalists have a licence whose 'sacred rule' is, respectively, 'this was made up' and 'none of this was made up'. What is noteworthy about these descriptions is that they are all metaphors and they all invoke solidity to the enterprise that, as Gérard Genette argues in discussing the related field of autobiography, 'is obviously highly optimistic as to the role of the reader who has signed nothing and who can take this contract or leave it' (1987, p. 11). All four writers know this, even as they wax metaphorical. McPhee is acutely aware of the importance his subjectivity plays in choosing a particular word or story structure, or even topic. Garner writes, a few sentences after those quoted above, that she feels a 'responsibility to the "facts" as you can discover them, and an obligation to make it clear when you have *not* been able to discover them' (1996, p. 7). Malcolm, too, soon after the passage just cited, writes: 'Of course, there is no such thing as a work of pure factuality, any more than there is one of pure fictitiousness' (1990, p. 154). And Hersey grants there is no such thing as 'absolute objectivity' and no way of presenting in words '*the* truth'. The absence of a laser-drawn line dividing fiction from non-fiction does not mean the two are indistinguishable or that practitioners are unable to make clear what they are offering readers. Mark Kramer, director of the Nieman Program on Narrative Journalism, acknowledges there is no Un-Literary-Journalistic-Activities-Committee to subpoena 'the craft's corner cutters' (1995, p. 23). It is another metaphor, but at least its use is ironic.

The practitioners' metaphors gesture towards something they all believe is important rather than provide a framework for understanding what happens between non-fiction writers and their readers. Does the law provide such a framework? Steven Brill argues that it does. In 2000 he reported on a false advertising lawsuit brought by a lawyer, Jeffrey Lerman, on behalf of an aggrieved reader against a series of financial self-help books. Written by a group of retired women known as the Beardstown Ladies, the books claimed to have achieved a 23 per cent annual rate of return, but media reports later showed they achieved the more modest rate of 9 per cent. Brill said the false advertising claim derived from the promotional copy on the books' dust jackets. Such a lawsuit was preferable to libel, which is only set in train when a person believes their reputation has been harmed by the book's contents. A false advertising suit:

> Does not threaten the author's right to write free of harassment suits (or real suits based on honest mistakes) or even a publisher's decision to publish a book that has material in it that's debatable or even wrong. And he's [Lerman] not using a libel law approach that requires that a victim of what's written undertake an expensive, long-shot courtroom battle. Instead, what he outlined in his legal papers is a structure that allows any consumer to sue but forces that consumer to clear some sensibly high hurdles (Brill 2000, p. 68).

These hurdles were that the material at issue was factually incorrect, that the publisher knew it was incorrect or could have found out if they made a good-faith effort and that the material in question was a significant part of the book's advertising. To Brill, consumer protection legislation is well suited to 'challenge America's leading consumer product: media', and in the context of narrative non-fiction, it makes sense to highlight the importance of supporting material, such as dust jacket copy.

Since the Beardstown Ladies case, Brill's ideas have borne fruit in the successful lawsuit brought in 2006 against James Frey over his 2003 memoir *A Million Little Pieces*. A memoir is not the kind of narrative non-fiction that is the subject of this book, but it does purport to be offering an account of a person's life. Frey's memoir became a bestseller, with the majority of its 3.5 million sales coming after television host and magazine publisher Oprah Winfrey selected it in 2005 for inclusion in Oprah's Book Club. Frey's memoir was written in a hairy-chested, take-no-prisoners style, retailing at length his drug-crazed clashes with police and his time spent in brutal jailhouses. Early in 2006, website The Smoking Gun revealed that *A Million Little Pieces* was fabricated in many ways, large and small. Frey initially denied the website's allegations and was supported by his publisher, Random House, but the documented weight of the website's six-week investigation forced Frey to acknowledge he had altered events and details throughout the book. 'A Note to the Reader' was included in later editions in which he admitted, among other things, that where he claimed to have been imprisoned for three months, he now agreed he had spent just five hours in jail while awaiting bail on a misdemeanour. 'I made other alterations in my portrayal of myself, most of which portrayed me in ways that made me tougher and more daring and more aggressive than in reality I was, or I am.' The unnumbered two-page note was inserted in the book on a loose sheet of paper that could easily fall out and be missed. The back of the book still carries the label 'memoir' and later reprints did not include the two-page note.

Class action lawsuits were lodged against Frey and in September 2006 lawyers representing readers and those representing the publisher agreed to a settlement in which readers who felt they had been defrauded by the book's claims could be refunded the purchase price. Late the following year, Associated Press reported that 1729 people were requesting reimbursement, which prompted commentators such as Lee Gutkind, editor of *Creative Nonfiction*, to suggest readers did not seem unduly worried about the factual reliability of memoirs. Gutkind may be right, especially as the publisher had agreed to set aside US$2.35 million and had spent only US$27,348 settling claims for refunds. But a reading of the Notice of Proposed Class Action Settlement posted by Random House on its website shows the figures are open to another interpretation. For a start, more than half the US$2.35 million was allocated to legal fees and costs associated with publicising and carrying out the settlement. Second, only those who bought the book before its fabrications were revealed could claim, and to do so they needed to provide proof of purchase, either a receipt for a book that may have been purchased up to three years beforehand or by supplying the book's front cover. Given the relatively low cost of the book—US$24 in hardback and US$15 in paperback—and the likelihood that the controversy would have made *A Million Little*

Pieces more valuable to collectors, I would argue that the figure of 1729 represents a substantial number of 'disgruntled readers'.

A clear-cut example of readers' anger at being deceived by a memoir is W.N.P. Barbellion's *The Journal of a Disappointed Man*, published in 1919. Its account of a talented young naturalist's gradual decline from a then largely unknown disease deeply moved readers (Abbott 2nd edn 2008). The book's final words are: 'Barbellion died on December 31 [1917]'. The memoir proved hugely popular, generating five printings in a few months, but when readers learnt that Barbellion had not died but had, as Abbott recounts, 'lived long enough to read the reviews of his life story, the feeling of betrayal was as deep as it was widespread, and the book fell into an obscurity from which it has rarely emerged' (2008, p. 31). Frey, two years after the furore sparked by *A Million Little Pieces*, was still ambivalent about accepting responsibility for his deception of readers (Peretz 2008). The gap between a book's content and its promotional claims is rarely as wide as Frey's memoir or the Beardstown Ladies' get-rich-quick books, as is evident in debate surrounding Binjamin Wilkomirski's disputed account in *Fragments* of growing up a Holocaust survivor (Lappin 1999). Capote's *In Cold Blood* has serious flaws, I have argued, but it is doubtful whether readers would have been able to bring a false advertising lawsuit against it on the ground, say, that Capote's portrait of Smith was distorted. The laws of libel, then, serve to remind practitioners of the care they need to take in representing people in books, and consumer protection laws underline the serious-ness with which at least some readers take a book's promotional copy and the need for practitioners to communicate clearly with them.

The law does not cover all the practitioner's ethical obligations to readers, however. Geoffrey Cowan, a professor of law and journal-ism, is well placed to weigh the interplay between the two fields. No contract between journalists and their readers is spelt out in law, and nor should it be because of the protection of free speech in the first amendment to the American constitution. But freedom of speech and, by extension, the news media, does not extend to inaccurate statements of fact that were made knowingly or with malice. Journalists have 'an ethical duty of care to their audience. Readers and viewers have a real but unenforceable right to rely on the accuracy of what they learn through those media that they expect or believe to be accurate' (Cowan 1998, p. 157). Cowan adds: 'All storytellers know the difficulty of telling a story truthfully; each details skews the description—and can, if desired, skewer the subject'. The most effective antidote to selective fact is more fact, an idea that underlies the first amendment. Beyond selection, though, fundamentally inaccurate portrayals of people in the media can be dangerous, he writes, citing a docudrama entitled *Hoodlum* in which Thomas Dewey, a racket-busting district attorney and New York governor in the 1930s, was shown as a corrupt prosecutor, taking bribes from gangsters. Dewey's outraged heirs complained but had no legal recourse, as the US Supreme Court had found in an earlier case that, in effect, the general public takes docudramas with a grain of salt.

Cowan does not propose a legal solution to these problems. Instead, he advocates the use of codes of ethics; these may be personal, corporate or industry-wide, and resemble Justin Oakley and Dean Cocking's regulative ideals (2001). He also proposes that works be seen existing along a hypothetical continuum of 'accuracy and balance'. At one end are 'entities that hold themselves out as reliable sources of information on the day's events', such as daily newspapers, news magazines and works of non-fiction and history. At the other end are docudramas, films and plays based on fact that could include, say, Shakespeare's histories. In the middle are opinion pieces, openly ideological magazines and books written with a clear point of view, such as Bill O'Reilly's and Christopher Hitchens's work. Cowan argues that even in docudramas, though, writers should not 'invent scenes that did not happen if they distort the essence of the characters or of the story', and have a moral, if not a legal, responsibility to disclose to the audience the nature and extent of the distortion. Narrative non-fiction sits within Cowan's framework and is held to a high standard of accuracy and balance.

Cowan's framework supports Hersey's argument that readers understand that in journalism there will be at least some selection and omission and so can 'hunt for bias', but 'the moment the reader suspects additions, the earth begins to skid underfoot, for the idea that there is no way of knowing what is real and what is not real is terrifying. Even more terrifying is the notion that lies are truths' (1989, p. 249). Cowan's framework also complements Doležel's use of possible worlds semantics discussed in Chapter 6; the latter provides a way of conceptualising boundaries between fictional and factual narratives while the former pays heed to readers' differing expectations. The next layer of complexity to add, as envisaged in Lehman's four-part framework of reading non-fiction, is that different readers respond to and engage with different works of narrative non-fiction in different ways.

Applying this thinking, I would argue that the majority of readers care a lot whether what they are reading is fiction or narrative non-fiction, but that some do not. I would argue most care about what they are reading if the people and events in the work are well known, even of historic importance, as in Woodward's books about various presidencies, and that fewer care if the people and events are publicly unknown or little known, as in John Berendt's *Midnight in the Garden of Good and Evil*. A variation on this theme occurs when works are read far from their origins in space or time; that is, Garner's *The First Stone* provoked passionate debates in Australia, and especially Melbourne, but was read through a different prism overseas, and probably would be read differently today, approaching two decades after publication. Where readers have firsthand knowledge of events and people depicted in a work, they care a great deal about whether the book is presented as fiction or non-fiction, I would suggest.

Non-fiction books have for many years comprised the majority of total books published in English-speaking countries, but there is limited empirical data about readers' expectations of non-fiction in general and narrative non-fiction in particular. There is not a lot of empirical evidence even about the ordinary reader's expectations of fiction, according to Andrew Milner. 'We know that people read and we know that they read novels. What seems much less clear, however, is what exactly it is that they make of the books they read' (2005, p. 184). Milner's focus is mainly on fiction, poetry and drama but, as he shows, four out of five books sold each year in the United Kingdom are non-fiction (2005, p. 101). Hillel Nossek and Hannah Adoni surveyed 520 representative adults in Israel in 2001 about how various media forms—books, newspapers, television and the internet—'helped them to fulfil psycho-social needs' (2006, p. 105). One of the needs expressed was 'to learn and enrich myself'; three out of four of those surveyed turned to books for this need, well ahead of the other forms, which were used in this way by just over half. The survey does not, however, distinguish between reading fiction and non-fiction books.

More recent empirical research conducted in Australia about attitudes towards deception in the news media is relevant here. Denis Muller, a former editorial executive at *The Sydney Morning Herald* and *The Age*, conducted quantitative surveys of 300 randomly chosen voters in Victoria, Australia, and nearly 170 self-selected journalists and journalism students for a doctoral thesis he completed in 2005 about accountability of the news media in a liberal democracy. Those surveyed were asked questions about five ethical scenarios, including 'Would you say it was always all right, never all right, or all right in some cases to pretend to be sympathetic to a person's situation in order to obtain an interview?'. Of the voters surveyed, only 3 per cent said it was always all right, 26 per cent said it was all right in some cases and 70 per cent said it was never all right. By comparison, 11 per cent of journalists said it was always all right, 57 per cent said it was all right in some cases and only 28 per cent said it was never all right. Muller comments: 'There is a very large gulf between journalists and the community on what is regarded as ethical. People in the community are far less likely than journalists to say that these ethical breaches are justifiable in some circumstances' (2005, p. 117). His finding provides empirical support for Sissela Bok's argument in her work *Lying* that in journalism 'deception is taken for granted when it is felt to be excusable by those who tell the lies and who tend also to make the rules' (1978, p. xvii). Muller's questions concerned journalism rather than narrative non-fiction, but they underscore the public's dislike of deception in general and by journalists in particular. Muller's research bears directly on the research phase of narrative non-fiction and indirectly on what practitioners offer readers and on what terms.

One way of gleaning the terms on which writers establish a relationship with their readers is to look at how narrative non-fiction is promoted. Genette's work about what he terms the paratext is relevant here. The paratext is material outside the body of the text, including titles, dedications, prefaces and notes. In *Paratexts*, Genette distinguishes between the peritext, which is paratextual material in the book, and the epitext, which takes in a potentially vast range of material that extends and comments on the text, such as the publisher's epitext (that is, promotional copy and posters), author interviews and reviews. Genette further distinguishes between the public and the private epitexts, which includes the author's correspondence and diaries. Genette's analysis of an element of writing practice that most take for granted or ignore entirely is primarily aimed at fiction, but it offers a rich and highly relevant framework for writers and critics of narrative non-fiction. Genette writes that the main function of the paratext is 'not to "look nice" around the text but rather to ensure for the text a destiny consistent with the author's purpose' (1987, p. 407). He nods to theoretical work, questioning whether authors can ever really know their purpose, but says the author's purpose sustains, inspires and anchors the paratextual performance. 'The critic is by no means bound to subscribe to that viewpoint. I maintain only that, knowing it, he cannot completely disregard it, and if he wants to contradict it he must first assimilate it' (1987, pp. 408–9).

Of particular relevance to narrative non-fiction is Genette's discussion of how historians use prefaces. The original aim of the preface was to ensure that the text was 'read properly', and even though he discusses various ways in which authors have inverted or played with this original aim, Genette writes that historians strive for truthfulness, or at the least sincerity, in their preface. Historians and autobiographers, such as Montaigne, pledge that their books have been written in good faith; historians reinforce their pledge by outlining their methods. Thucydides, for example, maintains that he relied only on direct observation and corroborated testimony. The similarity here between historians and those who write true stories is obvious. Genette's description of the author's view of publisher's promotional material appears snobbish, however—'most often he is satisfied just to close his eyes officially to the value-inflating hyperbole inseparable from the needs of trade' (1987, p. 347). Writing in the 1980s, in France, Genette's notion that authors are absolved from any responsibility, or at least interest, in the marketing of their book does not apply to many authors in the English-speaking world in the twenty-first century, but even as far back as the 1960s Capote defended the dust jacket copy for *In Cold Blood* as 'thoughtfully written' in its claims about the non-fiction novel, which implied that he had written it himself, or at the least approved it (ed. Inge 1987, p. 120).

I acknowledge promotional copy will not convey the work's complexity—that is what the actual content is for, after all—and that promotional copy is explicitly aimed at enticing a potential buyer, but I argue that promotional copy is a useful guide to the grounds on which the relationship between journalist and reader begins, or at least is proposed. Author interviews and other publicity for a work, such as appearances at writers' festivals, also help position the book in readers' minds, but not all books attract publicity, whereas all carry dust jacket copy. It needs to be remembered that, while a book is a product, many works of narrative non-fiction engage in revelation and debate about events, issues and people. These works are not a carton of eggs, as Steve Weinberg reminds us in an article about factual errors in narrative non-fiction, but a particular kind of product that plays an important role in sustaining the free flow of information and ideas in a democracy. Some genres of non-fiction books—such as true crime, sport, travel and biography—have their own drawing power for readers even before any particular marketing campaign is launched. With this in mind, I propose there are seven main grounds on which the relationship between writer and reader is proposed. These grounds have been gleaned from analysing the promotional copy on the covers of a range of works of narrative non-fiction, some of them prize winners, others bestsellers. Works of those interviewed by Boynton or by me have been examined, as well as a selection of those included in Sarah Statz Cords's readers' advisory, *The Inside Scoop*. The great majority of works examined have been published in the past two decades, but some earlier works, notably *In Cold Blood* and *The Final Days*, have also been examined. I looked at promotional copy for first editions, which represents the original promise to readers, but this has not always been possible, as university libraries generally remove dust jackets before making books available for loan. Some of the books

I own, however. Sometimes promotional copy for later editions uses a book's status as a 'classic', which may be an attraction for potential buyers, but does not add anything substantial to this analysis of promotional copy for narrative non-fiction.

The seven main grounds on which the relationship between writer and reader is proposed are, first, the book is true; second, it reads like a novel; third, it has new information; fourth, the book is about a major event, person or issue that is preoccupying the public; fifth, the book promises to take the reader 'inside' an event or issue; sixth, it is by a well-known individual journalist or author; and, seventh, it is about or in some way touches on celebrity. All but one of these grounds—it reads like a novel—is common in newspaper and magazine journalism. It is this ground, usually combined with the first (the book is true), that can make narrative non-fiction so readable and also pose the problems I have been discussing in this and earlier chapters. Sometimes books combine a perennially popular topic, such as crime or sport, with one of the seven grounds. For instance, Cramer's biography of Joe DiMaggio promises new information about the American baseball legend. The dust jacket copy of the first hardback edition, published in 2000, reads: 'This is the story Joe DiMaggio never wanted to tell—and never wanted anyone else to tell. It is the story of his grace—and greed: his dignity, pride—and hidden shame.'

To further explicate the seven grounds proposed, an example of the first is Jon Krakauer's *Into Thin Air*, published in 1997. Promotional copy from the book's 1998 paperback edition reads:

> On May 9th 1996, five expeditions launched an assault on the summit of Mount Everest. The conditions seemed perfect. Twenty-four hours later one climber had died and 23 other men and women were caught in a desperate struggle for their lives as they battled against a ferocious storm that threatened to tear them from the mountain. In all eight climbers died that day in the worst tragedy Everest has ever seen.

The proposal, or pitch, to use the language of marketing, is that the book is about extraordinary, dramatic or seemingly unbelievable events, as are Junger's *The Perfect Storm* and Blackburn's *Broken Lives*. An example of the second reason is Piers Paul Read's *Alive: The Story of the Andes Survivors*, an account of a plane crash in the Andes in 1972 where survivors were forced to choose whether to eat those who had died. The promotional copy for the original edition reads:

> How these young men finally sent out 'expeditionaries' to brave the Andean peaks and how, after appalling hardships, they achieved rescue and a return to civilization 72 days after the crash is one of the epic adventures of our time, a tale of human courage and triumph almost unequalled in this century. Piers Paul Read makes this deeply moving story *read like a great novel*, yet every word of it is true [emphasis added].

Examples of how the first two grounds can be combined are common: the tagline on the cover of the first edition of Preston's *The Hot Zone*, discussed in Chapter 9, reads: 'The most terrifying *true* story you will ever read', with the word 'true' in italics. Ken Follett's *On Wings of Eagles* recounts how an ex-Green Beret and a team of corporate executives from the company owned by billionaire Ross Perot, Electronic Data Systems, rescued two company executives taken hostage from the company's office in Iran in 1978. Originally published in 1983 and one of the top ten bestselling non-fiction books of that year, the dust jacket copy of the 1998 paperback edition begins: 'The story on these pages would have been incredibly exciting had it been fiction. But it is more than that—it is fact. It's a story that only Ken Follett, today's master of action and suspense, could do justice to'. In a preface, Follett, a bestselling novelist, declares: 'This is not a "fictionalization", a "non-fiction novel". Nothing has been invented. What you read is what really happened'. The promotional copy, which explicitly describes the events in the book as 'the stuff of Follett's fiction', promises the reader, then, they will be able to enjoy all the pleasures of fiction with none of what David Marr calls the 'raggedness' of non-fiction.

An example of the third ground is Ted Conover's *Newjack*, published in 2000. Promotional copy for the 2001 paperback edition reads:

When Ted Conover's request to shadow a recruit at the New York State Corrections Academy was denied, he decided to apply for a job as a prison officer himself. The result is an unprecedented work of eye witness journalism: the account of Conover's year-long passage into storied Sing Sing prison as a rookie guard, or 'newjack.'

New information may be conceived more broadly than new facts; that is, the appeal of some books is that they provide new information about a familiar issue that enables readers to see it afresh, such as Elizabeth Royte's 2005 work *Garbage Land: On the Secret Trail of Trash*, which provides an answer to a commonly asked question—what happens to rubbish after we put it out for collection? Alternatively, John Carlin, by casting his eye back a decade, was about to provide new information and understanding to the significance, both sporting and political, of events in South Africa. As the dust jacket of *Playing the Enemy* (which was later adapted for film) tells it:

> The Rugby World Cup final of 1995 was the last act of the most improbable exercise in mass seduction ever seen: Nelson Mandela's conquest of the hearts of white South Africa. When Mandela stepped onto the field at Ellis Park stadium, in Johannesburg, wearing the Springbok captain's jersey ... he captured the hearts of white South Africans, transforming that which divided black and white South Africa into a force for good.

New information may also take the form of a new approach to an old issue, as the dust jacket copy for Sandy Tolan's 2006 work *The Lemon Tree* shows:

> In 1967, Bashir Khairi, a twenty-five-year-old Palestinian, journeyed to Israel with the goal of seeing the beloved old stone house with the lemon tree behind it that he and his family had fled nineteen years earlier. To his surprise, when he found the house he was greeted by Dalia Eshkenazi Landau, a nineteen-year-old Israeli college student, whose family fled Europe for

Israel following the Holocaust. On the stoop of their shared home, Dalia and Bashir began a rare friendship, forged in the aftermath of war and tested over the next thirty-five years in ways that neither could imagine that summer day in 1967.

An example of the fourth ground proposed is William Langewiesche's *American Ground*, published in 2002. The promotional copy for the first edition published in England in 2003 reads:

William Langewiesche was the only journalist given unrestricted access to what became known as Ground Zero—the eleven stories of twisted metal and compressed concrete that had been 110 stories of the World Trade Center. He arrived within days of September 11 2001 and left after the final ceremony in May 2002.

Other examples of books about major events include English novelist John Lanchester's brilliantly lucid account of the global financial crisis, *Whoops: Why Everyone Owes Everyone and No One Can Pay*, Gordon Burn's exploration of the gruesome mass murders in Gloucester by Fred and Rosemary West, *Happy Like Murderers*, and Tom Watson and Martin Hickman's *Dial M for Murdoch*, about the phone hacking scandal that engulfed Rupert Murdoch's global media empire in existential crisis. The dust jacket of the last named picked up the value for readers of a book offering to make sense of complicated events, made doubly so for being obfuscated in the reporting of them in News Corporation outlets. 'Seeing the story whole, as it is presented here for the first time, allows the character of the organization it portrays to emerge unmistakeably. You will hardly believe it.'

The fifth ground proposed goes to the practitioner's promise to take the reader 'inside' an event or issue. This promise is the force driving almost every one of Woodward's books, up to and including his work on the Obama administration. Robert Saviano won global attention and acclaim for his 2006 work *Gomorrah: Italy's Other Mafia*. The dust jacket on the translated paperback edition reads:

Vigilante journalist Roberto Saviano compiled the most thorough account to date of the Camorra, the Neapolitan mafia, which exerts a malign influence on contemporary Italy. At great personal risk, Saviano worked undercover in his native city in Camorra—controlled factories, construction sites and even as a waiter at a mob wedding. Unforgettable and utterly compelling, *Gomorrah* is a nightmare journey into a world of devastating brutality.

Another example is Jonathan Franklin's *The 33*, billed on the front cover as 'The ultimate account of the Chilean miners' dramatic rescue' of thirty-three miners caught by accident in 'the longest underground entrapment in human history'. Franklin, a journalist who had worked in Chile for many years, made the most of his local knowledge to gain 'exclusive access' to the rescue operation and to the survivors. Where a novelist may offer to transport the reader to their imagined world, here the writer promises to take readers into parts of the actual world to which they do not have access. That world may be at the centre of an international event, like the Chilean mine disaster, but equally often it is to less dramatic but still significant worlds, such as Chandler Burr's exploration of cosmetics in *The Perfect Scent: A Year Inside the Perfume Industry in Paris and New York*.

The sixth ground proposed combines readers' following of particular authors and their enjoyment of true stories; with the exception of star journalists, such as retired war correspondent Kate Adie or darling of the corporate speaking circuit Malcolm Gladwell, this reason mainly turns on the drawing power of novelists writing narrative non-fiction. Didion and Mailer are obvious examples but there are many others, such as Gabriel Garcia Marquez (for *News of a Kidnapping*) or Helen Garner or Anna Funder. When *Joe Cinque's Consolation* was published in 2004, Garner's name was printed on the cover in type almost twice the size as that of the title. The promotional copy outlines the case concerning Joe Cinque but it, too, is in type half the size of the promotional tagline that reads: 'A masterwork from one of Australia's greatest writers'. Where writers are not well known it is common for publishers to highlight their role as a journalist, as in Karen Kissane's *Silent Death* and Kimina Lyall's *Out of the Blue*, or if they work for a well-known newspaper or magazine to draw attention to that association, as in *Cold New World* and *The Orchid Thief*, both of whose biographical notes prominently mention that William Finnegan and Susan Orlean are staff writers for *The New Yorker*.

Finally, the widespread phenomenon of celebrities in modern society is a particular ground most often found in biographies, especially of those celebrities alive when the book comes out. Prominent examples include Michael Crick's excoriation of the bestselling novelist and political figure Jeffrey Archer, entitled *Stranger than Fiction*, published in 1995, and Kitty Kelley's unauthorised biography of singer and friend of the Mafia Frank Sinatra, entitled *His Way*, published in 1986. The book's pitch was summed up in William Safire's excerpted review on the back cover of the 1987 paperback edition, which reads: 'The most eye-opening celebrity biography of our time'.

These examples show how the seven grounds can be identified quite readily, but what happens when writers are ambiguous about the terms of the relationship proposed with readers? Thomas Keneally recalls in *Searching for Schindler* that he was so worried his book on Oskar Schindler would be classified as Judaica and shelved at the back of bookshops that he asked for it to be classified as fiction. The promotional copy of the original hardback edition of *Schindler's Ark*, published in 1982, emphasises Keneally's background as a novelist and promises to take 'us back into Nazi-occupied Poland, from where an extraordinary tale emerges—of an extraordinary man's mission to save the Jewish people'. Inside, in an author's note, Keneally writes that his book is a true story and that he has 'attempted to avoid all fiction', but also that he has used 'the texture and devices of a novel'. *Schindler's Ark* is non-fiction, then, but it won the Booker Prize for fiction in 1982, which formalised the confusion even when there seemed little need for it. Keneally came to regret his decision when Holocaust deniers used the book's classification as evidence supporting their poisonous views.

To sum up, the grounds on which the relationship is proposed suggest readers of narrative non-fiction expect to learn something new and to be entertained, in roughly equal proportions. If their primary expectation is to learn something new, they would read a textbook; if their primary expectation is entertainment, the content of the book would be secondary. To the extent that the new information is a matter of urgent public interest (for example, how emergency workers dealt with the World Trade Center's destruction by a terrorist attack), the reader is better placed to fulfil their role as a citizen in a democracy. To the extent that the book is entertaining, that too is an important though often undervalued part of journalism's role—and appeal. To the extent that the book is emotionally as well as intellectually engaging, that may well shift readers' perspectives on an issue or event that, again, helps them fulfil their role as citizens. If there are some works of narrative non-fiction where the weight of expectation tilts towards the content and importance of the information, such as Langewiesche's *American Ground*, there are others, such as Berendt's *Midnight in the Garden of Good and Evil*, where the emphasis is on entertainment. The range of narrative non-fiction is an extension of the news media industry; both the news media and publishing industries publish work that is in the public interest, and both publish work that aims simply to entertain. The problems concerning a book's reception by the public may become visible more often if it is about a public interest issue and may be more urgent because a book about, say, a dishonest president concerns society as a whole, but issues can still arise in primarily entertaining books because they still purport to depict actual events and people, and these people merit ethical treatment as much as a world leader.

A prime example of such issues arising in an entertaining work of narrative non-fiction is in fact Berendt's *Midnight in the Garden of Good and Evil*, which combines a travelogue about Savannah, Georgia, and its eccentric, exotic inhabitants, with a courtroom drama about a murder trial. It is written in a narrative style that encourages the reader to read it as if it was a novel. The promotional copy of the front flap of the original hardback edition (1994) begins:

> Shots rang out in Savannah's grandest mansion in the misty, early morning hours of May 2, 1981. Was it murder or self-defense? John Berendt's sharply observed, suspenseful and witty narrative reads like a thoroughly engrossing novel, and yet it is a work of nonfiction ... It is a spellbinding story peopled by a gallery of

remarkable characters ... *Midnight in the Garden of Good and Evil* is a sublime and seductive reading experience.

The copy says the book is non-fiction, yet the weight of the pitch falls on the book's novel-like qualities—'engrossing', 'spellbinding' and a 'sublime and seductive reading experience'. In a three-sentence author's note, Berendt writes: 'Though this is a work of nonfiction, I have taken certain storytelling liberties, particularly having to do with the timing of events. Where the narrative strays from strict nonfiction, my intention has been to remain faithful to the characters and to the essential drift of events as they really happened'. This note appeared after the body of the book; in all likelihood, readers would not have seen it until after they finished the book and Berendt, an experienced magazine journalist and editor, gave readers no specific information about the 'certain storytelling liberties' he had taken. Later research revealed a number of factual errors, some minor, others more important. There was some fabricated dialogue, which Berendt terms 'rounding the corners to make a better narrative'; an undisclosed contract with Jim Williams, the man charged with, and eventually cleared of, murder; and accusations of Berendt using stories people told him without confirming details with others because they had the 'folkloric quality' he wanted for his book (Dufresne 1998).

These matters go to the research and writing phase of Berendt's work, but the most serious problem in how Berendt establishes his relationship with readers is that he places a version of himself in the book four years before he actually arrived in Savannah. He describes himself witnessing an argument between the main person in the book, Jim Williams, and the young hustler who worked for him, Danny Hansford. He describes himself attending the first two of the four trials of Williams for the murder of Hansford, and he describes himself at a midnight voodoo ritual with Williams, from which the book's title emerges. He even describes a sexual encounter between Hansford and a young woman in the most intimate detail: 'She breathed the salty smell of his T-shirt and felt his belt buckle rubbing against her stomach'. Questioned about this, Berendt says the woman, Corinne, recounted the event in every particular

(Ricketson 1995a). Not only does the ten-page scene rely on one person's memory, but it is also written to place the reader literally in the bedroom, and it reads like a bodice-ripping romance novel. All this appears to be what Berendt meant by 'certain storytelling liberties', but if the sex scene is tacky and its detail unnecessary, the time shifting is more accurately described as deception. A later film adaptation, starring John Cusack as Berendt and Kevin Spacey as Williams, perpetuated these deceptions on screen.

Midnight in the Garden of Good and Evil stayed on *The New York Times* non-fiction bestseller list for a then record 186 weeks and was shortlisted for a Pulitzer Prize in general non-fiction in 1995, but did not win. John Carroll, editor of *The Baltimore Sun* and a member of the Pulitzer board at the time, said: 'There's some fabrication in it' that meant 'as a journalist I'm not prepared to call it nonfiction'. Some people in Savannah were unconcerned by Berendt's 'story-telling liberties', including Williams's attorney, Sonny Seiler, who said the book would have been boring without them: 'Someone's got to put a spin on it'. Conversely, Williams's sister Dorothy Kingery, a sociologist, complained about the 'enormous liberties', about how Berendt 'grossly exaggerated' her brother's reliance on voodoo rituals and about the 'great blurring of fiction and nonfiction' in the book (Dufresne 1988). After the book's initial success and in response to some complaints, Berendt moved his author's note to the front of the book for later editions. In the new note, dated April 1996, he acknowledges some had read the book thinking it was fiction rather than non-fiction. His moving of the note put the reader 'on notice', but Berendt does not specify or discuss the central deception of his readers, namely writing as if he was present at events when he was not. In the revised note even his coy acknowledgement that he had taken 'certain storytelling liberties' is excluded, which means that in some ways he made matters worse.

The new note is almost two pages rather than three sentences, but is self-serving. Berendt affirms the existence of the exotic people he portrayed and that, despite publicity the book brought the city, Savannah somehow is both unspoiled and improved by the tourists flooding there in the book's wake, which sounds like a line from a PR agent. Berendt even points to the novelist Philip Roth's notion expressed by his narrator, a novelist in *The Counterlife*, that 'people don't turn themselves over to writers as full-blown literary characters. Most people are "absolutely unoriginal" and it is the novelist's job "to make them appear otherwise"'. By contrast, Berendt writes that he was blessed to find people in Savannah who were already 'full-blown literary characters' and 'absolutely compelling without any help from me'. Given that Berendt had already admitted to not checking details because his interviewees had the 'folkloric quality' he wanted, this is simply disingenuous. *Midnight in the Garden of Good and Evil* was and is labelled as non-fiction, though in later printings its back cover lists it with the slightly ambiguous label of 'crime/travel'. Much of the book's appeal is bound up with the reader's delight that so many exotic people telling so many outlandish stories could actually be living in the one city, and of the reader being drawn into the drama of events because they see them from the point of view of someone —Berendt—who says he was there as they unfolded.

Berendt, it seems, succumbed to what Kramer calls a 'moment of temptation', when the journalist realises that 'tweaking reality could sharpen the meaning or flow of a scene' (Kramer, 1995, p. 25). The book may have been written primarily as beguiling beach reading, but its fictionalising misrepresents several people and weakens its veracity; Berendt abuses the trust placed in him by readers. It may well be that some are unfussed whether the people and events described are factual or fictional, but Berendt treats all his readers as dupes, which is why his book has become something of a watchword for what not to do. What you can do to establish a strong relationship with your reader is the subject of the next chapter.

Chapter 12

Building a relationship of informed trust with readers

Rather more disturbing, however, was my gradual realisation that the press [publishing house] didn't share my perverse insistence on the distinction between history and fiction. It was unsettling enough to have my editor refer to the book as 'your novel', but I was shocked when he suggested plot enhancements without any historical warrant.

Iain McCalman, author of *The Seven Ordeals of Count Cagliostro*

In Chapter 5 we saw the value of writers drawing on elements of informed consent when negotiating access to their principal sources; that idea now needs to be matched by instilling in readers what I would call an informed trust for narrative non-fiction works. How you achieve such trust is the focus here, alongside consideration of issues that arise for those publishing book-length works, such as fact checking and avoiding potential lawsuits. Let's deal with the second issue first, as it is an important element that contributes to the reader's feeling of assurance about what they hold in their hands.

When journalists move from newspapers, magazines and online to books, they enjoy more freedom to shape their project, but they also take on more responsibility, as it is their name on the book's cover rather than their newspaper's or magazine's masthead. The paradox in publishing is that, while books, even in the digital age, carry cultural weight as a source of reliable information, most publishers do not fact check books, and the onus for verifying the contents falls mainly to the writer. A further paradox is that the time people spend on book-length projects means you would think their work should be more accurate than daily journalism, but most publishers are less experienced with prospective libel suits. These paradoxes go to the question of what is actually presented to readers. Vernacular expressions may suggest readers' preconceptions. The term 'journalese' not only rhymes with sleaze but also connotes threadbare or euphemistic language. The terms 'authority' and 'authoritative' derive from the word author, which is bound to books. Perceptions and vernacular expressions bear further scrutiny, however. Where newspaper, magazine and online journalism is produced by a team of practitioners that incorporates several layers of checking and editing (even if those layers are thinning as traditional media changes), books are primarily the work of one person, or occasionally two, as in David Marr and Marian Wilkinson.

Finding and verifying contentious information remains central to the operation of news organisations. Newsrooms have numerous experienced journalists and editors who have developed a keen sense of scepticism, because being baldly lied to is endemic to the practice of daily journalism. Newspapers retain the services of specialist media lawyers because they face the prospect of defamation actions daily. Publishing houses draw on lawyers too, but the threat of defamation, with its likelihood of sizeable payouts, is not as central to their business. Questions about the systems publishers use to verify book-length journalism and other non-fiction works, such as memoirs, have been raised for several years, notably in *Brill's Content* and *Columbia Journalism Review*.

Steve Weinberg surveyed book-length journalism and found book publishers tend to view writers as 'suppliers of information, which the publisher then markets, as a grocer markets the farmer's eggs' (1998, p. 52). Nicholas Lemann agrees, adding that many journalists are shocked to learn how little fact checking is done in publishing houses and publishers are 'surprised by that shock', as they 'seem to think of themselves as *purveyors* of literary material, not producers, assigners or shapers of it' (cited in eds Kramer & Call 2007, p. 192; see also Goldstein 2007). Errors made in newspapers and magazines reflect on the publication's credibility; errors made in books are more likely to reflect on the individual's credibility than on their publisher. Most journalists value their credibility and that, combined with the threat of libel suits, acts as an incentive to verify material in books, but the additional time devoted to a book project needs to be weighed against its scope—probably 90,000 words compared to 900—and the usually meagre support for fact checking.

Sarah Harrison Smith worked as a fact checker at *The New Yorker* before becoming head of fact checking at *The New York Times Magazine*. She has written a book entitled *The Fact Checker's Bible*, in which she argues that non-fiction books are not automatically rigorously checked; this even applies to some reference books. She quotes David Brock who, several years after writing a biography of now secretary of state Hillary Clinton, confessed:

All authors of big nonfiction books face the arduous task of generating headlines to spur book sales. Too often, authors succumb to market pressures by trafficking in rumour, using unreliable sources, or embellishing their material, all in the service of hype and buzz. Publishing houses are notoriously lax in fact-checking. Books are rarely retracted or even corrected (2004, p. 36).

In Australia, a similar minimalist approach to fact checking has been the norm, according to two experienced publishers I have spoken to: Michael Webster, principal consultant for Nielsen BookScan in Australia, and Sandy Grant, head of Hardie Grant. Controversies surrounding two memoirs, Norma Khouri's *Forbidden Love* in 2004 and Ishmael Beah's *A Long Way Gone* in 2007, have prompted at least some soul-searching and marginally more rigorous checking procedures. Even so, at Random House in Australia, publisher of Khouri's book, Margaret Seale, says ideally all facts would be checked but 'We are not journalists. We do not have the resources and books would be much more expensive if we did' (cited in Hope 2008). Some journalists, such as Richard Preston in *The Demon in the Freezer*, Ron Rosenbaum in *Explaining Hitler* and Eric Schlosser in *Fast Food Nation*, draw on the work of fact checkers, though it is not clear from the acknowledgements in their books whether they or their publishers paid for them.

There may be considerable overlap between readers of books and readers of newspapers and magazines (not to mention broadcast and online media), but readers are exposed to and perceive these industries differently. Newspapers and magazines are mass media that attract readers by their variety of offerings, by their being fresh daily, weekly or monthly, which creates a reading habit, and by a relatively cheap cover price that is subsidised by advertising. Books, by comparison, are one-off discretionary purchases that need to appeal to the reader then and there in the bookshop. They cost considerably more than newspapers, but they are to print media what 'pay-per-view' is to television, as Margaret Simons puts it in *The Content Makers*. That books are not reliant on paid advertising has provided an environment in which some of the best journalism in Australia has been published in book form, she argues, citing Masters's *Jonestown* and Marr and Wilkinson's *Dark Victory*. Susan Orlean, a long-time staff writer at *The New Yorker* and author of three works of narrative non-fiction, says: 'Books give you much more freedom, more of a chance to be unconventional. The book rises or falls on its own ability to appeal to an audience, rather than a magazine's need to sell itself to an advertiser'. Buyers and, for that matter, borrowers of books, then, do not have the kind of strong, pre-existing relationship with a work of narrative non-fiction that they customarily have with newspapers and magazines. With a few notable exceptions (such as Thompson, Wolfe and, in Australia, Garner) readers do not buy narrative non-fiction because it was written by a particular journalist, even though a few, such as Simon Winchester and Erik Larson, have forged international reputations specifically for their narrative non-fiction. Some works of narrative non-fiction were first published as magazine articles, but once put between the covers of a book their origins are forgotten by most or relegated to a note on the publication details page.

In this context, Garner's *The First Stone* illustrates the impact both of an author inexperienced in dealing with legal issues inherent in narrative non-fiction and of confusing readers about the nature of what they are reading. I remember reading the book soon after its publication and, like many people who knew little about the Ormond College case, was swept up in Garner's beautifully crafted prose, acutely observed details and engaging first-person style. Garner appeared to be taking the reader into her confidence, presenting herself as an honest, reflective middle-aged woman. She had really tried to get to the bottom of the Ormond case, but had been blocked by a succession of shrill, faceless, punitive feminists on campus. I did worry that it was the two young complainants who were accused of creating the problem rather than the university, whose procedures had so clearly failed them and, for that matter, Gregory. But as I read the book I found myself thinking: 'You're right, Helen; why couldn't all those feminists have been as reasonable as you?' On 8 August 1995 Garner delivered a speech about the response to her book at the Sydney Institute, and again attacked the women and their supporters for refusing to be interviewed. A key supporter of the women, Jenna Mead, then wrote an article that was published in *The Age* (1995, p. 17), revealing that Garner had disguised Mead's identity in *The First Stone*, splitting her into six or seven people. 'The effect is to suggest she is reporting the existence of a real conspiracy.' Reading this, I suddenly felt the book's power implode. Mead was in fact Dr Ruth V, Ms Vivienne S, Ms Rose H, Mrs Barbara W, Ms Margaret L, 'a thin-faced, thin-bodied woman in her forties' and perhaps two separate senior women in the college. There were, then, at least six conspiratorial feminists, variously described as a headmistress working over a fourth former and a rude, secretive woman who 'mined and ambushed' Garner's path to the complainants; describing Mead as thin-faced and thin-bodied invokes Julius Caesar's suspicion of Cassius's 'lean and hungry look' in Shakespeare's eponymous play.

A number of journalists and commentators, including me, began commenting on this in the news media. Later, for a book about *The First Stone* controversy edited by Mead and entitled *Bodyjamming*, I wrote an essay about Garner and journalism. Garner acknowledged in a letter to *The Age* on 23 September 1995 that she had given Mead half a dozen or so separate names in the book, and when the speech Garner had given about the Ormond case was reprinted in a selection of her journalism the following year, entitled *True Stories*, she added a paragraph saying she had been obliged to split up Mead by her publisher's lawyers, who feared a lawsuit. She had agreed with the greatest reluctance and regretted her actions because it had given some readers the idea that her book was 'fictionalised'. She wrote: 'It is not a novel. Except for this one tactic to avoid defamation, it is reportage'. When Garner's speech was printed in the Sydney Institute's journal, *The Sydney Papers*, she added a postscript defending her actions. She also replied to Mead's newspaper article saying that she did not believe Mead was the sole supporter of the two complainants but 'this does not mean that I think there was "a conspiracy" at work. At no point have I ever believed, nor have I suggested, that the Ormond events were fomented by "a conspiracy" of feminists'.

It is difficult to see how the chopping up of one woman into at least six different identities could not have an impact on how people read the book, especially as the issue had been made central to the book's narrative style. In any case, there are at least twenty-five passages that directly or indirectly suggest a feminist conspiracy in the Ormond case. The book is riddled with phrases like 'the faceless group of women in the wider university who supported the two complainants'. The rhetoric of some sentences is loaded: 'The warmth of her manner on the phone had congealed into the permafrost of a feminist who'd been shown my letter to Colin Shepherd [the pseudonym she gave Gregory in the book]', and her line about feminism not being the 'exclusive property of a priggish, literal-minded vengeance squad' who savage the gods' messenger, Eros. Garner's attempt to hold the feminist conspiracy charge at arm's length is misleading; she gives Gregory's allegation of a feminist conspiracy a sympathetic reading by remarking that, 'Whenever I've spoken to Colin Shepherd I've been struck by the absence of anger in his demeanour or tone'. A later passage contradicts the letter she had written in response to Mead's newspaper article: 'I asked him [the acting master of the college] if he thought that the feminist group in Ormond which had organized against Colin Shepherd might have formed in opposition to this blokish element in the college'.

A rereading of *The First Stone* allows the reader to see that perhaps in the original manuscript there was a sharper distinction drawn between the frustration Garner felt at being refused an interview by Mead and the repulsion she felt towards various women on campus, the so-called 'priggish, literal-minded vengeance squad'. But the effect of splitting Mead into at least six people in the text is to conflate these frustrations and imprint 'feminist conspiracy' on the reader's mind. The reader, therefore, is misled or, when Garner's action is revealed, the trust—or, to use Garner's term, the 'contract'—between writer and reader is ruptured. Garner deeply regrets acceding to the lawyer's advice. 'It was a flaw in my method. It shows that when the chips are down I was a coward and it distorted the nature of the story, just that bit, but it was a crucial bit.' I said that when I read that Mead had been split into six people I felt as a reader I had lost my bearings. She replied: 'That is the worst thing about it. That is the basis of my regret, that it violates the contract with the reader'. Garner also said there were a surprising number of women who would not speak to her for the book, but even if you accept her word, the addition of an extra half-dozen women made the conspiracy seem larger than it actually was. With the revelation of the splitting up of Mead, the rhetorical force of Garner's argument collapses, which, coupled with her unfair treatment of the two young women, seriously undermines the credibility of *The First Stone*, which is a pity because it is in many ways a powerful book.

The law's strictures on narrative non-fiction can hinder even those experienced in dealing with them, like Malcolm Knox, who was an experienced journalist with *The Sydney Morning Herald* when he decided to write about the experience of being a juror in a criminal trial, something rarely attempted in Australia where, unlike in some countries, it is a criminal offence for jurors to publicly discuss their deliberations during a trial and even afterwards. The case in which Knox was a juror ended in late 2001 and he finished his manuscript the following May, but the lawyers for Knox's publishers, Random House, opposed publication until all appeals had been heard, which took three years. Even then, the lawyers insisted Knox change names and details to make the case unrecognisable to general readers. The book was eventually published in 2005, selling around 5000 copies, and was critically well received. *Secrets of the Jury Room* toggles between three narrative threads: a firsthand account of serving on a jury, an account of a trial and an explanation of how the jury system works, along with suggestions for improving it. It is an informative, engaging work that, despite the nominally for-bidden nature of its contents, gives readers clear signposts about what is being read. There are nineteen pages of endnotes, a four-page bibliography, an eleven-page index and, at the front of the book, a nine-page author's note, of which the opening sentence proclaims 'Australians haven't read a book like this before' and then outlines Knox's predicament: how can journalists do what they want to—put as much interesting information into the public domain as possible—without falling foul of the law.

The secrecy surrounding the Australian jury system, and debate about that secrecy, gives Knox's work the force of acting in the public interest, but the law is explicit; he cannot write about deliberations and he cannot identify the accused for fear of prejudicing any trials in which the accused might appear that bear even the slightest resemblance to the original trial. Eventually Knox decides to blur the identities of both jurors and the accused:

> I must work on him with a novelist's skills: cobble him together out of ghosts, memories, fantasies, and little bits of real people. Consequently, he's become someone completely different. His life story is different. The context of the accusations against him is different, his lawyer is different, the witnesses for and against him are different. No future juror can recognize him or prejudge him because—dear hypothetical rogue juror—the man you will read about in these pages is not J [a pseudonym for the accused] at all. You don't know what is real and what I'm making up. He's become a character from a writer's imagination. And the discussions in the jury room that I'll talk about are also the magic lantern show of imagination (2005, p. xi).

Having tattooed this caveat on the reader's forehead, Knox writes: 'While the details are embroidered, however, what follows is an honest account of my own experience as a juror'. Honesty notwithstanding, the effect of the caveat is to make the reader think: how do I know which details are real and which are embroidered, and why would I care about a fictionalised case?

These questions begin to press on your mind as the book proceeds and the account unfolds. Knox relates the story of the trial in small sections, regularly digressing to discuss the jury system. To sustain reader interest, he keeps moving between the intrinsically less exciting material on the operation of the jury system to the story of the trial and to the view backstage in the jury room. This is a shrewd narrative strategy, but readers find themselves increasingly drawn to the details of the criminal trial—an attempted murder case in which a confident, appealing American film producer pursues his ex-wife and their young son to Tasmania, where the ex-wife has resumed a relationship with an aggressive gay woman. The film producer, whose moderately successful career has been sliding, devises a ploy of serving a subpoena on himself for the attempted kidnapping of his son so that he can remain in Australia and try and monitor his son while awaiting a Family Court custody hearing. While in gaol he conspires to hire a man to kill his wife and her lover. How is the reader to take this account? The reader has been encouraged to identify with Knox as an everyman juror and is mindful that the defining feature of the jury system is that, with few exceptions, any citizen can be called up and required to serve. If the account of the case is invented, it seems like pretty tacky stuff. If it is grounded in fact, the reader is beginning to think, 'This is amazing. It's like something out of a movie, but it is real. I wonder what it would have been like in that jury room?'

At this point readers may well recall Knox's note explicitly telling them they would not know what is real and what is imagined, and may well become frustrated. Knox acknowledged this when I put it to him, and said that he actually changed very few details of the case but, legally, he was unable to let readers know; this he found frustrating 'for exactly that sense of losing your moorings as a reader'. He said the book primarily concerned the jury system rather than an individual case, and that may well have been his intention, but what makes the book so absorbing is the interweaving of the three threads. 'It was a matter of damage control. It was not satisfactory but I was trying to make the unsatisfactoriness of it minimal.'

Knox's decision to abide by the law misled readers, but it protected those involved in the trial; conversely, Garner's decision to prevent any prospect of being sued for defamation misled readers because it overstated the number of 'faceless' feminists on campus and also misrepresented the two young women's chief supporter. The other difference is that, where Jenna Mead publicly identified herself, those involved in the *Secrets of the Jury Room* trial did not, though once the defendant in Knox's trial had exhausted his avenues for appeal he was able to be named, which Knox did, in passing, in an essay entitled *On Obsession*.

Where Garner misstepped, to her regret, and Knox misled readers, with relatively minor impact, Margaret Simons was keenly aware of the importance of checking and re-checking facts in *The Meeting of the Waters*, as the Hindmarsh Island bridge affair was a key site of the culture wars in Australia in the 1990s and she knew errors would be seized on. Simons drew on her experience as an investigative journalist writing about police corruption and worked closely with media lawyers to avoid defamation actions. Her achievement did not come without cost, not least to herself; she spent several months before and after publication of *The Meeting of the Waters* worried that if she were sued personally she would need to sell her house to fund a legal defence. Simons is a talented writer, but her express commitment to the integrity of the journalism meant that she felt the need to set out her interpretation of events and issues in exhaustive detail over more than 500 pages to ensure the book was defendable against its likely critics. It withstood the attacks of various commentators and participants in the case, and no lawsuits were launched, so the prudence of her decision was vindicated. It does mean the book is too long and, in parts, too dense for at least some of the readers Simons wanted to reach, which perhaps explains its sales of around 2000 copies, but Simons preferred this to weakening the book's underpinnings for the sake of pace or a simpler narrative style. And given what was at stake she was probably right. As Jack Fuller puts it: 'I would *always* sacrifice literary effects to the truth discipline' (1996, p. 143).

That is the point, of course: the writer of narrative non-fiction is not the master of their domain, which brings us back to the first issue mentioned at the beginning of the chapter—the relationship between writer and reader. That there are some readers who are unconcerned whether a work is fiction or non-fiction does not absolve writers of their obligations to readers, for two reasons: first, there are many readers who do care about the status of the work offered and, second, the writer's goal of veracity in their true stories predates the reader picking up the book.

If the notion of a contract between writer and reader is inaccurate and implausible, Gérard Genette's notion for autobiography that the 'genre or other indications *commit* the author' (1987, p. 11 footnote) does apply to narrative non-fiction. 'Commits' is a powerful word here, as it attests to the practitioner's obligations. They commit to present their work in a particular way to readers who, in turn, place their trust in the writer. Readers may not sign contracts with practitioners, but they do need to trust them if they care about the nature of what they are reading. Some readers will give (or withhold) trust regardless of what is presented, but for the majority, their trust can be nourished through materials provided by practitioners, some of which have already been discussed or alluded to in earlier chapters. These materials could be within the body of the book, through the narrative voice, or outside it in material such as endnotes, bibliographies, notes on sources, lists of interviewees and notes to the reader on whether writers witnessed events firsthand. This practice extends to providing information that would affect how readers weigh the work, such as any financial relationship between journalists and their principal sources. These practices amount to an informed or earned, rather than blind, trust.

Among Boynton's interviewees, twelve describe the relationship they seek to establish with readers as one of trust or something similar. They are Dash, Finnegan, Kotlowitz, Krakauer, Langewiesche, LeBlanc, Orlean, Rosenbaum, Schlosser, Trillin, Weschler and Wright. Langewiesche's view is representative; he says writers need to be honest with readers, sometimes brutally so, as writing is a 'private conversation' between practitioners and each individual reader: 'It is a very intimate communication, which relies on trust. So it is crucial to establish that trust by never tricking the reader, never playing cute, never cajoling, showing off, or wasting the reader's time' (Boynton 2005). Among the Australians, Bryson, Marr and Simons all invoke trust; Simons comments that the 'unreliable narrator', for years a source of rich interpretive interplay in fiction (Abbott 2008, 2nd edn; ed. Herman 2007), is inappropriate in narrative non-fiction precisely because readers need to trust the writer's narrative voice. This includes even the narrative voice of those like Didion, Mailer and Thompson, who call attention to the difficulty of representing people and events.

A series of scandals over accuracy or deception of readers by journalists, such as Stephen Glass at *The New Republic* in 1998 and Jayson Blair at *The New York Times* in 2003, has prompted intense self-scrutiny in the news media industry that has extended to book-length projects. It has become more common for writers to include endnotes, bibliographies, forewords and notes on sourcing to help readers weigh the veracity of their work. Lemann argues endnotes offer a way of attributing information without interrupting the narrative flow of the book, thereby making it more transparent and setting out the limits of their knowledge (eds Kramer & Call 2007, pp. 192–3). Of Boynton's nineteen interviewees, fourteen include some or all of these pieces of explanatory material. Of the fourteen, seven use endnotes; the other seven don't, but they do provide a detailed note to the reader on their methods. Five Boynton interviewees—Kramer, Langewiesche, Lewis, Orlean and Trillin—provide neither endnotes nor detailed notes to the reader. Of the Australians I interviewed, six of the seven include explanatory material, though Garner's is scant and, for *The First Stone*, misleading. The endnotes range from six and seven pages in Krakauer's *Under the Banner of Heaven* and Conover's *Newjack* respectively to forty-three and fifty-five pages in Wright's *The Looming Tower* and Schlosser's *Fast Food Nation* respectively. In addition, these authors provide bibliographies (eight pages in *Under the Banner of Heaven*, three in *Newjack*, six in *Fast Food Nation* and ten in *The Looming Tower*). Mark Bowden's *Black Hawk Down* has forty-five pages of notes on his sources and on his method for reconstructing an ill-starred military mission in Mogadishu, Somalia, that happened a few years beforehand. The scope of the endnotes and bibliographies in these works of narrative non-fiction approaches that found in academic books.

Some who eschew endnotes do offer detailed notes to the reader. Boynton's interviewees also use elements of the paratext to make explicit their attitude to what can be known about their subject. In the foreword to his book *Coyotes*, Conover draws a contrast between the many authors writing about illegal immigrants who probably would not recognise them if one came up and offered to shine their shoes and how, to gain an insight into their experience, he disguised himself as an 'illegal alien' and accompanied other Mexicans trying to cross the border into the United States. Despite this level of commitment, Conover is acutely aware 'This is not the whole story, but I have tried to make it their story'. Finnegan, in the introduction to his book about poverty in the United States, *Cold New World: Growing Up in a Harder Country*, is more explicit:

The moral authority of the social order that once might have allowed me to pass unambivalent judgments on the lives of poor Americans—an authority packed tight, at the best of times, with unexamined assumptions about power and virtue—has, in my view, simply grown too weak to support such exertions. A white, middle-class reporter inspecting the souls of poor African Americans is, given our history, an especially dubious proposition. So I've tried to keep one eye on my limitations as observer and analyst, and to reflect, where possible, the densely freighted power relations between me and some of my subjects (1998, p. xvi).

If it is difficult to imagine Woodward or Capote expressing such sentiments, even practitioners who present their works without drawing attention to their presence in the narrative are demonstrating a growing sophistication in dealing with issues arising in establishing a relationship with readers. Dina Temple-Raston, like Berendt, writes about a murder case in the American south in her work *A Death in Texas*, and like him she arrived in the city where the murder took place (in this case, Jasper, Texas) after the murder, but unlike him she did not place herself as an overt authorial figure in the book witnessing events that she had not seen. In a note on sources, though, she recounts how the father of one of the three white men accused of chaining a young African American man, James Byrd, to the bumper of a truck and dragging him to his death would not be interviewed, but did agree to deliver to her a statement from his son. When they met in a parking lot, he unexpectedly burst into tears, crying 'in such volume that his shirt was soaked'. He spoke to her for forty-five minutes, never taking his foot off the brake and never taking his car out of drive. 'He finally drove away, and I realized at that moment that the story of Jasper had yet to be told' (2002, pp. 278–9).

More narrative non-fiction works about national security and intelligence agencies are embracing a rigorous approach to sourcing and a transparency with readers. In an introduction to Seymour Hersh's *Chain of Command: The Road from 9/11 to Abu Ghraib*, David Remnick, Hersh's editor at *The New Yorker*, where his articles originally appeared, writes about how readers are, understandably, frustrated by the use of unnamed sources, especially as some reporters conceal names because it is easier or because it 'gives the piece the shadowy sense of a big-time investigation'. Anonymous sources are necessary in the areas Hersh writes about because they are risking their jobs or prosecution, but Remnick wanted to reassure readers that whenever Hersh mentioned anonymous sources in his copy, he had been asked by his editors who they are, what their motivations might be and if they can be corroborated. On the surface, it may seem a fine distinction to Woodward's practice, but where Woodward appears to be granting anonymity to senior officials in any given administration, Hersh is protecting people within intelligence agencies and the military who are providing information about corrupt, sometimes illegal, activities in their own organisations. He often has acquired, or been leaked, documentary evidence to support the allegations, such as the photographs of the torture of prisoners held at Abu Ghraib outside Baghdad and the internal report by Major General Antonio Taguba, which described in detail the beatings and sexual humiliation by Americans of prisoners in the gaol. Between the terrorist attacks on 11 September 2001 and the Abu Ghraib disclosures in mid-2004, Hersh wrote twenty-six articles for the magazine, ranging from the intelligence failures leading up to the attacks to the Bush administration's efforts to promulgate dubious intelligence on an Iraqi nuclear program, among others. In 2003, when Hersh wrote that the chairman of President Bush's Defense Policy Board, Richard Perle, also had business interests that stood to profit from a war in Iraq, Perle appeared on CNN and told Wolf Blitzer: 'Look, Sy Hersh is the closest thing American journalism has to a terrorist, frankly'. He threatened to sue Hersh and the magazine, but never did. What is clear from Remnick's introduction is that he and Hersh take seriously both the need to protect anonymous sources and the need to be as open as possible with readers. Their careful, principled decision-making helps them in their goal of making important disclosures in the national interest.

Where Hersh's work during this particularly testing period in American politics epitomises the maxim usually attributed to English newspaper proprietor Lord Northcliffe, 'News is what someone, somewhere wants to suppress. All the rest is advertising', Lawrence Wright's account of the rise of al-Qaeda manages to investigate an extremely difficult topic and to provide ample explanation of his methods and sources to readers. Wright lists by name more than 550 people he interviewed for *The Looming Tower*, which won the Pulitzer Prize for general non-fiction in 2007. In 'Acknowledgements and Notes on Sources', Wright addresses directly the problem of writing about intelligence operatives and jihadists. He notes the shoddiness of much early scholarship about al-Qaeda and the unreliability of sworn testimony of witnesses who have proven themselves to be 'crooks, liars and double-agents'. Some important documents on al-Qaeda have been seized by various arms of the United States government and used in court cases, but even these can be misleading, he writes, and cites several examples. He also offers an example of a 'tantalizing' piece of evidence that showed a high-ranking Saudi intelligence officer providing to the CIA in 1999 the names of two of the eventual hijackers of the planes flown into the World Trade Center on 11 September 2001, but Wright did not include it because he could not verify it to his satisfaction. He conducted his research 'horizontally' and 'vertically'; that is, by continually checking hundreds of sources against each other, and by interviewing people in depth, perhaps dozens of times. By outlining his methods he hopes 'the reader can begin to appreciate the murky nature of the world in which Al-Qaeda operated and the imperfect means I have sometimes employed in order to gain information' (2006). Wright dislikes seeing anonymous sources used in books and 'so I've dragged as many of my informants into the light as possible' (2006). Some sources habitually asked for an interview to be off the record, but Wright found they later approved specific quotations that he checked back with them. He concludes: 'Where there remain items that are not tied to specific individuals or documents, they represent vital information that I have good reason to accept as true' (2006). In his lengthy, candid note on sources, Wright acknowledges the difficulties of the journalist–source relationship, 'since trust and friendship go hand in hand. Knowledge is seductive; the reporter wants to know, and the more he knows, the more interesting he becomes to the source. There are few forces in human nature more powerful than the desire to be understood; journalism couldn't exist without it' (2006). Journalists cannot, however, protect sources from criticism in their work even though the sharing of secrets and unburdening profound feelings invites intimacy and a fellow feeling. 'By the conspicuous use of a tape recorder and extensive note-taking, I try to remind both of us that there is a third party in the room, the eventual reader' (Wright 2006). The level of care and attention Wright pays to verifying delicate and highly sensitive material, and his openness with his sources, are a shining example of a writer both enacting the virtue of truthfulness and carefully thinking his way through the complexities and competing demands of his role.

If there is a trend among practitioners towards more extensive use of paratextual material, it should be said that it is by no means universal, as the avoidance of such practices in five of Boynton's interviewees suggests. As to whether readers actually read the extensive notes directed at them, there is little firm evidence, but even if the majority of them pass readers by, that is not a good reason for their exclusion. There is a disconnection, though, between the poor reputation journalists have with many in their audiences and the depth of care and attention paid by many to ethical issues, both in narrative non-fiction, as exemplified in the work of some writers discussed in this book and, according to David Craig, in newspaper journalists, whose work he studied for *The Ethics of the Story*. For instance,

Sonia Nazario is a journalist with *The Los Angeles Times* who wrote a multi-part series about a sixteen-year-old Honduran boy's illegal journey into the United States to find his mother who had left him at home with her family when he was five years old. Nazario spent six months and filled more than one hundred notebooks researching her topic, and produced a powerfully written series for the newspaper in 2002 that included 7000 words of endnotes and won a Pulitzer Prize. She then expanded the series into a book entitled *Enrique's Journey*. Nazario has recounted the work undergirding her series at the Nieman Foundation conference on Narrative Journalism. She says that she received at least 1000 phone calls and emails from readers about the series. The newspaper's readers' representative, Jamie Gold, said reaction was overwhelmingly positive even though the series was about the controversial topic of illegal immigration. 'A lot of people did comment on the extensive footnotes, which is really unusual. But they appreciated that. And it might be as a result of that, that I didn't get a lot of questions about its veracity' (cited in Craig 2006, p. 67). This is worth underscoring because, for much of the series, Nazario had to reconstruct Enrique's journey. Nazario had been worried the endnotes would make the newspaper seem defensive:

> As it turned out, readers appreciated the transparency of the endnotes. They liked seeing the sources of all the information in the series. Surprisingly, they used them to follow the reporting process. They read the endnotes to figure out what I had done—how I had ridden the trains in Mexico and who I had interviewed. I never would have guessed that people would read endnotes for that purpose (cited in eds Kramer & Call 2007, p. 192).

If endnotes are becoming common in narrative non-fiction, they are still rare in newspapers, including their online editions, even though Wikipedia, whose entries can be updated as quickly as news websites, provides footnotes wherever possible and has been around since 2006. It is possible that new online technologies enabling readers to check sources of information and interact with media outlets is encouraging what appears to be a change in attitude to traditionally hidden practices, but further consideration is beyond the scope of this book other than to note that such transparency is a feature of the online world and that most mainstream news media outlets, initially slow to embrace it, are gradually catching up.

Principal sources for narrative non-fiction works read them in a very particular kind of way. Principal sources are as well placed as any to pick up inaccuracies, but they may also be so close as to lose perspective on how events and people are portrayed. Principal sources' responses, then, should be interpreted cautiously. Occasionally, though, their responses can illuminate the issues underlying the relationship between writer and principal source and between writer and reader. For instance, Julie Salamon was granted extraordinary access to the set of Brian De Palma's film adaptation of Tom Wolfe's best-selling novel *The Bonfire of the Vanities*, which was published in 1987. She extended Lillian Ross's *Picture* by writing a comprehensive book entitled *The Devil's Candy* that laid bare the process of how a major Hollywood studio film is made. Unfortunately for De Palma the film was a colossal flop, artistically and commercially.

But a decade after publication of *The Devil's Candy*, De Palma agreed to meet Salamon and be interviewed again for a reissuing of her book. She asked him if he regretted giving her unfettered access with no power of veto over the book. He replied: 'It's a book that even at 10 years distance is not particularly easy for me to read … I think it's very honest' (2002, 'Afterword: 10 years later', p. 421). Asked if he found the book upsetting to read, De Palma said: 'What can you say about something that was considered the greatest catastrophe of the day and then have a book written about it afterwards?'. So much of what is written about Hollywood is so false, though, he said, that he wanted someone to write something truthful. 'I don't think it changed anything, though it made people very aware of the real world we work in. It got a lot of people very angry', he said, probably referring to one of the film's stars, Bruce Willis, who told *Entertainment Weekly* in 1995 that he hoped that one night Salamon would finally understand 'the sick life she was living' and 'just put a gun in her mouth and blew [sic] her fucking brains out'. These responses are illuminating: Willis is revealed as an egotistical bully, De Palma is shown to have a stronger commitment to honesty in filmmaking than might have been expected from the director of such films as *Dressed to Kill* and Salamon is seen as a principled writer striving to balance her obligations to both her principal sources and her readers.

The nature of the relationship that writers aim to create with their readers is the third and final, and equally important, part of the three-part framework developed in this book. Most want readers to engage in a rich reading experience, whether they are moved to tears or laughter or outrage by a true story's contents. Writing in a narrative style is the way to achieve this, which means that the relationship writers create with readers can be as close as that created between novelists and their readers. The difference is that the relationship between readers and writers of narrative non-fiction is predicated on an understanding that what is being offered is a representation of actual people, events and issues. This understanding is not a formal contract, but is grounded in trust. Such trust is not naïve, but is informed by practitioners providing ways and means for readers to weigh the veracity of the truth-telling claims in the work. These may be through the narrative voice in the body of the work or in the paratext through a range of explanatory devices. The problems Woodward and Capote created for themselves in the writing phase of their works were aggravated by the scant means they gave readers to assess their book's truth-telling claims. Many current leading writers are acutely aware of their obligations to readers, especially when, pursuing Gardner's fiction dream state, they aim to enthral readers 'heart and soul'.

Conclusion

Here, at the end of this exploration into researching and writing true stories, I hope you will take with you three core points. First, narrative non-fiction is an important, vibrant and expanding area of writing. For years it has been held dockside in a literary cargo hold; it has not been included alongside the established literary genres of poetry, drama and fiction. It has sat apart—or been set aside—both from well recognised genres in non-fiction publishing such as history and biography and from the daily news media industries. Despite the absence of definitive data about the amount of narrative non-fiction published annually (precisely because it has not been an established genre), there is no doubt in my mind it is sizeable. I have been following this field for years, but when Sarah Statz Cords found 500 works of investigative non-fiction had been published in the United States in the first decade of the twenty-first century not only did the figure surprise me but so did the number of titles I had not even heard of let alone read. In the end all the arguments about what to call this area of writing, or whether it has won recognition from publishers, media companies or scholars, are less important than the simple fact that a good deal of it continues to be written and that it continues to be read by an appreciative audience.

Narrative non-fiction is an important genre because it sits on a continuum between newspaper, magazine and online journalism at one end and specialist academic study at the other. It fulfils a valuable social role because it retains the urgency and sense of connectedness with the general audience's interests that characterises daily journalism but has—or makes—the time and space to move beyond the superficial coverage inherent in the daily news media. Successful works approach the rigour of academic study but escape its theory-laden and eggbound prose; instead they are written in a narrative style to engage readers emotionally as well as intellectually. The creation of a body of deeply researched, vividly written books that provide fresh information and explore events in their complexity and people in their full humanity offers at least one part of a solution to problems that have beset the news media industries for many years.

Because narrative non-fiction dives deep into the grey areas of human experience and because it can make such a powerful impact on readers it necessarily prompts complex and knotty issues. This is the second core point. And it is not something to run away from; would you rather be writing something that had no stake in the world and left no imprint on your readers? You will necessarily come across critical ethical issues when you adopt a narrative approach to writing about actual people, events and issues for a broad audience. Some issues are similar to those experienced by people working in the daily news media, while other ethical issues take a particular form in book-length projects. I have not discussed all the sub-genres of narrative non-fiction, however; rather I have focussed on those areas of writing practice that have so far received less attention in the literature and which throw up the thorniest issues to be nutted out. By analysing these issues through a three part framework that separates the process into phases for research, writing and reception, I have identified the most distinctive and pressing ethical issues and have set them out in what I hope you have found to be an easily digestible form. These issues are: the difficulty faced by writers in developing close relationships with principal sources and maintaining a sense of editorial independence; representing actual people, events and issues in a narrative style; and developing a relationship of informed trust with readers.

Writing a true story at book length, then, creates an interlocking concentration of ethical issues. Those working in the daily news media sometimes develop close relationships with key sources, but they generally do not need to glean much personal, intimate information about these sources. And where they do need to do this, the journalists generally do not need to write about these sources in a narrative style. Sometimes, yes, they write in a narrative style but not as often as they write hard news reports. When they write in a narrative style their articles rarely extend beyond a few thousand words, and their work sits in a newspaper or magazine or online site amid a range of other articles, photographs, graphics, comics, listings and advertisements. Those working on book-length true stories need to negotiate and manage difficult and dynamic relationships with principal sources that can seem more than professional but less than personal. The majority of them choose to represent what they find in their research in a narrative style; that means they need to balance the demands of veracity inherent in a form making truth-telling claims with their desire to create a narrative that engages readers as fully as possible. Writers can be tempted to smooth over the gaps and bumps of confusion inherent in a serious investigation of the world and create the illusion of a seamless narrative. When writers choose to offer their work in books they learn that many readers associate books with novels, especially when they are presented with one that reads like a novel and offers little guidance that it is not a novel but a work of narrative non-fiction.

Many scholars make literary merit their criteria when choosing which works in this area of writing to study, which means Capote's *In Cold Blood* is included in most discussions of what is variously termed literary journalism, literary non-fiction or creative non-fiction, but Woodward's many works are not. As we have seen in earlier chapters, though, it is the initial decision to take a narrative approach to representing people, events and issues that triggers certain ethical issues. There is a relationship between the work of narrative non-fiction and the actual people and events it seeks to represent that cannot be gainsaid. If a writer is not aiming to represent actual people and events as fully and accurately as possible they are working in another genre of writing that looks pretty much like fiction. If they are aiming to represent people and events as truthfully as possible, no amount of artistry can dance away from the consequences of exploiting the people who are the subjects of the story, or falsely representing them, or deceiving readers about what they are being offered. The ethical issues are triggered, then, whether the true story is written by a fine writer like Capote or a pedestrian one like Woodward. Gardner's fiction dream state is not predicated on rare literary gifts but on baseline literary skills. This 'dream state' can be induced in romance novels and detective fiction as well as in novels conventionally seen as art, such as George Eliot's *Middlemarch*. Differing readers have differing reading levels; where one might be enthralled by a romance novel but be unprepared for the rigours of reading *Middlemarch*, another may be able, and willing, to engage with both books. Writers of narrative non-fiction have obligations to all their readers, regardless of differing reading levels. As discussed in earlier chapters, serious flaws were found throughout the three stages of research, writing and publication in narrative non-fiction works by writers of great literary skill (Capote) and those with less skill (Woodward).

Whatever their shortcomings, Capote and Woodward remain important figures in the historical development of narrative non-fiction. The third core point of this book is that numerous individual writers have reflected on their missteps and made significant advances towards resolving the ethical issues that arose in the work of Capote, Woodward and other New Journalists. Most of the writers interviewed by Robert Boynton and by me admire Janet Malcolm's work and thank her for prodding the hidden underbelly of the journalist–source relationship, but most have not accepted her view that it is an irredeemably flawed relationship. Individually, and on a project-by-project basis, writers have established practices for allowing principal sources to give informed consent for their involvement in books, and for finding and making clear the boundaries of their close working relationships. They have applied what Aristotle called 'practical wisdom' to clarify in their own minds the porous and shifting line between the worlds of fiction and non-fiction which equips them, as David Marr says, 'To deal with the raggedness of events without fictionalizing them, and still maintain the book's drama'. Many of the writers discussed in this book have come to the realisation that some narrative approaches, such as interior monologues, may be closed to non-fiction. Flowing from their understanding of the importance of distinguishing between fiction and

non-fiction, these writers take seriously the need to create a relationship with readers of what is termed in this book informed trust,
providing readers with the means by which they can weigh a work's
veracity even as they are drawn in by its contents.

In narrative non-fiction ethical issues arise with less immediate
urgency than in daily journalism, and they take a subtler form, but
they are no less important for that. The reflections of the writers
interviewed and studied here, as well as my own analysis, may
suggest that the relevant codes of ethics for journalists need extending to encompass the particular ethical issues arising in narrative
non-fiction; but perhaps that is a project for another time.

I trust that this book will prompt you to, first, seek out good
narrative non-fiction reading and, second and more importantly,
seek out a true story of your own to research and write. Every individual project has its own particular problems to solve. What I have
provided here is a roadmap to guide you in your own research and
writing. What you also find here are reflections and insights from
some of the smartest writers around and the encouragement that you
too can and should add to the rich storehouse of true stories roaming
around the world.

A checklist for writers of narrative non-fiction

This checklist should be used along with existing codes of ethics for journalists and with Bill Kovach and Tom Rosenstiel's core set of five concepts that form the foundation of the discipline of verification underpinning journalism (*The Elements of Journalism*, pp. 78–112):

- never add anything that was not there
- never deceive the audience
- be as transparent as possible about your methods and motives
- rely on your own original reporting
- and exercise humility.

The checklist provided below does not specifically cover issues that are common to both daily and long-form journalism. Nor are all points in the checklist relevant to all works of narrative non-fiction. For instance, in some works, writers do not need to develop particularly close relationships with their principal sources. Also, works of narrative non-fiction range from those written about ordinary people with little or no experience of the media to those written about media-savvy politicians and convicted criminals. Some works aim to gently explore an issue, others aggressively confront abuses of power. Codes of ethics for journalists have been developed with daily news media practice in mind rather than the issues that arise in projects that take months or even years to complete and (usually) are presented in book form. This checklist is specifically aimed at issues that arise in longer projects. It is drawn from my study over the years as well as my own experience. It draws on both mistakes made by writers as well as on their exemplary practices. All recommendations below are methods and behaviours practised by at least one writer whose work I've studied. Many recommendations are becoming accepted practice, while some are at the edge of current practice.

The research phase of narrative non-fiction

1. You should think carefully about the nature and the terms of any relationship developed with principal sources. It is understood that writers develop relationships with principal sources in a wide variety of circumstances, and that relationships do not have the kind of formal framework and institutional infrastructure that postgraduate students or working academics work with. However, it is worthwhile considering whether aspects of the protocols ethnographers establish with their 'hosts' can be used in telling true stories rather than falling into the pattern of 'seduction' and 'betrayal' that Janet Malcolm wrote about in *The Journalist and the Murderer*.

    There are three main issues to be considered: first, setting out in detail for the principal sources the nature of the project, the level of commitment anticipated, the potential benefits and any potential pitfalls for the source. Second, consider asking principal sources to sign an informed consent form; and third, understand that as relationships between writers and sources are dynamic, so the terms of the relationship may need to be renegotiated during the project. It is understood that for some works, especially investigative projects, obtaining informed consent from principal sources is inappropriate or irrelevant.

2. Be friendly without becoming friends. The closeness of the relationship between writers and their principal sources can be especially delicate to navigate. It is not possible to be precise about just how close you should become to the principal sources, as that will be determined by a range of elements, such as the nature of the project and the temperament of both the source and the writer. Here it is important for you to keep in mind the various and sometimes competing obligations which are primarily to

those about whom you write and to your readers, but also to your publishers and to yourself. The American Society of Professional Journalists' first two principles—maximise truth-telling and minimise harm—remain useful guidelines for book-length projects. The boundaries between ethical and unethical behaviour in the relationship between writer and source may differ from project to project: the important point to grasp is that there *are* boundaries to the relationship and that you find out where they are and keep within them. When socialising with sources as a way of developing the source's trust, you should keep in mind the reason you are spending time with the source—to gather material for publication. It is also worth remembering that socialising is not the only way to develop the source's trust. Malcolm Knox and Lawrence Wright both testify to the importance of genuine curiosity and seriousness of purpose on the writer's part in building a source's trust.

3. Don't deceive sources about your views on the issue you are writing about. This stems from the problems Joe McGinniss had when he did not tell Jeffrey MacDonald that he had changed his mind about MacDonald's guilt over murder charges. The majority of practitioners interviewed by Robert Boynton for *The New New Journalism* favour being open if they disagree with their sources about an issue critical to the project, first because they believe in being honest with sources and, second, because disagreement can be seen as a way of continuing to ask probing questions. I acknowledge there will be some circumstances in writing, as there are in life, where total honesty between writer and source is inappropriate or unnecessary.

4. Consider carefully about entering into any financial relationship with principal sources. It is acknowledged that payment of sources or royalty sharing agreements will usually be seen by readers as tainting the value of the source's testimony. But some of the circumstances of book-length projects differ from daily journalism. If a principal source is going to voluntarily provide many hours of their time over months or even years, it may be worth considering some level of compensation for their time and energy. In the case of Gitta Sereny's book about Mary

Bell, *Cries Unheard*, there were clear grounds for compensating her, even though the arrangement between author and subject created a storm of controversy. In most biographies of people still living it is important for the independence of the project that there is no financial relationship; it is also apparent that a full-length biography affords the subject a rare level of publicity. A good question to ask is what the source stands to gain by the project; weigh that against the level of commitment required of them. Chequebook journalism is widely, and usually rightly, condemned but it is rarely examined. Media organisations already pay for material, whether that be in extracts from books, reprinting of articles from magazines or in paying a newsmaker to write an article about a topic, and then asking a staff journalist to use the article as the basis for a news report.

5. Consider showing sources what has been written about them before publication, or at least checking quotations with them. Again, this practice is frowned upon in daily journalism, and with good reason, but contrary to newsroom lore even in daily journalism it is not universally followed. Given that a book is researched and written over a much longer period, has a much longer shelf life and is expected to be more accurate than daily journalism, I recommend considering checking material with sources for accuracy. Whether sources check everything that has been written about them in the book or only quotations attributed to them, and whether they are shown material at draft stage or after the manuscript has been edited, will depend on the nature of the book and the importance of the source. Even if sources are allowed to look at the manuscript their role should be limited to questions of accuracy or to putting their point of view if they disagree with the writer's interpretation of events or actions. Sources should not have power of veto over a project.

6. Dealing with principal sources after the project is finished. Sometimes writers do become friends with their principal sources. Given what has been written above this could be seen as a problem but it would be puritanical, not to mention unrealistic, to believe that when people work intensely over a long period on a project—not together but side by side, as it were—friendship

will never result. Friendship should not be the goal of a work of narrative non-fiction but should not be outlawed either. It may disqualify the journalist from writing extensively about that person in the future, though, as it did with John McPhee and Bill Bradley. It may also depend on the nature of the relationship. Alex Kotlowitz, in a 'Note on Reporting Methods' for his book about two years in the lives of two poor young African American boys, *There Are No Children Here*, told Robert Boynton how he helped pay for them to attend private schools and set up trusts for them but did this after he finished writing the book. 'I'll always remember, in those first few months with Lafeyette and Pharoah, all they wanted to know was "was I going to leave after I finished the book". They asked me that repeatedly. And eventually I did promise them that I would not move, and I didn't.'

Representing people and events in narrative non-fiction

1. Writers and even scholars commonly talk about using the 'techniques' of fiction in narrative non-fiction. Such thinking perpetuates the mistaken belief that journalists deal always and only in objective, verifiable facts and that when they come to write books they will apply the techniques of fiction to facts. This in turn encourages practices such as imagining dialogue or recreating scenes that the journalist did not witness. If journalists reproduce dialogue in their books it should be dialogue that they themselves reported or that has been recalled in official documents such as court transcripts. The reconstruction of scenes is discussed below. The point I'm making here is that in writing narrative non-fiction you do more extensive research than is possible in daily journalism and then you represent what you find quite differently from the narrowly framed form of the news report. Long-form narrative conveys a broader and deeper account of people and events, one that incorporates facts, atmosphere, emotions, context, texture and meaning. This narrative approach will draw on elements of literary practice that are customarily associated with but not owned by fiction, such as characterisation, dialogue, scene-setting and authorial voice, among others. As Tracy Kidder has said: 'They belong to storytelling'.

2. The act of representing people and events and issues in narrative non-fiction involves ethical as well as linguistic choices. Narrative non-fiction that reads like a novel may induce in the reader John Gardner's 'fictional dream state' so it is important to balance the compelling reading experience with a clear sense that while the book may read like a novel it is about real people, events and issues—and be clear that it is intended as such. This can be achieved either in the body of the book or in the paratext; that is, in the material that surrounds and adds to the body of the work. If the writer takes the first approach, they may draw the reader's attention to the nature of what they are reading by saying of a particular scene that while one person recalled it happening in one way, another remembered it differently. Or they may quote remembered dialogue but preface it by writing that 'it went something like this'. You foreground the writer's active choice in representing a situation in a certain way. If you take the second approach, that is using the paratext to foreground the factual nature of the narrative, you may want the work to read as if it were a novel but use endnotes, appendices and indexes to signal clearly the book's status as non-fiction.

3. Most journalists coming to books from the news media are trained to focus on the events they are writing about rather than to draw attention to their presence in the book. You need to consider carefully the kind of authorial presence you want to project because removing your overt presence from the narrative and creating an omniscient authorial voice runs the risk of persuading readers that the version of events presented is the only possible version. Most journalists of even a few years experience are all too aware of the difficulty of establishing exactly what happened in any major newsworthy event. There are gaps in the record, they cannot get access to some of the sources, there are several conflicting accounts and some people appear to be lying. Writers who choose to withdraw as an overt presence from their book should include paratextual material to remind readers of the nature of what they are reading. You cannot claim to be master of your non-fictional universe. In this context, Jack Fuller, a Pulitzer Prize-winning journalist and author of five

novels, advises: 'I would *always* sacrifice literary effects to the truth discipline'.

4. Underlying the previous two points in the checklist is the notion that good practice requires writers to balance the desire to offer a readable work with the obligation to be transparent with readers about the limits of our knowledge of the events and people we write about. As part of that transparency, acknowledge your presence in some or many of the events you describe. I do not intend to be prescriptive about the approach writers take to finding a suitable narrative style for their subject; some may opt to remove themselves as an overt presence in the narrative, others will choose the opposite, and others still will find alternative ways of telling the story they want to tell. Having said that, writers who acknowledge their presence openly and draw attention to gaps and questions about the subject of their book make it easy for the reader to identify these complex issues.

5. Writers need to find a balance between their obligations to those they write about and to their readers. Vivid, pungent descriptive writing may be painfully honest or may simply inflict pain. Novelists can describe their fictional characters any way they choose; journalists, however, are representing real people rather than creating characters so they need to posit several questions to guide their ethical choices. Is the description relevant to the book? Is the description of a person's actions representative of their overall behaviour? Are you trying to use description as a substitute for argument? Finding the point where truth-telling tips over into cruelty is not always straightforward but it is important. Of course, sometimes truth-telling is brutal but at least one should avoid gratuitous cruelty.

6. In reconstructing scenes they did not witness, writers need to balance their desire to write in a dramatic narrative style with their obligation to veracity in their account. Several questions need to be considered: how long ago did the events occur? How important are they to the book? Are the events in the scene strongly contested or is there likely to be broad agreement about them? It is important to get an account of the event from all those involved or from as many sources as possible. It may be useful to

visit the place where the events took place or ask sources to revisit it with you. Alternatively, take photographs of the physical scene and show them to sources to help them recall events. Having done as much as possible to verify the events and words spoken by participants, it is equally important to be aware of the fallibility and vagaries of memory and to signal to readers that you have reconstructed the events in question rather than witnessed them. Such signalling can be done in endnotes or in the body of the work.

7. I strongly recommend you consider carefully before attempting to write interior monologue for a source. You cannot know with any degree of precision what a person was thinking or feeling at a given moment. But it is tempting to include interior monologue. Presenting a person's thoughts and feelings is an intimate and deeply involving literary device that gives the reader the sense that they are close to or can truly understand the person in the narrative. There are three complex issues for writers to consider: first, is the person for whom they are writing an interior mono-logue cooperating or are they hostile or unavailable; second, even if the person is cooperative, how honest and self-aware are they; and, finally, how in-depth are the thoughts and feelings being conveyed. There are some instances where practitioners have successfully and ethically written interior monologues, but in my assessment these are rare. It requires saturation interviewing and deep wells of empathy to draw from people their innermost thoughts and feelings. David Finkel did so in his 2013 book about traumatised veterans returning from the Iraq War, *Thank You for Your Service*, but his book is a rare achievement. Most writers oppose the use of interior monologue or are suspicious of it. Some writers, such as David Marr, say that just as there are some things that can be achieved in narrative non-fiction that cannot be done in fiction, so there are some elements of fiction that are virtually outside the scope of non-fiction.

The terms of the relationship with the reader

1. Ensure the book is accurately labelled, both on the cover and inside the book. The precise phrasing is less important than that a

statement signals that the work is about actual people and events and issues, and aims to represent them as accurately as possible. The book may be labelled current affairs, journalism, non-fiction, reportage or even creative non-fiction. It may also fall into one of several non-fiction genres, such as true crime, biography or travel writing. If the work is a combination of fiction and non-fiction, make that clear too, as Anna Funder did in her 2011 novel, *All That I Am*, when she included a note on sources and when she wrote in her acknowledgements: 'My story, of course, lifts off from the facts as known; I have made connections and suppositions, a plot and characters which cannot be justified solely by reference to the historical record, and for that I take full responsibility'.

2. Avoid sending misleading signals to readers by referring to 'characters' in your narrative non-fiction or by providing a list of 'dramatis personae' as Jon Krakauer did for *Into Thin Air*, his account of the tragic deaths of eight people in a climbing expedition to Mount Everest. These terms refer to works of fiction or theatre. Would you refer to, say, Richard Nixon, as a 'character'? Obviously not, which is why Woodward and Bernstein's listing of a 'cast of characters' in *All the President's Men* and *The Final Days* signals their determination to render the Nixon presidency as a racy narrative digestible by those with a casual interest in politics. Referring to actual people as characters compounds the confusion readers may face when journalism is written in a narrative style and presented in the form most commonly associated with fiction—the book. I have lost count of the number of student assignments I've read that refer to any work of narrative non-fiction as a novel.

3. I recommend the use of paratextual material to help build a relationship of informed trust with your readers. Just as attribution of sourcing is essential in journalism, so too is setting out the nature and range of source material essential in narrative non-fiction. This may include a preface, endnotes, a bibliography, an index, a chronology, maps, illustrations, acknowledgements, notes to the reader on methods and so on. These paratextual elements provide transparency about how material in the book came to be included, and this, in turn, builds trust with readers. The effective

use of paratextual material gives you greater freedom in the range of narrative styles you can choose.

4. For those writing book-length projects, establish whether the publisher uses fact checkers. This is not common in publishing and in light of the industry's squeezed circumstances as it adapts to e-books is not likely to become so despite concerns among readers about accuracy in narrative non-fiction. It is important you understand that when writing a book you carry primary responsibility for the veracity of its contents. This contrasts with daily news media where colleagues, sub-editors, section editors and in-house lawyers all provide layers of checking and counsel.

Acknowledgements

This book has been a long time coming. I seem to remember saying that for the previous book Allen & Unwin published, *Writing Feature Stories*, and for reasons good and bad it is true again. I won't tell you the whole story as it's not that interesting but it probably began when I read Helen Garner's *The First Stone*, which confirmed for me that non-fiction was a much more supple form of writing than it is given credit for and then, when controversy erupted over how Garner had chopped up the two young women's chief supporter, Dr Jenna Mead, into six or more people, I began to see just how thorny writing narrative non-fiction could be. I wrote about these issues, both journalistically and academically, but eventually realised they needed in-depth study and so enrolled in a PhD at Monash University, which I completed in 2010. I would like to thank again my two supervisors, Dr Chris Worth and Dr Nina Philadelphoff-Puren, who were invaluable guides in the rigorous pursuit of knowledge and sanctioned form of obsessive-compulsive disorder that is the doctoral thesis. I would also like to acknowledge study support from the RMIT School of Applied Communication where I was working early in my candidature, from *The Age* which granted me a leave of absence while I was their Media and Communications editor, and from my current employer, the University of Canberra, which provided me with a period of time to complete the thesis.

Many colleagues and friends have helped me over the years in nutting out the particular qualities and problems of writing true stories. They include former colleagues from RMIT's Journalism program, Sybil Nolan, Muriel Porter and Nick Richardson, as well as former students, especially Kimina Lyall and Sophie Vorrath. Thanks to Mitchell Stephens for advice when I decided to transplant his Best American Journalism of the Twentieth Century list to Australia, and for his collegiality. Thanks to Bruce Shapiro who I met through the Dart Center for Journalism and Trauma and who has shown keen interest and offered valuable advice. In my last stint in the news media industry at *The Age*, I was fortunate to work alongside many fine journalists who between deadlines shared their thoughts with that blend of incisiveness, street-savvy and unexpected wells of knowledge that seems unique to newsrooms. They include: Paul Austin, Garry Barker, Shaun Carney, Kate Cole-Adams, Gordon Farrer, Daniel Flitton, Peter Hanlon, Ian McIlwraith, Mal Maiden, Katharine Murphy, Jim Schembri, Michael Short, Kirsty Simpson, Ruth Williams and Leonie Wood. They also include John Langdon, Frank Prain and Michelle Stillman in the editorial library.

I would like to thank those writers I interviewed for this project for their time and their insights: John Bryson, Helen Garner, Chloe Hooper, Malcolm Knox, David Marr and Margaret Simons. I also benefited from conversations with Estelle Blackburn about her book, *Broken Lives*.

Portions of this book appeared in different form in the following journals: *Australian Journalism Review*, *Meanjin* and *Text*; and in proceedings from an Australian Association of Writing Programs and an Australian and New Zealand Communication Association conference. I thank the respective editors for permission to draw on these articles. I would like to thank my colleagues at the University of Canberra—especially Simon Brady, Glen Fuller, Crispin Hull, Kerry McCallum and Jason Wilson—for covering for me when I took a leave of absence to complete this book after I had already been away working on the Independent Media Inquiry with Ray Finkelstein QC. At Allen & Unwin thanks to Belinda Lee for her fine editing work and to publisher Elizabeth Weiss who was again a delight to work with. Finally, to my wife, Gill, and our three (all growed up!)

children, Gemma, Hayley and Josh, thank you, thank you for your love and forbearance. Gill, especially, offers this when her own day job carries a modicum of responsibility and does get, from time to time, a tad busy. Thank you once again darling.

Selected bibliography

PRIMARY SOURCES: Writers' papers and interviews

The New York Public Library, Manuscripts and Archives Division, Truman Capote Papers, c. 1924–84, Boxes 7, 8, 11 and 23.

John Bryson, interviewed on 2 July 2007.

Helen Garner, interviewed on 29 January 2007.

Chloe Hooper, interviewed on 16 March 2009.

Malcolm Knox, interviewed on 3 July 2007.

David Marr, interviewed on 28 February 2007.

Margaret Simons, interviewed on 29 November 2006 and 19 March 2007.

NARRATIVE NON-FICTION

Barry, P. 1993, *The Rise and Rise of Kerry Packer*, Bantam, Sydney.

Berendt, J. 1994, *Midnight in the Garden of Good and Evil*, Vintage, New York.

——1996, 'Preface to this edition', *Midnight in the Garden of Good and Evil*, Vintage, New York, pp. vii–viii.

Bernstein, C. and Woodward, B. 1974, *All the President's Men*, Simon & Schuster, New York.

Blackburn, E. 1998, *Broken Lives*, Stellar, Claremont.

Bowden, M. 1999 (2000), *Black Hawk Down: A Story of Modern War*, Corgi, London.

Brien, S. 1984, *Azaria: the trial of the century*, QB Books.

Brooks, G. 1994 (2003), *Nine Parts of Desire: The Hidden World of Islamic Women*, Anchor, Sydney.

Bryson, J. 1985, *Evil Angels*, Viking, Melbourne.

——1988, 'Afterword', *Evil Angels*, Bantam, New York, pp. 525–36.

Buford, B. 1991, *Among the Thugs*, Secker & Warburg, London.

Capote, T. 1965, 'Annals of Crime: In Cold Blood' in *The New Yorker*, 25 September, 2 October, 9 October and 16 October, pp. 57–166, 57–175, 58–183 and 62–193.

——1966, *In Cold Blood: A True Account of a Multiple Murder and Its Consequences*, Hamish Hamilton, London.

Carlin, J. 2008, *Playing the Enemy: Nelson Mandela and the Game That Made a Nation*, Atlantic Books, London.

Cassidy, J. 2002, *Dot.Con: The Greatest Story Ever Sold*, HarperCollins, New York.

Conover, T. 1987, *Coyotes: A Journey through the Secret World of America's Illegal Aliens*, Vintage, New York.

——2000 (2001), *Newjack: Guarding Sing Sing*, Vintage, New York.

Cramer, R. 1992 (1993), *What It Takes: The Way to the White House*, Vintage, New York.

——2000, *Joe DiMaggio: The Hero's Life*, Simon & Schuster, New York.

Crick, M. 1995 (1996), *Jeffrey Archer: Stranger than Fiction*, 2nd edn, Penguin, London.

Crouse, T. 1973 (1993), *The Boys on the Bus*, Ballantine, New York.

Cullen, D. (2009), *Columbine*, Old Street, London.

Danner, M. 1993 (2005), *The Massacre at El Mozote*, Granta Books, London.

——2009, *Stripping Bare the Body: Politics, Violence, War*, Black Inc, Melbourne.

Didion, J. 1968 (1974), *Slouching Towards Bethlehem*, Penguin, Middlesex.

——1983, *Salvador*, Vintage-Random, New York.

Dover, B. 2008, *Rupert's Adventures in China: How Murdoch Lost a Fortune and Found a Wife*, Viking, Camberwell, Victoria.

Ehrenreich, B. 2001, *Nickel and Dimed: On (Not) Getting By in America*, Metropolitan-Holt, New York.

——2005, *Bait and Switch: The (Futile) Pursuit of the American Dream*, Metropolitan-Holt, New York.

Finkel, D. 2013, *Thank You for Your Service*, Scribe, Brunswick.

Finkel, M. 2005, *True Story: Murder, Memoir, Mea Culpa*, Chatto & Windus, London.

Finnegan, W. 1998 (1999), *Cold New World: Growing Up in a Harder Country*, Macmillan, London.

Flanagan, B. 1995, *U2 at the End of the World*, Bantam, London.

Follett, K. 1983 (1998), *On Wings of Eagles*, Macmillan, London.

Funder, A. 2002, *Stasiland*, Text, Melbourne.

Garner, H. 1995, *The First Stone: Some Questions of Sex and Power*, Pan Macmillan, Sydney.

——2004, *Joe Cinque's Consolation: A True Story of Death, Grief and the Law*, Pan Macmillan, Sydney.

Gellman, B. 2008, *Angler: The Shadow Presidency of Dick Cheney*, Penguin, New York.

Gladwell, M. 2000, *The Tipping Point: How Little Things Can Make a Big Difference*, Little Brown, New York.

Gordon, H. 2003, *The Time of Our Lives: Inside the Sydney Olympics*, University of Queensland Press, St Lucia.

Gourevitch, P. 1998, *We Wish to Inform You That Tomorrow We Will Be Killed with Our Families: Stories from Rwanda*, Farrar, New York.

Gourevitch, P. and Morris, E. 2008, *Standard Operating Procedure*, Penguin, New York.

Guttenplan, D.D. 2001, *The Holocaust on Trial: History, Justice and the David Irving Libel Case*, Granta Books, London.

Haigh, G. 1993, *The Cricket War: The Inside Story of Kerry Packer's World Series Cricket*, Text, Melbourne.

Halberstam, D. 1979, *The Powers That Be*, Knopf, New York.

Hersey, J. 1946a (1985), *Hiroshima*, Penguin, London.

——1946b, 'A Reporter at Large: Hiroshima' in *The New Yorker*, 31 August, pp. 15–68.

Hersh, S. 1970, *My Lai 4: A Report on the Massacre and Its Aftermath*, Random House, New York.

——2004, *Chain of Command: The Road from 9/11 to Abu Ghraib*, Allen Lane, Camberwell, Victoria.

Hooper, C. 2008, *The Tall Man: Death and Life on Palm Island*, Hamish Hamilton, Camberwell, Victoria.

Hyland, A. 2011, *Kinglake–350*, Text, Melbourne.

Jordan, J. 2005, *Savage Summit: The True Stories of the First Five Women Who Climbed K2, the World's Most Feared Mountain*, William Morrow, New York.

Junger, S. 1997 (2000), *The Perfect Storm: A True Story of Men Against the Sea*, Fourth Estate, London.

Kapuscinski, R. 1993 (1994), *Imperium*, trans. K. Glowczewska, Granta Books, London.

Keneally, T. 1982, *Schindler's Ark*, Hodder & Stoughton, London.

Kidder, T. 1989 (1990), *Among Schoolchildren*, Picador, London.

Kissane, K. 2006, *Silent Death: The Killing of Julie Ramage*, Hodder, Sydney.

Knox, M. 2005, *Secrets of the Jury Room*, Random House, Sydney.

Kotlowitz, A. 1991, *There Are No Children Here: The Story of Two Boys Growing Up in the Other America*, Doubleday, New York.

Krakauer, J. 1997 (1998), *Into Thin Air: A Personal Account of the Mount Everest Disaster*, Macmillan, London.

Kram, M. 2001, *Ghosts of Manila: The Fateful Blood Feud between Muhammad Ali and Joe Frazier*, HarperCollins, New York.

Lahr, J. 1991, *Dame Edna Everage and the Rise of Western Civilisation*, Bloomsbury, London.

Langewiesche, W. 2002 (2003), *American Ground: Unbuilding the World Trade Center*, Scribner, London.

LeBlanc, A.N. 2003 (2004), *Random Family: Love, Drugs, Trouble, and Coming of Age in the Bronx*, HarperPerennial, New York.

Lemann, N. 1991, *The Promised Land: The Great Black Migration and How It Changed America*, Knopf, New York.

——1999, *The Big Test: The Secret History of American Meritocracy*, Farrar, New York.

Lewis, M. 2003, *Moneyball: The Art of Winning an Unfair Game*, W.W. Norton, New York.

——2006, *The Blind Side: Evolution of a Game*, W.W. Norton, New York.

Lukas, J.A. 1976, *Nightmare: The Underside of the Nixon Years*, Viking, New York.

Lyall, K. 2006, *Out of the Blue: Facing the Tsunami*, ABC Books, Sydney.

McGinniss, J. 1983, *Fatal Vision*, New American Library, New York.

——1985, 'The 1985 Afterword' in *Fatal Vision*, New American Library, New York, pp. 654–59.

——1989, 'The 1989 Epilogue' in *Fatal Vision*, New American Library, New York, pp. 660–84.

McLarney, T. 2006, 'Case Closed' in *Homicide: A Year on the Killing Streets*, Owl Books, New York, pp. 643–46.

McPhee, J. 1967 (1991), *Oranges*, Noonday Press, New York.

——1968 (1988), *The Pine Barrens*, Noonday Press, New York.

——1999, *A Sense of Where You Are: A Profile of Bill Bradley at Princeton*, 3rd edn, Farrar, New York.

Mailer, N. 1968, *The Armies of the Night: History as a Novel, the Novel as History*, Weidenfeld & Nicolson, London.

——1975 (1991), *The Fight*, Penguin, Harmondsworth, Middlesex.

Malcolm, J. 1981, *Psychoanalysis: The Impossible Profession*, Knopf, New York.

——1984, *In the Freud Archives*, Papermac, London.

——1989, 'Reflections: The Journalist and the Murderer' in *The New Yorker*, 13 and 20 March, pp. 38–73 and 49–82.

——1990, 'Afterword' in *The Journalist and the Murderer*, Bloomsbury, London, pp. 147–63.

——1993, *The Silent Woman: Sylvia Plath and Ted Hughes*, Picador, London.

——1994, 'Note to the British Edition' in *The Silent Woman: Sylvia Plath and Ted Hughes*, Picador, London, pp. 209–13.

——1997, 'Afterword' in *In the Freud Archives*, Papermac, London, pp. 166–70.

——1999, *The Crime of Sheila McGough*, Knopf, New York.

Marquez, G.G. 1996 (1997), *News of a Kidnapping*, trans. E. Grossman, Knopf, New York.

Marr, D. and Wilkinson, M. 2003, *Dark Victory*, Allen & Unwin, Crows Nest.

Masters, C. 2006, *Jonestown: The Power and the Myth of Alan Jones*, Allen & Unwin, Crows Nest.

Mayer, J. 2008, *The Dark Side: The Inside Story of How the War on Terror Turned into a War on American Ideals*, Doubleday, New York.

Orwell, G. 1933 (1974), *Down and Out in Paris and London*, Penguin, Harmondsworth, Middlesex.

——1938 (2003), *Homage to Catalonia*, Penguin, London.

Orwell, G. and Davison, P. (ed.) 2001, *Orwell's England: 'The Road to Wigan Pier' in the Context of Essays, Reviews, Letters and Poems selected from 'The Complete Works of George Orwell'*, Penguin, London.

Plimpton, G. 1977 (1989), *Shadow Box*, Simon & Schuster, London.

Powers, W. 2010, *Hamlet's Blackberry: A Practical Philosophy for Building a Good Life in a Digital Age*, Scribe, Melbourne.

Preston, R. 1994, *The Hot Zone*, Doubleday, New York.

——2002, *The Demon in the Freezer: The Terrifying Truth about the Threat from Bioterrorism*, Random House, New York.

Price, R. 2006, 'Ante Mortem' in *Homicide: A Year on the Killing Streets*, Owl Books, New York, pp. xi–xv.

Read, P.P. 1974, *Alive: The Story of the Andes Survivors*, HarperPerennial, New York.

——2005, 'A Discussion with Piers Paul Read Three Decades Later' in *Alive: The Story of the Andes Survivors*, HarperPerennial, New York, PS section, pp. 1–5.

——2005, 'Introduction' in *Alive: The Story of the Andes Survivors*, HarperPerennial, New York, pp. xi–xiv.

Remnick, D. 1998, *King of the World: Muhammad Ali and the Rise of an American Hero*, Random House, New York.

Rich, F. 2006, *The Greatest Story Ever Sold: The Decline and Fall of Truth—The Real History of the Bush Administration*, Viking, New York.

Ricketson, M. 2000, 'Afterword: Looking for Demons' by Paul Jennings, in *Paul Jennings: 'The Boy in the Story is Always Me'*, Viking, Ringwood, pp. 294–300.

Ricks, T. 2006, *Fiasco: The American Military Adventure in Iraq*, Penguin Press, New York.

Rosenbaum, R. 1998, *Explaining Hitler: The Search for the Origins of His Evil*, Random House, New York.

Ross, L. 1952 (1962), *Picture*, Penguin, Harmondsworth, Middlesex.

——1966, *Reporting*, Mayflower Books, London.

Salamon, J. 1991, *The Devil's Candy: 'The Bonfire of the Vanities' Goes to Hollywood*, De Capo Press, Massachusetts.

——2001, *Facing the Wind: A True Story of Tragedy and Reconciliation*, Random House, New York.

——2002, 'Afterword: 10 years later' in *The Devil's Candy: 'The Bonfire of the Vanities' Goes to Hollywood*, De Capo Press, Massachusetts, pp. 421–32.

Saviano, R. 2006 (2007), *Gomorrah: Italy's Other Mafia*, trans. V. Jewiss, Pan, London.

Schlosser, E. 2001, *Fast Food Nation: What the All-American Meal Is Doing to the World*, Penguin, Harmondsworth, Middlesex.

Sereny, G. 1998 (1999), *Cries Unheard: The Story of Mary Bell*, Pan Macmillan, London.

Simon, D. 1991, *Homicide: A Year on the Killing Streets*, Owl Books, New York.

——2006, 'Post Mortem' in *Homicide: A Year on the Killing Streets*, Owl Books, New York, pp. 623–42.

Simons, M. 1999, *Fit to Print: Inside the Canberra Press Gallery*, UNSW Press, Sydney.

——2003, *The Meeting of the Waters: The Hindmarsh Island Affair*, Hodder, Sydney.

——2007, *The Content Makers: Understanding the Media in Australia*, Penguin, Camberwell, Victoria.

Stone, G. 2007, *Who Killed Channel 9? The Death of Kerry Packer's Mighty TV Dream Machine*, Macmillan, Sydney.

Suskind, R. 2006, *The One Percent Doctrine*, Simon & Schuster, New York.

Talese, G. 1969 (1971), *The Kingdom and the Power*, Calder & Boyars, London.

——1971, *Honor Thy Father*, Souvenir Press, London.

Temple-Raston, D. 2002, *A Death in Texas: A Story of Race, Murder, and a Small Town's Struggle for Redemption*, Henry Holt, New York.

Thompson, H.S. 1966 (1967), *Hell's Angels*, Penguin, Harmondsworth, Middlesex.

——1971 (1993), *Fear and Loathing in Las Vegas: A Savage Journey to the Heart of the American Dream*, Flamingo, London.

——1973 (1994), *Fear and Loathing on the Campaign Trail '72*, Flamingo, London.

Tolan, S. 2006. *The Lemon Tree: An Arab, a Jew and the Heart of the Middle East*. Bloomsbury, New York.

Wallace, C. 1997, *Greer: Untamed Shrew*, Macmillan, Sydney.

Watson, S. and Hickman, M. 2012. *Dial M for Murdoch: News Corporation and the Corruption of Britain*. Allen Lane, London.

White, T. 1961 (1964), *The Making of the President 1960*, Jonathan Cape, London.

Wilkinson, M. 1996, *The Fixer: The Untold Story of Graham Richardson*, William Heinemann, Port Melbourne.

Williams, P. 1997, *The Victory: The Inside Story of the Takeover of Australia*, Allen & Unwin, St Leonards.

Wolfe, T. 1968 (1981), *The Electric Kool-Aid Acid Test*, Bantam, New York.

——1979 (1991), *The Right Stuff*, Picador, London.

Wolff, M. 2008, *The Man Who Owns the News: Inside the Secret World of Rupert Murdoch*, Knopf, New York.

Woodward, B. 1987, *Veil: The Secret Wars of the CIA, 1981–1987*. London, Simon & Schuster.

——2002 (2003), *Bush at War*, Simon & Schuster, New York.

——2004, *Plan of Attack*, Simon & Schuster, New York.

——2005, *The Secret Man: The Story of Watergate's Deep Throat*, Simon & Schuster, New York.

——2006, *State of Denial: Bush at War, Part III*, Simon & Schuster, New York.

Woodward, B. and Bernstein, C. 1976, *The Final Days*, Simon & Schuster, New York.

Wright, L. 2006, *The Looming Tower: Al-Qaeda and the Road to 9/11*, Penguin, New York.

SECONDARY SOURCES

Abbott, H.P. 2002 (2008), *The Cambridge Introduction to Narrative*, 2nd edn, Cambridge University Press, Cambridge.

Anderson, C. 1987, *Style as Argument: Contemporary American Nonfiction*, Southern Illinois University Press, Carbondale.

Applegate, E. 1996, *Literary Journalism: A Biographical Dictionary of Writers and Editors*, Greenwood Press, Connecticut.

Associated Press, 2006, 'Frey, Publisher Settles Suit over "Pieces"', 12 September, <www.msnbc.msn.com/id/14715706/> [6 February 2008].

——2007, 'Judge Approves *A Million Little Pieces* Refund Settlement for Disgruntled Readers', 2 November, <www.foxnews.com/story/0,2933,307837,00.html> [6 February 2008].

Aucoin, J. 2007, 'Journalistic Moral Engagement: Narrative Strategies in American Muckraking' in *Journalism*, vol. 8, pp. 559–72.

Bak, J. and Reynolds, B. (eds) 2011, *Literary Journalism Across the Globe: Journalistic Traditions and Transnational Influences*, University of Massachusetts Press, Amherst and Boston.

Baker, C. 1969, *Ernest Hemingway: A Life Story*, Penguin, Harmondsworth.

Bates, S. 1995, 'Who Is the Journalist's Client?' in *Media Ethics*, Fall, pp. 3, 14–16.

Berner, R.T. 1986, *Literary Newswriting: The Death of an Oxymoron*, Journalism Monographs 99, October, Association for Education in Journalism and Mass Communication, Columbia, South Carolina.

Birkerts, S. 1987, 'Docu-fiction' in *An Artificial Wilderness: Essays on Twentieth Century Literature*, S. Birkerts, William Morrow, New York, pp. 265–70.

Black, J., Steele, B. and Barney, R. 1997, *Doing Ethics in Journalism: A Handbook with Case Studies*, 3rd edn, Allyn & Bacon, Florida.

Blackburn, E. 2007, *The End of Innocence: The Remarkable True Story of One Woman's Fight for Justice*, Hardie Grant, Melbourne.

Blundell, W. 1988, *The Art and Craft of Feature Writing*, Plume, New York.

Bok, S. 1978, *Lying: Moral Choice in Public and Private Life*, Pantheon Books, New York.

Booth, W. 1988, *The Company We Keep: An Ethics of Fiction*, University of California Press, Berkeley.

Borden, S. 1993, 'Empathic Listening: The Interviewer's Betrayal' in *Journal of Mass Media Ethics*, vol. 8, pp. 219–26.

Boynton, R. 2005, *The New New Journalism: Conversations with America's Best Nonfiction Writers on Their Craft*, Random, New York.

Brill, S. 1999, 'How Woodward Goes Wayward' in *Brill's Content*, September, pp. 29–34.

——2000, 'Selling Snake Oil' in *Brill's Content*, February, pp. 66–9.

Brill, S. and Woodward, B. 2000, 'Rewind' in *Brill's Content*, November, pp. 22–3, 122–6.

Bromley, D. and Carter, L. (eds) 2001, *Toward Reflexive Ethnography: Participating, Observing, Narrating*, JAI, Amsterdam.

Campbell, K. (ed.) 2000, *Journalism, Literature and Modernity: From Hazlitt to Modernism*, Edinburgh University Press, Edinburgh.

Capote, T. 1980 (1981), 'Preface' in *Music for Chameleons*, Signet, New York, pp. xi–xviii.

——1987, 'A Beautiful Child' in *A Capote Reader*, Penguin, London, pp. 578–89.

——1987, 'The Duke in His Domain' in *A Capote Reader*, Penguin, London, pp. 517–44.

Carey, J. 1986, 'The Dark Continent of American Journalism' in *Reading the News*, eds R. Manoff and M. Schudson, Pantheon, New York, pp. 146–96.

——1987, 'Introduction' in *The Faber Book of Reportage*, J. Carey, Faber, London, pp. xxix–xxxviii.

Carroll, E.J. 1993, *Hunter: The Strange and Savage Life of Hunter S. Thompson*, Plume, New York.

Chadwick, P. 2008, *Sources and Conflicts: Review of the Adequacy of ABC Editorial Policies Relating to Source Protection and to the Reporting by Journalists of Events in Which They Are Participants*, ABC Director of Editorial Policies, July <www.abc.net.au/corp/pubs/documents/200806_confidentialsources_final report_july2008.pdf>. [1 May 2009].

Chamberlain-Creighton, L. 1990 (2004), *Through My Eyes: The Autobiography of Lindy Chamberlain-Creighton*, East Street Publications, Bowden, South Australia.

Chance, J. and McKeen, W. 2001, 'Introduction' in *Literary Journalism: A Reader*, J. Chance and W. McKeen, Wadsworth, Belmont, California, pp. vii–xiv.

Cheney, T. 1991, *Writing Creative Nonfiction: How to Use Fiction Techniques to Make Your Nonfiction More Interesting, Dramatic—and Vivid*, Ten Speed Press, California.

Christians, C., Fackler, M. and Rotzoll, K. 1995, *Media Ethics: Cases and Moral Reasoning*, 4th edn, Pearson, Boston.

Clarke, G. 1988 (1993), *Capote: A Biography*, Abacus, London.

——(ed.) 2004, *Too Brief a Treat: The Letters of Truman Capote*, Vintage International, New York.

Cohen, E. and Elliott, D. (eds) 1997, *Journalism Ethics: A Reference Handbook*, ABC-CLIO, Santa Barbara, California.

Connery, T. (ed.) 1992, *A Sourcebook of American Literary Journalism: Representative Writers in an Emerging Genre*, Greenwood, New York.

Cords, S. 2006, *The Real Story: A Guide to Nonfiction Reading Interests*, Libraries Unlimited, Connecticut.

——2009, *The Inside Scoop: A Guide to Nonfiction Investigative Writing and Exposés*, Libraries Unlimited, Connecticut.

Cowan, G. 1998, 'The Legal and Ethical Limitations of Factual Misrepresentation' in *Annals of the American Academy of Political and Social Sciences*, vol. 560, pp. 155–64.

Craig, D. 2006, *The Ethics of the Story: Using Narrative Techniques Responsibly in Journalism*, Rowman & Littlefield, Maryland.

Cramer, J. and McDevitt, M. 2004, 'Ethnographic Journalism' in *Qualitative Research in Journalism: Taking It to the Streets*, Lawrence Erlbaum, New Jersey, pp. 127–43.

d'Alpuget, B. 2008, *On Longing*, Melbourne University Press, Carlton.

De Bellis, J. 1979, 'Visions and Revisions: Truman Capote's *In Cold Blood*' in *Journal of Modern Literature*, vol. 7.3, pp. 519–36.

Didion, J. 2001 (2002), 'Political Pornography' in *Political Fictions*, Vintage International, New York, pp. 191–214.

Doležel, L. 1999, 'Fictional and Historical Narrative: Meeting the Postmodernist Challenge' in *Narratologies: New Perspectives on Narrative Analysis*, ed. D. Herman, Ohio State University Press, Columbus, Ohio, pp. 247–73.

Dufresne, M. 1998, 'Why *Midnight* May Be Darker Than You Think' in *Columbia Journalism Review*, May–June, pp. 78–9.

Dunn, S. 2007, '*Rolling Stone*'s Coverage of the 1972 US Presidential Election' in *Asia-Pacific Media Educator*, vol. 18, pp. 31–43.

Eagleton, T. 1983 (1996), *Literary Theory: An Introduction*, 2nd edn, Basil Blackwell, London.

Eisenhuth, S. and McDonald, W. 2007, *The Writer's Reader: Understanding Journalism and Non-fiction*, Cambridge University Press, Sydney.

Elliott, D. and Culver, C. 1992, 'Defining and Analyzing Journalistic Deception' in *Journal of Mass Media Ethics*, vol. 7, pp. 69–84.

Emery, F. 1994, *Watergate: The Corruption of American Politics and the Fall of Richard Nixon*, Times Books, New York.

Epstein, J. 2004, 'A Lad of the World: Truman Capote and the Cost of Charm' in *The Weekly Standard*, 6 December, pp. 21–5.

Fakazis, E. 2002, 'Janet Malcolm: Constructing a Journalist's Identity', PhD dissertation, Indiana University.

——2003, 'How Close Is Too Close? When Journalists Become Their Sources' in *Desperately Seeking Ethics: A Guide to Media Conduct*, H. Good, Scarecrow Press, Lanham, Maryland, pp. 45–59.

Felt, M. and O'Connor, J. 2006, *A G-Man's Life: The FBI, Being 'Deep Throat' and the Struggle for Honor in Washington*, Public Affairs, New York.

Fisher Fishkin, S. 1985, *From Fact to Fiction: Journalism and Imaginative Writing in America*, Johns Hopkins University Press, Baltimore.

Flippo, C. 1980, 'Tom Wolfe: *The Rolling Stone* interview' in *Rolling Stone*, 21 August, Issue 323–24, pp. 52–60.

Forché, C. and Gerard, P. 2001, *Writing Creative Nonfiction*, Story Press, Cincinnati, Ohio.

Frank, R. 1999, '"You Had to Be There" (and They Weren't): The Problem with Reporter Reconstructions' in *Journal of Mass Media Ethics*, vol. 14.3, pp. 146–58.

——2004, 'The Trickster in the Newsroom' in *Points of Entry*, vol. 2, pp. 45–58.

Franklin, J. 1986, *Writing for Story: Craft Secrets of Dramatic Nonfiction by a Two-Time Pulitzer Prize Winner*, Plume, New York.

Frayn, M. 1965 (1966), *The Tin Men*, Fontana, London.

Frey, J. 2003 (2006), 'A Note to the Reader' in *A Million Little Pieces*, John Murray, London.

Friend, T. 2001, 'Notes on the Death of the Celebrity Profile' in *Lost in Mongolia: Travels in Hollywood and Other Foreign Lands*, T. Friend, Random House, New York, pp. 40–8.

Frus, P. 1994, *The Politics and Poetics of Journalistic Narrative: The Timely and the Timeless*, Cambridge University Press, Cambridge.

Fuller, J. 1996, 'News and Literary Technique' in *News Values: Ideas for an Information Age*, J. Fuller, University of Chicago Press, Chicago, pp. 131–64.

Gardner, J. 1983, *The Art of Fiction: Notes on Craft for Young Writers*, Vintage, New York.

Gare, S. and Wilson, P. 2008, 'Twist in the Tale of a Sierra Leonean Child Soldier as Dates and Facts Begin to Unravel' in *The Weekend Australian*, 19 January, pp. 1, 8, 15, 22–23.

Garner, H. 1995, 'Sticks and Stones' (letter) in *The Age*, 23 September, p. 22.

——1996, 'The Art of the Dumb Question' in *True Stories: Selected Non-fiction*, H. Garner, Text, Melbourne, pp. 1–12.

Geertz, C. 1973, *The Interpretation of Cultures*, Basic Books, New York.

Genette, G. 1987 (1997), *Paratexts: Thresholds of Interpretation*, trans. J. Lewin, Cambridge University Press, Cambridge.

——1991 (1993), *Fiction and Diction*, trans. C. Porter, Cornell University Press, Ithaca.

Glass, I. (ed.) 2007, 'Introduction' in *The New Kings of Nonfiction*, I. Glass, Riverhead Press, New York, pp. 1–14.

Glover, S. (ed.) 1999, *Secrets of the Press: Journalists on Journalism*, Allen Lane, London.

Goldstein, T. 2007, *Journalism and Truth: Strange Bedfellows*, Northwestern University Press, Evanston, Illinois.

Goldsworthy, K. 1996, *Helen Garner*, Oxford University Press, Melbourne.

Gottlieb, M. 1989, 'Dangerous Liaisons: Journalists and Their Sources' in *Columbia Journalism Review*, July–August, pp. 21–35.

Greenberg, D. 2003, *Nixon's Shadow: The History of an Image*, Norton, New York.

——2005, 'Beyond Deep Throat' in *Columbia Journalism Review*, September–October, pp. 51–3.

Gutkind, L. 1997, *The Art of Creative Nonfiction: Writing and Selling the Literature of Reality*, John Wiley, New York.

——2005, 'The Creative Nonfiction Police?' in *In Fact: The Best of Creative Nonfiction*, ed. L. Gutkind, W.W. Norton, New York, pp. xix–xxxiii.

Hackett, A. and Burke, J. 1977, *80 Years of Bestsellers*, R.R. Bowker, New York.

Harrington, W. 1997, 'Prologue: The Job of Remembering for the Tribe' and 'A Writer's Essay: Seeking the Extraordinary in the Ordinary' in *Intimate*

Journalism: The Art and Craft of Reporting Everyday Life, ed. W. Harrington, Sage, Thousand Oaks, pp. xi–xlvi.

——2004, 'The Writer's Choice' in *River Teeth: A Journal of Nonfiction Narrative*, vol. 5.2, pp. 77–89.

Harrison Smith, S. 2004, *The Fact Checker's Bible: A Guide to Getting it Right*, Anchor, New York.

Hart, J. 2011, *Storycraft: The Complete Guide to Writing Narrative Nonfiction*, University of Chicago Press, Chicago.

Hartsock, J. 2000, *A History of American Literary Journalism: The Emergence of a Modern Narrative Form*, University of Massachusetts Press, Amherst.

Havill, A. 1993, *Deep Truth: The Lives of Bob Woodward and Carl Bernstein*, Birch Lane, New York.

Helliker, K. 2013, 'Capote Classic *In Cold Blood* Tainted by Long-lost Files' in *The Wall Street Journal*, 8 February, <http://online.wsj.com/article/SB10001424127 887323951904578290341604113984.html> [27 March 2013].

Herman, D. (ed.) 2007, *The Cambridge Companion to Narrative*, Cambridge University Press, Cambridge.

Herman, D., Jahn, M. and Ryan, M. (eds) 2005, *Routledge Encyclopedia of Narrative Theory*, Routledge, London.

Hersey, J. 1980, 'The Legend on the License' in *Killing the Messenger: 100 Years of Media Criticism*, (1989) ed. T. Goldstein, Columbia University Press, New York, pp. 247–67.

Heyne, E. 1987, 'Toward a Theory of Literary Nonfiction' in *Modern Fiction Studies*, vol. 33.3, pp. 479–91.

——2001, 'Where Fiction Meets Nonfiction: Mapping a Rough Terrain' in *Narrative*, vol. 9.3, pp. 322–33.

Hoffman, J. 1995, *Theodore H. White and Journalism as Illusion*, University of Missouri Press, Columbia, Missouri.

Holland, M. 2012, *Leak: Why Mark Felt Became Deep Throat*, University Press of Kansas, Lawrence, Kansas.

Hope, D. 2008, 'Loose with the Truth' in *The Australian*, 25 January, p. 13.

Howarth, W.L. 1976, 'Introduction' in *The John McPhee Reader*, ed. W.L. Howarth, Farrar, New York, pp. vii–xxiii.

Howe, A. (ed.) 2005, *Lindy Chamberlain Revisited: A 25th Anniversary Retrospective*, LhR Press, Canada Bay, New South Wales.

Hulteng, J.L. 1976, *The Messenger's Motives: Ethical Problems of the News Media*, Prentice-Hall, Englewood Cliffs, New Jersey.

Hurst, J. 1988, *The Walkley Awards: Australia's Best Journalists in Action*, John Kerr, Melbourne.

Hurst, J. and White, S. 1994, *Ethics and the Australian News Media*, Macmillan, Melbourne.

Hursthouse, R. 1999, *On Virtue Ethics*, Oxford University Press, Oxford.

Hutton, G. and Tanner, L (eds) 1979, *125 Years of Age*, Nelson, Melbourne.

Inge, M.T. (ed.) 1987, *Truman Capote: Conversations*, University Press of Mississippi, Jackson.

Isaacson, W. 1992 (2005), *Kissinger: A Biography*, Simon & Schuster, New York.

Jack, I. 1993 (1998), 'Introduction' in *The Granta Book of Reportage*, ed. I. Jack, Granta, London, pp. v–xiii.

Jackson, S. 2009, 'Hacks Find Escape between the Covers' in *The Australian*, Media, 11 May, pp. 35–6.

——2009, 'Prizes That Buy Time for Thinking', *The Australian*, Media, 11 May, pp. 35–6.

Johnson, M. 1971, *The New Journalism: The Underground Press, the Artists of Nonfiction and Changes in the Established Media*, University Press of Kansas, Lawrence.

Jones, D. 1992, 'John Hersey' in *A Sourcebook of American Literary Journalism: Representative Writers in an Emerging Genre*, ed. T. Connery, Greenwood, New York, pp. 213–21.

Joseph, S. 2007, 'Retelling Untellable Stories: Ethics and the Literary Journalist' in *Asia-Pacific Media Educator*, vol. 18, pp. 125–39.

Keeble, R. and Wheeler, S. (eds) 2007, *The Journalistic Imagination: Literary Journalists from Defoe to Capote and Carter*, Routledge, London.

Keeble, R. and Tulloch, J. (eds) 2012, *Global Literary Journalism: Exploring the Journalistic Imagination*, Peter Lang, New York.

Kelliher, L. 2004, 'Ties That Bind' in *Columbia Journalism Review*, May–June, pp. 40–3.

Keneally, T. 2007, *Searching for Schindler: A Memoir*, Knopf Australia, Sydney.

Kennamer, D. 2005, 'What Journalists and Researchers Have in Common About Ethics' in *Journal of Mass Media Ethics*, vol. 20, pp. 77–89.

Kerrane, K. and Yagoda, B. (eds) 1997, *The Art of Fact: A Historical Anthology of Literary Journalism*, Scribner, New York.

Koenig, B. 2003 (1903), 'Introduction' in *The People of the Abyss*, J. London, Pluto Press, London, pp. v–xi.

Kornstein, D. 1989, 'Twisted Vision: Janet Malcolm's Upside Down View of the *Fatal Vision* Case' in *Cardozo Studies in Law and Literature*, vol. 1.2, pp. 127–56.

Kovach, B. and Rosenstiel, T. 2001 (2007), *The Elements of Journalism: What Newspeople Should Know and the Public Should Expect*, 2nd edn, Three Rivers, New York.

Kramer, M. (1995), 'Breakable Rules for Literary Journalists', in N. Sims and M. Kramer, *Literary Journalism: A New Collection of the Best American Nonfiction*, Ballantine, New York, 21–34.

Kramer, M. and Call, W. (eds) 2007, *Telling True Stories: A Nonfiction Writers' Guide from the Nieman Foundation at Harvard University*, Plume, New York.

Kunkel, T. 1995, *Genius in Disguise: Harold Ross of* The New Yorker, Random House, New York.

——(ed.) 2000 (2001), *Letters from the Editor:* The New Yorker's *Harold Ross*, Modern Library, New York.

Lappin, E. 1999, 'The Man with Two Heads' in *Granta*, Summer, pp. 7–65.

Legge, K. 2008a, 'The Secret Life of Blanche' in *The Weekend Australian Magazine*, 2 August, pp. 10–14.

——2008b, 'Truly Helen' in *The Weekend Australian Magazine*, 29 March, pp. 16–21.

Lehman, D.W. 1997, *Matters of Fact: Reading Nonfiction over the Edge*, Ohio State University Press, Columbus.

——2001, 'Mining a Rough Terrain: Weighing the Implications of Nonfiction' in *Narrative*, vol. 9.3, pp. 334–42.

Lifton, R. and Mitchell, G. 1995, *Hiroshima in America: Fifty Years of Denial*, Grosset/Putnam, New York.

Lodge, D. 1992, *The Art of Fiction*, Penguin, London.

Long, B. 1966, 'In Cold Comfort' in *Esquire*, June, pp. 124, 126, 128, 171–3, 175–81.

Lorenz, A. 2005, 'When You Weren't There: How Reporters Recreate Scenes for Narrative' in *River Teeth: A Journal of Nonfiction Narrative*, vol. 7.1, pp. 71–85.

Lounsberry, B. 1990, *The Art of Fact: Contemporary Artists of Nonfiction*, Greenwood, New York.

Ludtke, M. 2008, 'The Ties That Bind: Newspapers and Nonfiction Books' in *Nieman Reports*, Winter, <www.nieman.harvard.edu/reportsitem.aspx ?id=100716> [3 March 2009].

Lule, J. 2001, *Daily News, Eternal Stories: The Mythological Role of Journalism*, Guilford Press, New York.

McCalman, I. 2004, 'Flirting with Fiction' in *The Historian's Conscience: Australian Historians on the Ethics of History*, ed. S. Macintyre, Melbourne University Press, Carlton, pp. 151–61.

McKeen, W. 1995, *Tom Wolfe*, Twayne's United States Authors Series No. 650, Twayne, New York.

——2008, *Outlaw Journalist: The Life and Times of Hunter S. Thompson*, W.W. Norton, New York.

McPhee, J. 2009, 'Checkpoints: Fact-checkers Do it a Tick at a Time' in *The New Yorker*, 9 and 16 February, pp. 56–63.

Masters, C. 2002, *Not for Publication*, ABC Books, Sydney.

Mead, J. 1995, 'A Player in the Ormond Drama Defends her Cause in *The Age*, 16 August, p. 17.

——(ed.) 1997, *Bodyjamming: Sexual Harassment, Feminism and Public Life*, Random, Milsons Point, New South Wales.

Media Entertainment and Arts Alliance 1997, *Ethics in Journalism: Report of the Ethics Review Committee, Media Entertainment and Arts Alliance, Australian Journalists' Association Section*, Melbourne University Publishing, Melbourne.

Meilaender, G. 1984, *The Theory and Practice of Virtue*, University of Notre Dame Press, Notre Dame, Indiana.

Milner, A. 2005, *Literature, Culture and Society*, 2nd edn, Routledge, London.

Mindich, D. 1998, *Just the Facts: How 'Objectivity' Came to Define American Journalism*, Oxford University Press, New York.

Mitchell, J. 1993, 'Author's Note', *Up in the Old Hotel and Other Stories*, Vintage, New York, pp. ix–xiii.

Morris, Edmund 1999 (2000), 'Publisher's Note', *Dutch: A Memoir of Ronald Reagan*, HarperCollins, London, pp. vii–xvi.

Morris, Errol 2012, *A Wilderness of Errors: The Trials of Jeffrey Macdonald*, Penguin Press, New York.

Muller, D. 2005, 'Media Accountability in a Liberal Democracy: An Examination of the Harlot's Prerogative', PhD thesis, University of Melbourne.

Murphy, J. 1974, *The New Journalism: A Critical Perspective*, Association for Education in Journalism, Kentucky.

Nance, W. 1970, *The Worlds of Truman Capote*, Stein and Day, New York.

'Narrative Journalism: Reporting and Writing in a Different Voice' 2000, *Nieman Reports*, vol. 54:3, Fall, pp. 4–44.

Neill, R. 1995, 'Garner Hype Goes too Far' in *The Australian*, 17 August, p. 11.

Nell, V. 1988, *Lost in a Book: The Psychology of Reading for Pleasure*, Yale University Press, New Haven.

The New York Times 1959, 'Wealthy Farmer, 3 of Family Slain', November 16, <www.nytimes.com/books/97/12/28/home/capote-headline.html>

New York University Journalism Department 1999, 'Best American Journalism of the Twentieth Century', <www.infoplease.com/ipea/AO777379.html> [16 February 2006].

Nielsen BookScan 2012, 'The Top 100 Bestselling Non-fiction Books for the years 2002–2012', provided by Michael Webster, principal consultant for Nielsen BookScan in Australia.

Nossek, H. and Adoni, H. 2006, 'The Future of Reading as a Cultural Behavior in a Multi-channel Environment' in *The Future of the Book in the Digital Age*, eds B. Cope and A. Phillips, Chandos Publishing, Oxford, pp. 89–113.

Nuttall, N. 2007, 'Cold-blooded journalism: Truman Capote and the Non-fiction Novel' in *The Journalistic Imagination: Literary Journalists from Defoe to Capote and Carter*, eds R. Keeble and S. Wheeler, Routledge, London, pp. 130–44.

Oakley, J. and Cocking, D. 2001, *Virtue Ethics and Professional Roles*, Cambridge University Press, Cambridge.

O'Connor, J. 2005, 'I'm The Guy They Called Deep Throat' in *Vanity Fair*, July, pp. 84–7, 127–31.

O'Donnell, M. 2007, 'Special Issue: Narrative and Literary Journalism' in *Asia-Pacific Media Educator*, ed. M. O'Donnell, vol. 18, pp. 1–154.

Peretz, E. 2008, 'James Frey's Morning After' in *Vanity Fair*, June, <www.vanityfair.com/culture/features/2008/06/frey200806?printable=true&current> [16 May 2008].

Plimpton, G. 1987, 'The Story Behind a Nonfiction Novel' in *Truman Capote: Conversations*, ed. M.T. Inge, University Press of Mississippi, Jackson, pp. 47–68.

——1998 (1999), *Truman Capote: In Which Various Friends, Enemies, Acquaintances, and Detractors Recall His Turbulent Career*, Picador, London.

Publishers Weekly 2006, 'Frey's Agent Goes on the Record with "PW"', 31 January, <www.publishersweekly.com/article/CA6303378.html?text=evashevski> [6 February 2008].

Quinn, A. 2007, 'Moral Virtues for Journalists' in *Journal of Mass Media Ethics*, vol. 22.2, pp. 168–86.

Random House 2007, 'Notice to Customers Regarding *A Million Little Pieces* by James Frey', media release, 14 June, <www.randomhouse.biz/media/pdfs/ ClassNoticeFin.pdf> [6 February 2008].

Reed, K. 1981, *Truman Capote*, Twayne's United States Authors Series No. 388, Twayne, Boston.

Remnick, D. 1996, 'Introduction' in *The Second John McPhee Reader*, ed. P. Strachan, Farrar, New York, pp. vii–xvii.

Richards, I. 2005, *Quagmires and Quandaries: Exploring Journalism Ethics*, UNSW Press, Sydney.

Ricketson, M. 1995a, 'After Midnight' in *The Herald Sun*, Weekend, 4 November, p. 9.

——1995b, 'The Demidenko-Darville and Garner Controversies', *The Media Report*, ABC Radio National, 24 August.

——1997, 'Helen Garner's *The First Stone*: Hitchhiking on the Credibility of Other Writers' in *Bodyjamming: Sexual Harassment, Feminism and Public Life*, ed. J. Mead, Random House, Milsons Point, New South Wales, pp. 79–100.

——2000, 'The Reporting Is All: The Nature and Role of the Reporting Process in a Piece of Book-length journalism', MA by project and exegesis, RMIT University.

——2001a, 'Freedom of Information and Authors: An Unsung Treasure Trove' in *FOI Review*, vol. 94, pp. 26–9.

——2001b, 'True Stories: The Power and Pitfalls of Literary Journalism' in *Journalism: Theory in Practice*, eds S. Tapsall and C. Varley, Oxford University Press, Melbourne, pp. 149–65.

——(ed.) 2004, 'Introduction' in *The Best Australian Profiles*, Black Inc, Melbourne, pp. 1–21.

——2004, *Writing Feature Stories: How to Research and Write Newspaper and Magazine Articles*, Allen & Unwin, Crows Nest.

——2007, 'In Search of the Real Capote' in *The Age*, A2, 26 May, p. 20.

——2008, 'Drawn to Trouble' in *The Age*, A2, 16 August, pp. 26–7.

——2009, 'Accidental Outlaw' in *The Age*, A2, 10 January, p. 14.

——2009, 'Ethical Issues in the Practice of Book-length Journalism', dissertation, Monash University.

——2010, 'Truman Capote and the World He Made' in *Meanjin*, vol. 69.3, pp. 89–101.

——2011, 'The Blind Side' in *Griffith Review*, vol. 33, pp. 161–8.

RMIT University Journalism Program, 'The Best Australian Journalism of the Twentieth Century', 9 December 1999, <http://fifth.estate.rmit.edu.au/

Febo4/106.html> [11 March 2008]. (Also published as 'Century's Top 100' 1999, *The Australian*, Media, 9 December, pp. 6–7.)

Rodden, J. 1989, *The Politics of Literary Reputation: The Making and Claiming of 'Saint George' Orwell*, Oxford University Press, New York.

Ross, L. 2002, *Reporting Back: Notes on Journalism*, Counterpoint, New York.

Rubie, P. 2009, *The Elements of Narrative Nonfiction*, Quill Driver Books, Fresno, California.

Rule, R. and Wheeler, S. 2000, *True Stories: Guides for Writing from Your Life*, Heinemann, Portsmouth.

Sanders, D. 1990, *John Hersey Revisited*, Twayne's United States Authors Series No. 569, Twayne, Boston.

Sanders, K. 2003, *Ethics and Journalism*, Sage, London.

Sanders, S. 2007, 'Introduction' in *Touchstone Anthology of Contemporary Creative Nonfiction: Work from 1970 to the Present*, eds L. Williford and M. Martone, Touchstone, New York, pp. xv–xvi.

Schudson, M. 1978, *Discovering the News: A Social History of American Newspapers*, Basic Books, New York.

——1995, *The Power of News*, Harvard University Press, Cambridge, Massachusetts.

——2005, 'News as Stories' in *Media Anthropology*, eds E. Rothenbuhler and M. Coman, Sage, Thousand Oaks, California, pp. 121–9.

Schultz, J. 1998, *Reviving the Fourth Estate: Democracy, Accountability and the Media*, Cambridge University Press, Cambridge.

Schultz, T. 2011, *Tiny Terror: Why Truman Capote (Almost) Wrote 'Answered Prayers'*, Oxford University Press, New York.

Seligman, C. 2000, '*Salon* Brilliant Careers: Janet Malcolm' in *Salon*, 29 February, <www.salon.com/people/bc/2000/02/29/malcolm/print.html> [28 September 2005].

Serrin, J. and Serrin, W. 2002, 'Introduction' in *Muckraking! The Journalism That Changed America*, eds J. Serrin and W. Serrin, The New Press, New York, pp. xix–xxii.

Shafer, J. 2006, 'Newsbooks: The Triumph of a Journalism Genre' in *Slate*, 11 October, <www.slate.com/toolbar.aspx?action=print&id=215127> [15 May 2007].

Shapiro, B. 2003, 'Introduction: Striking Through the Mask' in *Shaking the Foundations: 200 Years of Investigative Journalism in America*, ed. B. Shapiro, Thunder's Mouth Press, New York, pp. xiii–xxvi.

Shelden, M. 1991 (1992), *Orwell: The Authorised Biography*, Minerva, London.

Shepard, A.C. 2007, *Woodward and Bernstein: Life in the Shadow of Watergate*, John Wiley, New Jersey.

Sherman, S. 2003, 'The Avenger: Sy Hersh, Then and Now' in *Columbia Journalism Review*, July–August, pp. 34–44.

Shields, C.J. 2006 (2007), *Mockingbird: A Portrait of Harper Lee*, Owl Books, New York.

Sifton, E. 2007, 'The Second Draft of History' in *Columbia Journalism Review*, September–October, pp. 54–7.

Silvester, C. 1993, 'Introduction' in *The Penguin Book of Interviews: An Anthology from 1859 to the Present Day*, ed. C. Silvester, Penguin, Harmondsworth, Middlesex, pp. 1–48.

Simons, M. 2004, 'An Exercise in Creative Non-fiction and Investigative Journalism: *The Meeting of the Waters: The Hindmarsh Island Affair*', dissertation by project and exegesis, University of Technology, Sydney.

Sims, N. (ed.) 1984, *The Literary Journalists*, Ballantine, New York, pp. 3–25.

——(ed.) 1990, *Literary Journalism in the Twentieth Century*, Oxford University Press, New York.

——2007, *True Stories: A Century of Literary Journalism*, Northwestern University Press, Evanston, Illinois.

Sims, N. and Kramer, M. (eds) 1995, *Literary Journalism: A New Collection of the Best American Nonfiction*, Ballantine, New York.

The Smoking Gun 2006, 'A Million Little Lies: Exposing James Frey's Fiction Addiction', 8 January, <www.thesmokinggun.com/archive/0104061james frey1.html> [20 April 2006].

Stanton, R. 1980, *Truman Capote: A Primary and Secondary Bibliography*, G.K. Hall, Boston.

Starkman, D. 2010, 'The Hamster Wheel' in *Columbia Journalism Review*, September–October, pp. 24–8.

Stephens, M. 1988 (2007), *A History of News*, 3rd edn, Oxford University Press, New York.

Stone, I.F. 1968, 'A Louis XIV—in all but Style' in *In a Time of Torment*, I.F. Stone, Jonathan Cape, London, pp. 62–8.

Talese, G. 1970 (1993), 'Author's Foreword', *Fame and Obscurity*, Ivy Books, New York.

Talese, G. and Lounsberry, B. (eds) 1996, *Writing Creative Nonfiction: The Literature of Reality*, HarperCollins, New York.

——1999, 'The Silent Season of a Hero' in *The Best American Sports Writing of the Century*, series ed. G Stout, Houghton Mifflin, Boston, pp. 3–22.

——2003, 'Frank Sinatra Has a Cold' in *Esquire's Big Book of Great Writing: More than 70 Years of Celebrated Journalism*, ed. A. Miller, Hearst, New York, pp. 583–622.

Tanner, S., Kasinger, M. and Richardson, N. 2009, 'Book-length Writing: Creative Non-fiction' in *Feature Writing: (Telling the Story)*, S. Tanner, M. Kasinger and N. Richardson, Oxford University Press, Melbourne, pp. 344–57.

Tapsall, S. and Varley, C. (eds) 2001, *Journalism: Theory in Practice*, Oxford University Press, Melbourne.

Taylor, A. 2005, 'Stones, Ripples, Waves: Refiguring *The First Stone* Media Event', dissertation, University of New South Wales.

Tebbel, J. and Zuckerman, M.E. 1991, *The Magazine in America 1741–1990*, Oxford University Press, New York.

Thompson, H.S. 1997 (1998), *The Proud Highway: Saga of a Desperate Southern Gentleman 1955–1967*, ed. D. Brinkley, Bloomsbury, London.

——2000, *Fear and Loathing in America: The Brutal Odyssey of an Outlaw Journalist 1968–1976*, ed. D. Brinkley, Bloomsbury, London.

Tompkins, P.K. 1966, 'In Cold Fact' in *Esquire*, June, pp. 125, 127, 166–8, 170–1.

Toohey, B. 1995, 'Stone's Bad-throw: Six-into-one Doesn't Go' in *The Australian Financial Review*, 5 September, p. 17.

Tynan, K. 1967, *Tynan Right and Left*, Longmans, London.

Van Maanen, J. (ed.) 1995, *Representation in Ethnography*, Sage, London.

Wakefield, D. 1966, *Between the Lines: A Reporter's Personal Journey Through Public Events*, Little Brown, Boston.

Weber, R. (ed.) 1974, *The Reporter as Artist: A Look at the New Journalism Controversy*, Hastings House, New York.

——1980, *The Literature of Fact: Literary Nonfiction in American Writing*, Ohio University Press, Athens.

Weinberg, S. 1992a, 'The Secret Sharer' in *Mother Jones*, May–June, pp. 52–9.

——1992b, *Telling the Untold Story: How Investigative Reporters are Changing the Craft of Biography*, University of Missouri Press, Missouri.

——1998, 'Why Books Err So Often' in *Columbia Journalism Review*, July–August, pp. 52–6.

——2007, 'The Book as an Investigative Vehicle for News' in *Nieman Reports*, Spring, <www.nieman.harvard.edu/reports/07–1NRspring/p104–0701-weinberg.html> [17 December 2007].

——2008, *Taking on the Trust: The Epic Battle of Ida Tarbell and John D. Rockefeller*, W.W. Norton, New York.

Weingarten, M. 2005, *From Hipsters to Gonzo: How New Journalism Rewrote the World*, Scribe, Carlton. (Published in the United States under the title *The Gang That Wouldn't Write Straight*.)

Weisberg, J. 2006, 'The Decline of Rumsfeld' in *Slate*, 4 October, <www.slate.com/toolbar.aspx?action=print&id=2150953> [15 May 2007].

Wenner, J.S. and Seymour, C. (eds) 2007, *Gonzo: The Life of Hunter S. Thompson*, Sphere, London.

White, H. 1978, 'The Historical Text as Literary Artifact' in *Tropics of Discourse: Essays in Cultural Criticism*, Johns Hopkins University Press, Baltimore, pp. 81–100.

——1987, *The Content of the Form: Historical Discourse and Historical Representation*, Johns Hopkins University Press, Baltimore.

——1992, 'Historical Emplotment and the Problem of Truth' in *Probing the Limits of Representation: Nazism and the 'Final Solution'*, ed. S. Friedlander, Harvard University Press, Cambridge, Massachusetts, pp. 37–53.

Wilkins, L. and Christians, C. (eds) 2009, *The Handbook of Mass Media Ethics*, Routledge, New York.

Williford, L. and Martone, M. (eds) 2007, *Touchstone Anthology of Contemporary Creative Nonfiction: Work from 1970 to the Present*, Touchstone, New York, pp. xi–xiv.

Windham, D. 1987, *Lost Friends: A Memoir of Truman Capote, Tennessee Williams, and Others*, William Morrow, New York.

Wolfe, T. 1973 (1975), 'The New Journalism' in *The New Journalism*, eds T. Wolfe and E.W. Johnson, Picador, London, pp. 15–68.

——1987 (1988), 'Stalking the Billion-Footed Beast' in *The Bonfire of the Vanities*, T. Wolfe, Picador, London, pp. vii–xxx.

——2000, '*The New Yorker* Affair' in *Hooking Up*, T. Wolfe, Jonathan Cape, London, pp. 247–93.

Yagoda, B. 2000, *About Town: 'The New Yorker' and the World It Made*, Scribner, New York.

——2004, *The Sound on the Page: Great Writers Talk about Style and Voice in Writing*, HarperCollins, New York.

Zavarzadeh, M. 1976, *The Mythopoeic Reality: The Postwar American Nonfiction Novel*, University of Illinois Press, Urbana.

Zelizer, B. 2004, *Taking Journalism Seriously: News and the Academy*, Sage, Thousand Oaks.

Index